Andrew Wilson

Leaves from a Naturalist's Notebook

Andrew Wilson

Leaves from a Naturalist's Notebook

ISBN/EAN: 9783743324589

Manufactured in Europe, USA, Canada, Australia, Japa

Cover: Foto ©ninafisch / pixelio.de

Manufactured and distributed by brebook publishing software (www.brebook.com)

Andrew Wilson

Leaves from a Naturalist's Notebook

LEAVES

FROM

A NATURALIST'S NOTE-BOOK

BY

ANDREW WILSON, F.R.S.E. F.L.S. ETC.

AUTHOR OF "LEISURE-TIME STUDIES," ETC.

London

CHATTO AND WINDUS, PICCADILLY

1882

[The right of translation is reserved]

TO

P. S.

I DEDICATE THESE SKETCHES

IN

REMEMBRANCE OF

MANY PLEASANT HOURS OF FRIENDSHIP.

PREFACE.

THE present series of sketches has been compiled chiefly because of the existence of a growing taste on the part of the cultured public, for a knowledge of the objects in which the naturalist professes an interest. The papers, written under divers moods and circumstances, possess at least the merit of variety. I have not hesitated to include under the designation of a biologist's studies, such diverse topics as a diatribe against the unlawful practice of medicine, and a visit to the great emporium of wild zoology in the East End of London. Similarly, I have regarded as interesting enough in a general sense, and have accordingly included in this volume two papers on the aids which Science is prepared to give to the legal Nemesis in the pursuit of the criminal. If the book may be found capable of imparting in some degree a taste for higher natural history studies; or if it may succeed even in profitably whiling away the tedium of a lengthy journey, or an hour wherein there is "nothing to do," I shall feel that its highest aim has been fulfilled. In this light, I offer it respectfully to the great and appreciative audience of which that "patient omnivore" the "general reader" is the typical representative.

CONTENTS.

	PAGE
SCIENCE AND CRIME	1
LOST AND MISSING	22
IN SOME MEDICAL BY-WAYS	43
AT JAMRACH'S	64
JELLY-FISHES	71
THREADS AND THRUMS IN LOWER LIFE	96
WHALES AND THEIR NEIGHBOURS	118
FOOD AND FASTING	138
SCIENTIFIC GHOSTS	148
THE EARLIEST KNOWN LIFE-RELIC	159
SKATES AND RAYS	168
THE AUTOBIOGRAPHY OF A BARNACLE	176
LEAVES	187
THE AUTOBIOGRAPHY OF A FLY	194
ABOUT KANGAROOS	203
ON GIANTS	215
THE POLITY OF A POND	232

LEAVES

FROM

A NATURALIST'S NOTE-BOOK

SCIENCE AND CRIME.

THE scientific study of criminals, and the philosophic study of crimes, form not merely an interesting, but a highly warrantable exercise of intellect. Only through some such investigation into these subjects can a knowledge of the nature, cause, and cure of crime be attained—if, indeed, such knowledge in its perfect phases be ever reached in human history. And only when aided by the skilled expert—the chemist, surgeon, physiologist, or engraver—and by the deductions and inductions science is able or prepared to draw from any given set of circumstances, is justice enabled to enter upon the pursuit of crime, and to make her name a terror to evildoers. It is not our intention to follow, at present, such experimenters as Mr. Francis Galton in his remarkable researches into the conformation and configuration of the criminal head, amongst other types of human character. Readers interested in knowing what may be done in the way of a scientific study of character should peruse Mr. Galton's address to the Anthropological Section of the British Association for 1877. In that address will be found embodied some curious facts and inferences relative to the classification of groups and types of men, based on their habits of mind and physiognomy. Through the application of an ingenious method of observation, in which, by an arrangement of mirrors, four views of a person's head can be simultaneously photographed, the full and complete comparison of types of head-conformation can be effected. As the result of investigations conducted on this basis, Mr. Galton mentions that by physiognomy, together with the general contour of the head, a practical arrangement of criminal types becomes possible. Provided with a large number of photographs of criminals, and by familiarising himself with this collection, certain natural classes of criminals became discernible; and thus a scientific study of character may assist in the determination of the results of criminal tendencies, and, through these, towards the amelioration of the race.

Thus much for the part science promises to play in determining the causes of crime and criminals. With the results of crime, however, science at present concerns herself much more nearly; and it is with the ways and means science brings to bear on the detection of crime that we purpose chiefly to concern ourselves in the present paper. Our newspapers familiarise us, day by day, with instances of the application of scientific methods to criminal investigation. Not a case of forgery is tried but the expert in caligraphy and engraving is appealed to in order to aid the cause of justice, by the detection, through scientific means, of likenesses or differences in handwriting, or of alterations and erasures in disputed deeds or manuscripts. Every case of homicide brings its array of medical and surgical evidence, or its quota of chemists, prepared to do battle for the truth. Even the identification of a *corpus delicti* may be a matter in which medical science alone has absolute sway, and in which the skill of the medical jurist, with his testimony to the probable time and circumstances of death, may first point the way in which detective science should travel. A bloodstain, and its nature, when interpreted by the microscopist, may convict the suspected, or may, on the other hand, set him free. And, in many other ways and diverse fashions, the art of the detective may be shown to owe more to science than most people unacquainted with the routine of criminal investigation could readily imagine.

To select a simple case, and one, nevertheless, regarding which much popular misconception exists, let us try to discover the place and power of the microscope in medical jurisprudence. In such a study we may discover that certain powers, popularly imagined to be at the beck and call of the microscopist, are grossly exaggerated; whilst it may also be shown that the actual extent of the microscopist's ability fully outweighs the fallacies just alluded to. Chief among the cases in which the microscope becomes of paramount importance as an agent in the detection of crime, are those in which blood-stains, or marks of allied characters, and fragments of clothing or hairs, require to be examined and referred to their exact source. An actual case may be related by way of exemplifying the conditions demanding inquiry. A man was tried in 1857 at one of our English assizes for the supposed murder of a companion. The dead man's throat had been cut in such a fashion as to preclude the idea of suicide. The prisoner had been last seen in the company of the deceased, and in his possession a knife stained with blood was found. This knife was alleged by the prosecution to be that with which the murder was committed, and the stains thereupon were alleged to be those of human blood. The defence explained the presence of these stains by asserting that they were produced by cutting raw beef. Now, it may be asked, in what position is science placed in such an issue as the present? Could the chemist and microscopist, placed in the witness-box, swear to the identity of the stain with blood? and could either testify to its being human blood as distinguished from that of the ox? To the first query, an affirmative answer must be returned. Chemical tests of great delicacy are known whereby the presence of blood can be infallibly detected. Mr. Sorby tells us that spectrum analysis will reveal the presence of blood where the stain is only the tenth of an inch in diameter, or where a quantity of the red colouring matter of blood, not exceeding the one hundredth part of a grain, can be obtained. In so far as blood itself, and its mere presence is concerned, there are no scientific difficulties in the way of its exact determination and separation from all other red-coloured stains. But when we turn to the question of the exact source of the blood-stains, we find the powers of science to be limited in some degree. In the case just alluded to, in which the defence rested upon a statement that the blood-stains were obtained from beef, the fallacies of that description of evidence which grossly departs from a scientific standard were exemplified. A chemist gave evidence in which he alleged that the knife in question had been immersed in living blood to its hilt, and that the blood was certainly not that of the ox or sheep. This testimony was offered, despite the fact, known to every physiologist, that there exists no appreciable differences between the stain of living blood and of blood from a recently killed animal; and that the microscopist is as yet unable to detect differences between the blood of man and that of the ox or sheep sufficiently clear to enable him to decide their exact and specific nature. Even spectrum analysis, with all its subtlety of method and delicacy of research, cannot decide upon exact differences between new and old blood-stains; nor can it enable the experimenter to say if the blood be human or that of a lower animal. Fortunately for the cause of justice in the foregoing case, the crime was brought home to the prisoner by evidence other than that of the chemist in question, and by testimony which depended on no fallacies of microscopic testimony.

To discover the limitations of science in such a case, we must make ourselves familiar with the details of an elementary study in physiology. When a thin film of human blood is examined under a high power of the microscope, it is seen to present the appearance of a clear watery fluid—the "serum" or "plasma" of the physiologist—in which float an immense number of small round bodies, the blood corpuscles. These latter are of two kinds, red and white; the red being by far the more numerous, and imparting, through their immense numbers, the red hue to the blood. The red corpuscles of human blood are round and biconcave in form, each measuring from the one three-thousandth to the one four-thousandth of an inch in diameter. The white corpuscles are a little larger, and attain a diameter averaging the one two thousand five-hundredth part of an inch. Thus it may be safely asserted that when the microscopist is able to discern in any liquid those characteristic blood-globules, he may positively allege that the liquid in question is blood. When the further and equally important question of the kind of blood is submitted to the scientific observer, his answers must savour of caution. The red corpuscles of man, unlike the white, do not possess a central particle or nucleus. They are therefore in physiological language said to be "non-nucleated." But it is noteworthy that, in this latter feature, man's blood-globules agree with those of all other mammals or quadrupeds. Every quadruped, in short, possesses red blood-globules which want a central spot or nucleus. Moreover, all quadrupeds, except the camel tribe, possess red blood-globules of circular shape; those of the camel being elliptical in form. But when we descend in the animal scale and pass to the birds, as most nearly approaching quadrupeds, and from the birds to reptiles and fishes, the blood-globules are found, in these lower classes, to be not merely oval or elliptical in shape, but to be invariably nucleated—that is, possessing each a central particle.

With this zoological information at hand, we may be able to appreciate the power of the microscope as a detector of crime. In 1851, the defence, in a case of murder tried at the Essex Assizes, rested partly on the statement that the blood-stains on the clothes of the prisoner were derived from chicken's blood. In such a case the microscopic evidence is invaluable; since the blood of the bird will contain oval and nucleated globules. From an examination of these blood-stains the prisoner's statement in the case referred to was proved to be false, the corpuscles being those of some mammal. Similarly, when the late Professor Hughes Bennett, of Edinburgh, was confronted with a patient supposed to be troubled with chest-disease of serious type, an examination of the fluid blood supposed to have come from the lungs, revealed the presence of oval blood-globules. The patient's wonder may be better imagined than described, when her imposture was thus declared plain. Seeing, then, that the blood of quadrupeds is distinguishable from that of all other animals, the question yet remains, how far does microscopical evidence proceed in determining human blood from that of other mammals? Here, leaving aside the singular and exceptional case of the camels and their neighbours with oval but non-nucleated globules, the chief, and indeed the only, guide to the microscopist must be size. This guide, it may be further noticed, is by no means a certain or exact test; since even in one and the same animal the blood-globules may vary in dimensions. In some quadrupeds, it is true, the excessively minute nature of the globules would of itself form a feature distinguishing them from those of man. Thus the blood-corpuscles of the musk-deer measure the one twelve thousand three hundred and twenty-fifth part of an inch in diameter—such a size being infinitesimal when compared with those of man. When, however, we compare the blood of ordinary domestic animals with human blood, the difficulties in the way of exact determination increase in a very marked fashion. It is known as a fact that the blood-globules of the horse, ox, ass, mouse, cat, pig, and bat are nearly of the same size; the dimensions of the blood-globules bearing no reference to the size of the animal to which they belong.

The blood-globules which approach most nearly to those of man in size are found in the dog, rabbit and hare. Supposing, therefore, that in a case of suspected murder a blood-stain were declared to be that of a dog, he would be a worse than foolish scientist who would even venture to hazard his reputation by stating in a witness-box his ability to distinguish the stain as that of human blood. Cases in illustration of the foregoing facts are abundantly met with in the records of criminal jurisprudence. A medical witness, giving evidence some years ago at an English assizes in a case of suspected homicide, was sharply rebuked by the presiding judge for the enunciation of speculative niceties regarding blood; and in no eyes does such a witness seem more foolish than in those of scientific men, who know best the fallible ground on which he is treading. In another case a scientific witness alleged his ability to distinguish certain stains as those of horse's blood, and others as those of human blood—such evidence being inadmissible on scientific grounds, and being therefore morally and legally wrong.

The power and value of the microscope as an aid to the discovery of the truth in criminal cases is, however, by no means limited to the determination of blood-stains. On weapons alleged to have been used with homicidal intent or effect, the merest traces of various substances may occasionally be found, and may serve in the hands of the man of science as important clues. A Dr. Lyons has left on record a case, in which the supposition of a person's guilt as a murderer appeared to be materially strengthened by the discovery, beneath a bed, of a hatchet to which clotted blood and hairs were adherent. The hair, submitted to microscopical examination, was discovered to belong to some animal; and this fact helped to turn the tide of evidence in favour of the accused; although had this case occurred before the day of the microscope and its use in medicine, it is not difficult to predict what would have been the result of the trial in question. Cotton fibres, proved by microscopical research to be such, served as a link in the chain of evidence adduced against a prisoner tried for homicide at an Essex Assizes in 1852. On the boots of another man charged with a like crime at Maidstone in 1863, Doctors Taylor and Pavy discovered some hairs corresponding with those taken from the head of the deceased, who had been fatally assaulted by kicking; whilst some red woollen fibres also found on the boots of the accused corresponded with those of a woollen comforter with which the deceased had been provided. So also in a case of much mystery, in which a young woman was found brutally murdered, a knife which had been placed in the hand of the deceased—presumably for the purpose of simulating death by suicide—bore on its blade amidst a small blood-clot a number of woollen fibres of a peculiar hue. These fibres exactly corresponded with those of a woollen jacket worn by the accused, who was convicted, and duly confessed his crime. Such examples certainly serve to show the exceeding importance in medical jurisprudence of the veriest trifles, and to demonstrate how the most insignificant clues may, when welded into the chain of circumstances, literally form "confirmations strong as proofs of holy writ." By aid of the microscope, linen fibres may be distinguished from those of cotton, and both from those of wool; whilst marked differences are observable in the hairs of different animals.

Shreds and patches may thus literally piece out evidence of importance for or against an accused person. And not less clearly is this fact shown when the trifling details on which grave discoveries often hinge are illustrated. One Sellis, who had attacked the Duke of Cumberland, thereafter destroyed himself. Sellis committed suicide by cut-throat, and on the left side of the bed on which he was found a razor was laid. This otherwise suspicious circumstance, which laid the late Duke of Cumberland under some suspicion in 1810, was clearly explained when Sellis was proved to be equally dexterous in the use of both hands. A man was found dead in 1865 in London under similar circumstances to Sellis, the left hand having been used to inflict the fatal injury. The unusual situation of the wound was explained when the deceased was proved to be a woodcarver by trade, and to have been accustomed to use both hands when at work. A singular and shrewd observation of Sir Astley Cooper's was the means of detecting a criminal of no ordinary type. A Mr. Blight, of Deptford, was fatally wounded by a pistol-shot in 1806, and Sir Astley was called in to see the sufferer. Proceeding to the scene of the assault, Sir Astley, from an examination of the locality and the position of the wounded man, together with the situation of the wound, came to the conclusion that the assassin must have been a left-handed man. A Mr. Patch answered to the latter description. He was near the locality at the time of the murder, and, hitherto unsuspected, he was arrested. On being asked to hold up his hand to plead to the indictment, Patch at once raised his left hand. He was tried and convicted for the offence, fully confessing his guilt before his execution.

The case of Bolam, who was tried at the Newcastle Summer Assizes in 1839 for the murder of a man named Millie, presents some features worthy of note as showing the difficulties against which the medical jurist may have to contend. The circumstances of the case were altogether of a peculiar kind. Millie was killed by direct violence done to the head, and, when discovered, Bolam was found lying close by in a state of insensibility, real or pretended, whilst the apartment in which both were found had been set on fire. Bolam stated that he had been attacked by some person, and had been knocked down by a blow on the head. Attempting to escape, he was again thrown to the ground, and then became aware of an attempt being made to cut his throat, although by his own showing he did not use his hands to prevent the injury, and no wounds or cuts were found upon his hands. The only injury Bolam appeared to have sustained was a wound on the left side of the neck, but this wound was neither considerable in extent nor in depth; it had involved no deep tissue, and had caused but little bleeding. His coat and other garments were cut in many places, but the incisions were entirely unrepresented upon his body. The case really turned upon the nature of these injuries, and the solution of their infliction. If they were likely to have been inflicted by a third person, then this third party might have also murdered Millie. If Bolam were the self-inflictor of these wounds, the theory of the prosecution that they had been caused with the view of screening his own crime became, on the other hand, highly probable. The scientific evidence, aided by a full consideration of all the circumstances of this case, was given decidedly against the prisoner. The case terminated in a verdict of manslaughter against Bolam, who was accordingly sentenced for that crime. Equally interesting, as showing the complex nature of the cases which await solution, and of the occasionally simple fashion in which such solution may dawn upon the investigators, is an instance related as having occurred at Nottingham in 1872. In this case a young man preferred a charge of assault and wounding against a person whose motives for committing such an offence were undiscoverable. As evidence the prosecutor submitted his wounded arm, his coat, and his shirt-sleeve. He showed that they had indeed been cut, but a more careful examination revealed the interesting fact that the lining of the coat-sleeve was intact. No clearer proof was required to show that the charge was false, and the accused person was at once liberated.

No more interesting details in the annals of criminal science can be presented than those which bear upon cases in which the evidence for suicide, as against homicide, has to be weighed and determined. Allusion has already been made to cases, such as those of Sellis and the wood-carver, in which a knowledge of the peculiarities of the deceased served to explain the cause of death. An historical instance, illustrating this phase of our subject, is that of the Prince of Condé, whose death occurred in 1830. On the 27th of August in that year, the prince was found dead in his bedroom under somewhat unusual, and it may be added suspicious, circumstances. The body was suspended from the window sash by a linen handkerchief, which was in turn attached to a cravat round the neck of the deceased. An important feature in this case, and one which certainly lent an air of mystery thereto, was found in the fact that the toes of both feet rested on the ground, the heels being elevated, and the knees bent forward. A chair stood near the deceased, and the only marks of violence discernible were a few slight abrasions on the lower limbs; such, indeed, as might have been produced by contact with the chair. It may be added, that the handkerchief was attached to the window at a height of about six and a half feet above the floor. The discovery of the manner of death, added to the circumstances attending the decease, gave rise to uncomfortable suspicion that the case was one of murder. Living in unsettled times, it was contended that the prince had been killed by assassins, and that his body had been placed in the position in which it was found in order to suggest suicide by hanging as the cause of death. The abrasions on the limbs, certain peculiarities attending the mark left by the ligature on the neck, and the fact that the feet of deceased rested on the floor, were urged as so many facts supporting the theory of homicide. Certain other circumstances, such as a want of power in one arm, and the fact that the handkerchiefs were tied in knots of a complicated character, were duly urged in support of the latter view. But the experience of medical science gave powerful support to the opposite conjecture—that of suicide. Every medical jurist can point to cases of suicide by hanging, in which the mere position of the body at first appears strongly suggestive of its having been placed in that position with a view of simulating self-destruction. So far from persons suspending themselves in a free posture in such an act of suicide, it is comparatively rare to find their bodies in other positions than those from which it would appear they could have readily released themselves. Persons have been found dead almost in a sitting posture, and suspended in a position which at first sight would seem strongly to invalidate the theory of suicide. A man has been known to commit suicide by hanging himself from a hook in the top of a tent bedstead, being found with his knees well-nigh resting on the bed; and one hospital patient was actually discovered resting on his knees by the side of his bed, having hanged himself from the top of the bedstead. It is, in fact, exceedingly rare to find the suicide imbued with sufficient determination to take a leap into space; and the explanation of the readiness with which death may take place under these seemingly unfavourable circumstances may be held to rest on the fact that suspension in any position in which the weight of the body is gently thrown on the neck, induces at first a state of insensibility, which, as it gradually deepens, causes increased pressure on the windpipe, and consequent death. In some few cases, the suspicious elements in the cases before us have been strengthened by the observation that the limbs of the deceased persons have been found to be firmly secured. Not merely may the hands be secured in a case of veritable suicide, but the weight of the body may actually be intentionally increased (as was found in a case of suicide occurring in 1844 at Worcester) by the attachment of a couple of flat irons to the wrist! Thus much for the curiosities of suicide; and when it is added that the blind have been known to destroy their own lives, and that the act of suicide has been perpetrated by a boy of nine, and by a man of ninety-seven years of age, as representing opposite extremes, little is wanting to invest the subject with more than ordinary interest in the eyes of the psychologist.

Passing somewhat from the domain of actual crime, we may find an interesting study in the details of cases relating to the "presumption of death," and to questions of "survivorship." Both subjects present some of the gravest puzzles of both science and law. In the quiet course of ordinary existence it seems hardly possible that even the "presumption" of death should require to be legally established. But the romance of life teems with tales stranger even than that of Enoch Arden, and which show that the possibilities of a person's decease may require to be duly argued and decided upon by our courts of law. "The fact of death," says that eminent authority on medical law, Dr. Alfred S. Taylor, "may be proved by presumptive, as well as by direct evidence." Thus the question of decease may fall to be determined by a jury; and when the *corpus delicti* is not forthcoming, as in all cases of the kind referred to, "the legal presumption" is in favour of life, and the burden of proof rests on the plaintiff's case.

As most readers are aware, seven years' unexplained absence from home and friends constitutes the period at the expiry of which the presumption of death may legally be inquired into. With the caution which everywhere marks the footsteps of legal procedure, an English court once held itself incompetent to pronounce judgment confirming the presumption of death in a case in which a woman had left her father's house in 1810, and had not, for a period of thirty-four years, been seen or accounted for; and, according to Best, in his "Presumptions of Law and Fact," the Court of Queen's Bench held that it could not assume "judicially" that a person who was alive in the year 1034 was dead in the year 1827! From which statement, the non-legal mind may reasonably enough regard the "judicial" faculty as decidedly opposed both to the logical and scientific. In the suit of Church *versus* Smith, tried in London in 1853, the husband of the plaintiff was proved to have been unheard of for twelve years, and the question for decision was whether she could sue, as a widow, in her own right. The husband, however, ultimately appeared in the witness-box; but the presiding judge remarked to the jury that in the face of the twelve years' absence, he should have directed them, but for the sudden appearance of the missing spouse, to return a verdict for the plaintiff, on the presumption that her husband was dead. Missing husbands thus occasionally crop up under awkward circumstances. Four months after marriage a husband deserted his wife, and disappeared for seven years; the woman meanwhile contracting another marriage in her maiden name. She was indicted for bigamy and convicted, but her conviction was quashed on appeal. In another case, an application for probate was made to the Probate Court in 1858, by the relatives of a ship-captain who had sailed from Southampton in December, 1856; arrived in Calcutta in October, 1858; and thence sailed for Port Louis, but had never reached his destination. Here the presumption of death was strong enough to cause the Court to grant probate of the will, although a modern Robinson Crusoe or Alexander Selkirk would naturally feel rather chagrined at the course of events, on a possible return home after rescue from enforced residence abroad as a castaway.

The subject of "presumption of death" may, in some cases, join issue with the criminal side of character. A curious and somewhat mysterious case in point was tried in London. A man had insured his life against accident for a sum of two hundred and fifty pounds on the 6th of September, 1856. This person was single, and was aged twenty-six. A week after insuring his life, he took a return ticket to Brighton; leaving London on Saturday, September 13th, 1856, by an evening train. The succeeding Sunday and Monday were spent in the company of his friends. He bathed in the sea on the morning of Monday (the 15th), and in the evening intended to return to London, announcing, however, to his friends, when he left at seven p.m., his intention of again bathing before his departure. He was traced to the sea-beach, but was not again seen alive. A suit of clothes was found on the steps of a bathing-machine, the owner of the garments being missing. The police could discover no clue to the identity of the owner, save a purse containing part of a return ticket. Ultimately, the clothes were identified as those of the intending bather, who was duly searched for and advertised for, but without success. Forty-five days after his disappearance, and on the 30th of October, a dead body, completely divested of clothing, was found on the beach at Walton-on-the-Naze, in Essex, situated about one hundred and sixty miles from Brighton. The evidence of medical men showed that the body had been in the water from six to seven weeks. The features were unrecognisable, but a brother of the missing man maintained that, to the best of his belief, the body was that of the bather who had disappeared from Brighton on the 15th of September. The brother accordingly entered an action against the insurance company, who had refused payment of the policy on the ground of want of identification; and the defence also rested upon the assumption that the assured person was alive, and that, in short, the report of his death was merely a ruse to obtain money from the insurance office. The alleged deceased, it was proved, had been declared bankrupt in 1855, and he had further effected in 1856 insurances in different offices. His will ordered that the money due under the policies should be applied to the discharge of his debts. In such a case the conflicting features of the evidence, and the uncertainty of identification, resulted in the disagreement of the jury and in their consequent discharge. Clearer in all its details was the case of Vibal Douat, a Bordeaux merchant, who insured his life in Paris for one hundred thousand francs, and was shortly thereafter declared a fraudulent bankrupt. Douat next disappeared suddenly, and his wife lodged in Paris a certificate of the death and burial of her husband in England, and claimed the payment of his policy of insurance. That the case was one of fraud, however, was clearly proved. Douat had actually ordered his own coffin, had registered his own death, and had actually attended his own funeral—or rather that of the mass of lead which was found to be enclosed in the coffin. He was arrested, and, in due course, convicted of the fraud.

The subject of "survivorship," in its obvious and important relations determining succession to property, presents us with features no less remarkable than those involved in the preceding topic. Some dread calamity overwhelms, it may be, an entire family circle, and it may be left to science to decide from the circumstances of the case which member probably survived the others. Such a case came before the Rolls Court in London in 1854. The circumstances of the suit in question are given by Dr. Taylor as follows. A Mr. Underwood, aged forty-three, and his wife, aged forty, being about to sail for Australia, and being each entitled to certain property, made their wills before their embarkation. By these wills each testator gave to the other, absolutely, the whole property he and she possessed respectively. Each will also declared that "if the one to whom the same was given should die in the lifetime of the donor," the property should be divided among their three children on the latter attaining their majority. It must be mentioned that the family of the testators included three children—two sons, aged fifteen and thirteen respectively, and a daughter, aged eighteen. In case all of the children died before reaching the age of twenty-one years, the wills directed that a mutual friend, a Mr. Wing, should receive the entire property. The parents and children embarked on board the ill-fated ship *Dalhousie*, which sailed from London on October 13th, 1853, and which foundered off Beachy Head. Only one survivor, a seaman named Read, escaped; his testimony showing that the ship foundered on the morning of October 19th, 1853, lay on her beam-ends for about twenty minutes, and finally disappeared in the deep. After the ship lay over, the Underwoods, with the exception of the girl, escaped through the cabin window and clung to the side of the vessel, but whilst in this position a heavy sea swept them from their hold, and Read declared that they must have perished thereafter. Not a single trace of them was found. But an important addendum to this information was contributed by Read, who said that not only did the daughter appear on the deck after her parents and brothers had been swept away, but also that he had lashed her to a spar and cast her adrift as her sole hope of safety. He stated also that he saw Miss Underwood alive in the sea lashed to the spar. Mr. Underwood, it may be added, was described as a tall man of powerful build, and his wife as of small stature and of delicate constitution.

The suit before the Rolls Court turned on the question which of the testators—husband or wife—survived the other? The testimony of Read established the fact that the daughter had unquestionably survived her relatives. The Master of the Rolls inclined to believe that death was simultaneous in the case of the parents and brothers, and the result of his decision was that the property must pass to the next of kin of the daughter. Mr. Wing, the mutual friend who was entitled to succeed, had thus no claim, owing to the simultaneous death of the testators, and judgment was accordingly given for the plaintiff Underwood as next of kin.

The case was taken on appeal to the Lord Chancellor's Court, and was finally carried to the House of Lords. Medical evidence was now sought to substantiate the appellant's case. All the children having died under the age of twenty-one years, the case of the daughter's survival was not made a part of the pleadings. The question submitted for consideration to the medical experts related to the probabilities of the husband having survived the wife, it might be even for a very brief period of time. As the stronger of the two, the appellant contended Mr. Underwood should be held to have survived his wife, in which case Mr. Wing would claim the property of deceased under the terms of the will. Even if the latter had survived her husband—the more unlikely alternative—Mr. Wing would in that case also gain his case. Medical and physiological evidence went to show that, in face of the facts that Mr. Underwood was known to be a good swimmer, and that he was a strong and powerfully-built man, the probability was that he survived his wife. The difference in age, sex, and strength, said the experts, rendered it highly improbable that death by drowning or asphyxia, depending on cessation of the heart's action amongst other things, would take place exactly at the same moment, and in this view the more robust subject would therefore in all probability be the longest liver. The medical testimony was therefore in favour of Wing. Upon technical grounds the Lord Chancellor, in February, 1855, affirmed the judgment of the Master of the Rolls, and the House of Lords confirmed these decisions, one of the judges dissenting. Dr. Taylor's remarks upon this case are so apt and interesting that they may bear quotation by way of commentary on this singular case. This authority remarks: "The difficulty was created by the legal rule which threw the onus of proof on the claimant (Wing) under the two wills. The case of the next of kin, who was not mentioned in the will, was that the husband and wife died at the same instant of time; but this was a physiological impossibility; and had the proof of this been thrown upon the plaintiff (Underwood) the case must have failed. The contention of the defendant was that the testator and testatrix could not have died at the same instant. This negative proposition could not of course be proved by direct evidence; it simply became a medical inference; but when the law declares that in the absence of evidence the property shall go in the same way as if the parties had expired at the same instant—*i.e.* as if they had died intestate—this is deciding such questions by a rule which is as arbitrary in its operation as that of the Code Napoleon. In Underwood *versus* Wing," concludes Dr. Taylor, "this rule of law practically affirmed that an event took place which was physiologically impossible, and upon that event the wills of husband and wife were set aside, and the property was handed to one whose name was intentionally excluded from the wills of both."

An analogous case, tried in November, 1856, in the Rolls Court, presents the melancholy interest of having arisen out of the untoward fate of Sir John Franklin's expedition to the Polar Seas in 1845. The issue depended upon the determination of the survivorship of a father (James Couch) or son (Edward Couch). It was not disputed that the father died at home, in January, 1850. Edward Couch went as mate of the *Erebus* in August, 1845, and it had to be determined whether Edward had pre-deceased his father, or had survived him. Dr. Rae deposed that in 1854 some Esquimaux informed him that in April or May, 1850, a party of white men were seen dragging a boat across the ice, and that these men killed birds which were never found in those regions before the month of May. Of course, no evidence was at hand to show that Edward Couch was one of these survivors of 1850; but the law in this case declared for the probability of the son's survival; this course being adopted with a view to avoid further litigation.

A somewhat notorious case occurred in London, in 1870, which gave rise to the question of survivorship, complicated with the additional interest of criminal procedure. A person named Huelin had made a bequest to his housekeeper, with whom he lived at Brompton. In May, 1870, both were murdered by a man named Millar, who was tried for the crime. The body of Huelin was buried by way of concealment; that of the woman was packed by the prisoner in a box, which he requested a carrier to rope and cord. During the performance of his task, the carrier noticed that blood was oozing from the box, and this circumstance excited suspicion and led to the discovery of the crime. In 1871, a suit was raised to decide the disposal of Huelin's belongings. If the housekeeper were proved to have survived the master, then the bequest to her would take effect; whilst, assuming the opposite view, the heirs of Huelin would claim the entire property. Here medical evidence assisted the decision of the Vice-Chancellor's Court, by declaring that the signs of death were more recent in the case of the woman than in that of Huelin; and circumstantial evidence lent its aid towards substantiating that of the experts. The court decided in favour of the heirs of the unfortunate housekeeper. A case has also been related in which, during a quarrel between husband and wife, the latter, in an ungovernable passion, rushed from the house across a lawn and flung herself into a pond. Her husband tried to rescue her, but both were drowned. Evidence failed to elicit any satisfactory details regarding the priority of death, and the suit which had been entered into was compromised accordingly.

Little need exists for expatiation on the curious nature of such studies in 'the shady paths of life, or on the singular blending of fact and romance in certain phases of human existence. But one idea may be fairly expressed by way of conclusion: namely, that science and law together, whilst often achieving veritable triumphs in the patient pursuit and discovery of the truth, are yet unable to save humanity from one of its worst enemies—its contorted and debased self.

LOST AND MISSING.

Amongst the many curious phases of human existence, none are invested with a greater degree of interest than those which relate to the occasional disappearance of society's units, and which deal with the circumstances attending their absence from the circle or sphere in which they have lived and moved. Statisticians tell us that a surprising number of individuals disappear mysteriously each year from the circle of their acquaintance; and police records similarly inform us of the large proportion of such cases in which no clue is obtained to the whereabouts or existence of missing men and women. Indeed, from all accounts it seems a tolerably easy matter to get lost beyond recognition or finding; and the annals of detective science are no better prepared with an answer to the query about missing persons than ordinary society would be to reply to the familiar question, "What becomes of the pins?" It will be understood that we are referring to those cases of inexplicable disappearance in which no adequate reason can be assigned, in the first instance at any rate, for the mystery of absence. True, as we shall presently note, this mystery may be explained in the plainest but saddest fashion by the discovery of the missing body; although, as the sequel will show, the records of medical jurisprudence teem with examples wherein the identity of the lost individual becomes a matter of the gravest doubt and uncertainty. And thus we note that amongst the unwonted phases of human life there stand forth prominently those in which, first, a case of disappearance gives rise to the vain search or to the discovery of the missing body, and in which, secondly, science appears to assist in the work of identification—this latter being in many cases a difficult and sometimes a hopeless labour, impeded, as we shall see, by the grim and even ludicrous force of circumstances. The well-worn adage that "truth is stranger than fiction" finds nowhere a better illustration than in the histories stored up in the note-book of the medical jurist. And the notice-boards of a police-station may in their own way furnish the imagination with a more fertile field than has yet been encompassed by the most facile pen of a Hugo or a Sue.

Allusion has just been made to the difficulty experienced in the work of identification, even by the most intimate relations and friends of the missing person. Many examples of this difficulty may be cited; the indefinite nature of the task arising probably as much from the alteration in appearance produced by the "chilly hand" which sets the features in repose, as from any other cause. The lapse of a few hours after death may effect grave change in the cast or *pose* of the human face, as every doctor knows; and police authorities who have to do with the identification of the dead as well as of the living are accustomed to receive with justifiable care and caution the statements made by most persons in cases of disputed identity.

A comparatively short time ago an instance of this fact was afforded in a northern city. The body of a woman of dissolute habits was found under circumstances which rendered the theory of her having been murdered an extremely probable hypothesis. The question naturally arose as to the name and identity of the victim. Several persons were found ready to declare that the body in question was no other than that of M. N., with whom they had daily associated. Interrogated closely upon this point, they still adhered to the exact statement they had made; and their opinion was supported by at least one fact, namely, that M. N. had not been seen in her usual haunts for some days prior to the discovery of the body. Identification in this case seemed to be little short of a certainty, when it occurred to a shrewd police-officer to make assurance doubly sure by visiting the city prison, with the view of ascertaining whether the person in question might not be incarcerated within its walls. His search was duly rewarded by the discovery that M. N. was there undergoing a short term of imprisonment, ignorant of the circumstances under which, like some notabilities of our day, she was credited with being "with the majority" whilst still alive and well. A suggestion gravely made in connection with this case, that the body was that of a certain person A. B., was indignantly refuted by A. B. herself walking into the police-station and confronting her anxious friends.

But the apparent impossibility of identifying even near relations may be aptly illustrated by a reference to a case decided in the Vice-Chancellor's Court so recently as 1866. This latter was a suit in which the plaintiffs, Holliss, wished to establish the death of a person named William Turner. Turner was last seen alive on the 7th of May, 1865, when he was entertained at Guildford. He then presented an emaciated appearance; his mind was unsettled and weak; he was unshaven and suffering from boils and sores, which were dressed at the last-named place. On the 17th of May a drowned body was found in the river Wey, and at the inquest, which was summoned on the 17th, two men named Etherington swore to the corpse as that of their father, who was missing at the period in question. The friends who had entertained Turner at Guildford, on the other hand, declared their belief that the body was that of William Turner; but it was nevertheless duly interred as that of Philip Etherington. On the neck of the drowned man a coloured neckerchief was found; this article assisting in the ultimate identification of the body, which was effected some months afterwards, on Philip Etherington, the supposed drowned subject, walking into his daughter's house. The question who was the drowned man was then revived. The proofs were clearly brought out at last. William Turner had left behind him at Guildford a fragment of a handkerchief; this fragment being found to correspond exactly with the article removed from the neck of the drowned body, and the fact that the sores of William Turner had been dressed at Guildford, recalled to mind the fact that similar traces of disease were discernible on the drowned man. To the Vice-Chancellor's mind the chain of evidence was complete and satisfactory, and judgment was given establishing the identity of William Turner and the drowned man. Yet the two sons of Etherington were positive as to the identity of the body with their father, who in his turn must have remained utterly ignorant, during his absence from home, concerning the quandary into which that absence had led his friends and others.

The medical jurist would inform us that the common notion that the human body rapidly decomposes in water is contrary to fact. Especially in winter, and if the body remains below the surface, are the structures well preserved. Identification may therefore be tolerably easy, when otherwise free from embarrassing circumstances, in cases of drowning taking place in winter, and even after some weeks have elapsed. It may also, in some cases, be of positive importance, either as an aid to identification, or for other purposes, to fix accurately the date of the death of an individual. Such a case was tried at the Warwick Assizes in 1805, where a suit was entered by the relatives of a drowned man to annul a commission of bankruptcy on the ground that, being already drowned when the commission was issued, it was void in law, and the creditors would therefore have no power to seize the property of the deceased. The drowned man was last seen alive on the 3rd of November; the commission was taken out a few days after this date, and on the 12th of December his body was discovered in a river. Five weeks and four days had therefore elapsed between his departure from home and the discovery of the body. No doubt was cast upon the identification in this case, and the question before the court turned upon the date of death by drowning. How could the date be fixed? Nature in this case afforded a means of at least approximating to the date in question. As part of the chemical changes which the human body undergoes in the course of its decomposition in water or in damp soil, a peculiar substance called *adipocere* is formed. This substance is, in fact, a kind of soap, ascertained to result from the union of the fatty acids of the body with the ammonia also derived therefrom; and when thus converted into adipocere the body may retain its condition for lengthened periods of time. The Warwickshire case of the drowned bankrupt exhibited in part the chemical changes resulting in the production of adipocere, and the natural question, "How long does this substance take to form?" came to be raised. Medical evidence adduced at the trial tended to show that a period of about six weeks was, at the very least, necessary for the production of adipocere, whilst a very much longer period was required, as a rule. This evidence tended naturally to cause the jury to extend as far as possible, and as far as was consistent with facts, the time the body had lain in the water; an opinion which led to a verdict for the plaintiff, carrying with it the statement that deceased must have been dead during the whole period of nearly six weeks.

Perhaps no chapter in the grim romance of life presents events of more fascinating and mysterious kind than that containing the records of scientific speculation regarding the nature of human remains, which are occasionally brought to light as the first, and it may be the only, witnesses of a grave crime. Here science and the criminal officer go hand-in-hand to ferret out the dead secrets of crime, often with an ingenuity worthy a Vidocq, and with the calculating mind and balancing theories of a Poe. Nor is the mysterious in crime unrelieved by touches of humour, and sometimes of even ludicrous perplexity. In 1838 the authorities at the Mansion House were concerned over the supposed discovery of a human hand in a City dust-bin—the sad relic of humanity proving, after medical examination, to be merely the fin of a turtle, which had doubtless perished in a manner well understood in the halls of judicial examination. The thigh-bone of a horse or ox has, ere now, also formed the subject of grave inquiry, until the doubts of law and justice were duly solved by an appeal to the comparative anatomist.

More astounding, because absolutely true, and in the highest degree perplexing as illustrating the curious and remarkable coincidences of human life, are cases in which a confusion of identity, and even of name, may assist in blindfolding justice in the most singular and bewildering fashion. In December, 1831, a woman named Elizabeth Ross was tried at the Old Bailey for the murder of an Irishwoman named Caroline Walsh. After much solicitation on the part of Ross and her husband, Walsh had consented to live with them, and, on the evening of the 19th of August, 1831, the deceased went to the residence of Ross in Goodman's Fields, taking with her as her belongings, a bed and a basket. The latter contained the tapes and other odds and ends which Walsh was accustomed to sell by way of earning a scanty livelihood. All traces of Caroline Walsh disappeared on the evening of the 19th of August. When Ross was interrogated respecting her visitor and lodger, she at first replied in an unsatisfactory fashion; but ultimately stated that Walsh had left her house on the 19th, and that nothing had been heard of her lodger since. Circumstances, however, came to the knowledge of the police, which resulted in Ross being duly arraigned for the murder of Caroline Walsh, and it was proved by the testimony of Ross's son that his mother had suffocated Walsh on the evening of the 19th of August, and had disposed of her body for anatomical purposes.

Now appears, however, a most singular element in the case. On the evening of the 20th of August an old woman, giving her name as Caroline Welsh, was found lying in the neighbourhood of Goodman's Fields in a state of squalor and filth, and was duly conveyed to the London Hospital. There it was discovered that she had sustained a fracture of the hip, and after a few days' residence in the hospital the patient died and was duly interred. At the trial it was argued on behalf of Ross that the Caroline Welsh of the London Hospital was in reality her late lodger; and hence it became important to settle the marvellous identity which had thus arisen between the missing lodger and the hospital patient. The former, as has been stated, was an Irishwoman; but so also was Caroline Welsh. It was found out, however, that Caroline Walsh came from Kilkenny, whilst the hospital patient hailed from Waterford.

This first point of difference was speedily followed by the discovery of other distinctions fatal to the prisoner's case. Caroline Walsh was described as being about eighty-four years of age, tall, of a pale complexion, and had gray hair. Caroline

Welsh, who died in hospital, was about sixty years of age; she was also tall, but was of dark complexion. Further, Caroline Walsh was cleanly in person, and exhibited no defect in physical conformation. Caroline Welsh was dirty and emaciated, and her feet were so covered with corns and bunions as to present the appearance of being deformed. In dress, however, the two women were very much alike; and more curious still, both possessed baskets of similar make, that of Welsh having a cover, which the basket of Walsh wanted.

It may be said that, with the evidence as to the difference between the women in question, and with positive evidence as to the death of Walsh, little doubt could have existed as to the identity of each. But the confused identity of name, dress, and occupation was effectually set at rest by one remarkable observation, namely, that Caroline Walsh, the murdered woman, was known to possess very perfect front teeth; a fact sufficiently remarkable in a woman of her age to attract the attention even of unscientific observers. Now, Caroline Welsh was found to possess no front teeth, and the medical evidence given at the trial proved that the sockets of the front teeth had been obliterated in the hospital patient for a very lengthened period. This latter difference between Caroline Walsh and Caroline Welsh was too typical to be combated by the ingenuity of counsel or by the circumstances which favoured the prisoner's defence; and Elizabeth Ross was found guilty, and duly executed for her crime. It formed a notable fact of this inquiry, that the body of Caroline Walsh was never discovered, although the London dissecting-rooms were duly searched. But the case against Ross was rendered the more conclusive when the grand-daughters of Caroline Walsh, on being shown the remains of Welsh, distinctly alleged that the body was not that of their relative.

The difficulty of exactly identifying the remains of a particular person after mutilation has been added to the crime of murder, has unfortunately been more than once fully illustrated by some of the most prominent crimes of recent years. Several historical instances exist, all unfamiliar to the present generation, in which the triumph of science over crime has been signally illustrated. The case of Eugene Aram has formed subject-matter for poem and story, it is true; but the exact details of the crime for which Aram suffered are by no means perfectly or generally understood. Aram was born at Ramsgill, Yorkshire, in 1704. Settling at Knaresborough as a schoolmaster, he became acquainted with Daniel Clark, a shoemaker, who was possessed of certain valuables, and who was alleged to have been murdered by Aram and another. Clark disappeared in February 1745, and Aram was shortly thereafter arrested on suspicion of having been concerned in his disappearance, but was acquitted from want of evidence. Eventually, Aram became usher at Lynn Academy, Norfolk, and whilst there engaged, his accomplice confessed that certain bones discovered in a cave near Knaresborough in 1758 were those of Daniel Clark. Aram was brought to trial at York in 1759. In his elaborate defence he laid great stress on the difficulties besetting the identification of human remains after such an interval as had elapsed since Clark's death. His pleas in defence were founded on the alleged impossibility of determining the exact nature, sex, and other particulars regarding a skeleton after the lapse of many years. The fracture of the temporal bone found in the skeleton proved nothing; for was it not probable that the cave may have been a place of burial in olden times, and that the injury might have been produced after death in the spoliation to which graves were frequently subjected? These and like pleas Aram urged in his defence with singular ability; but the confession of his accomplice and the facts of the case overruled his pleas, and he was found guilty and executed, having previously confessed his crime; whilst with strange philosophy he wrote a defence of suicide, and endeavoured practically to defeat justice by carrying his theories into effect.

Two very marked cases in which the lost and missing were the subjects of legal and scientific examination have occurred within the memory of every reader of middle age. These cases are the Parkman tragedy of America and the famous Waterloo Bridge murder amongst ourselves. Both cases illustrate very typically not merely the difficulties which beset the question of identification, but also the aid which science may afford in deciding the fate of the lost and missing.

Dr. Parkman, a Boston (U.S.) physician of standing, was traced, on the 23rd of November, 1849, to the laboratory of a Professor Webster, a lecturer on chemistry, of that city. Thereafter all traces of Dr. Parkman were lost, and the excitement regarding his fate became intense. It would appear that certain pecuniary transactions had taken place between the two persons just named, that Webster was considerably in Parkman's debt, and was, moreover, in embarrassed circumstances. On Webster's laboratory and its precincts being searched, the haunch-bones, the right thigh, and the left leg of a human body were discovered. Associated with these remains were several laboratory towels bearing Webster's name. In the refuse and slag of a chemical furnace were found fragments of bones of the skull and of the spine-bones, along with the blocks of artificial teeth and a little melted gold. A further search in the laboratory brought to light a tea-chest in which, disposed among tan, and covered over with mineral matters, the trunk of a human body along with the left thigh were contained. These latter parts and the parts previously discovered were found to belong to one and the same body. Pieced together, these relics showed that they formed part of a body of which the head, arms and hands, both feet, and the right leg from the knee to the ankle were missing, but which at the same time corresponded with the frame of the missing man in every particular. Dr. Parkman, at the time of his disappearance, was sixty years of age. The examination of the skeleton pointed to its being the remains of a man of about the age referred to. Parkman's height was 5 ft. 11 in., and the skeleton pieced out and proportionately measured was found to indicate a height of 5 ft. 10½ in. In these points, therefore, the identity of the remains seemed to be clearly shown. But, as in the case of Caroline Walsh, there were special points in Dr. Parkman's case which served to place the identification well-nigh beyond a doubt. It was quite evident that an attempt to destroy the head by fire had not only been made, but had well-nigh succeeded. The evidence of Dr. Keep, the missing man's dentist, came to the rescue in a very remarkable fashion, after an examination of the remains of the artificial teeth which had escaped the action of Webster's furnace. Keep's evidence was, that four years before the disappearance of Dr. Parkman he fitted artificial teeth in blocks for that gentleman in both upper and lower jaws. The dentist could also speak with certainty to seeing these teeth in Dr. Parkman's mouth about a fortnight before his disappearance, when he had fitted the teeth with a new spring. The artificial teeth rescued from Webster's furnace were sworn to by Keep as those he had made for Dr. Parkman from their fitting the moulds in which the teeth of the latter had been made, and from peculiarities of make. The left side of the lower jaw of Dr. Parkman exhibited a certain irregularity, which was recognised by Keep in the form of the gold plates recovered from the furnace of Webster. Other circumstances combined to weave the evidence strongly around the latter as the perpetrator of a heinous crime. That the remains had not been used for anatomical purposes was abundantly proven by medical evidence; and that murder had been committed was evident from an examination of the chest, which revealed a wound on the left side. Webster was duly convicted by a chain of circumstantial evidence of the most complete kind, and was executed. As an eminent authority in matters medico-legal has remarked on the Parkman tragedy, even the refinements and appliances of science may fail in the attempt to destroy a body, or so to mutilate it as to prevent its identification.

Better known from its occurrence in the teeming metropolis of the world, and from the unsolved mystery which still enshrouds the deed, is the Waterloo Bridge murder. A carpet-bag was discovered on a buttress of Waterloo Bridge, London, in the beginning of October, 1857. On being examined, this bag was found to contain portions of a human frame, which had been so treated as to present a veritable illustration of the disposition of Cassim Baba by the robbers in the "Forty Thieves." In all, some twenty-three portions of the frame were discovered, these being parts of one and the same body. The portions missing were the head, the greater part of the spine, the hands, feet, and left side of the chest; whilst the internal organs were also wanting. The questions submitted to the medical inspectors for the guidance of the police in the investigation of the crime had reference to the sex, age, and height of the deceased; the cause of death; the period which had elapsed between the occurrence of death and the finding of the remains; the state of the body as indicative of its having formed the subject of anatomical research or not; and the presence of any peculiarity, normal or acquired, the discovery of which might lead towards the identification of the body.

These queries were on the whole answered with an accuracy

and fulness which bespoke volumes for the patience and skill of the medical inspectors. The remains were those of a man who, judging from the full development of the skeleton, must have attained the age of between thirty and forty years, and must have measured about five feet nine inches in height. The person was probably dark haired, judging from the colour of the hair of the wrists and knee. The cause of death was plainly apparent. A stab had been inflicted between the third and fourth ribs on the left side of the chest, and in such a situation as to have penetrated the heart, whilst the appearance of the wound led the inspectors to declare that it must have been inflicted during life, or immediately after death; the former alternative being that most consistent with the facts of the case. The cause of death was, therefore, seen to be perfectly consistent with the theory of murder, and that of a very deliberate type. Equally important for the purposes of the detective was it to fix the probable date of the commission of the crime; but on such a point speculative rather than actual evidence alone could be offered. It was noticed that, from the perfect state of preservation of the remains, they must have undergone some preservative process, probably with the view of preventing discovery through their decomposition. They must, in fact, have been boiled and salted, and this latter feature alone may serve to indicate the cold-blooded and deliberate nature of the crime. The fact that the remains had thus been artificially preserved rendered the calculation of the period of death difficult, and in any case uncertain. But from an examination of those portions of the remains which were least affected by the process of preservation, the examiners came to the conclusion that the person might have been dead for three or four weeks prior to their examination of the remains; or, in other words, that the subject of the Waterloo Bridge murder was probably alive in the latter part of September, or even at the beginning of October, 1857.

Not a particle of evidence was forthcoming to show that the remains had been used for anatomical purposes. On the contrary, the manner in which the parts had been separated, and the clumsy fashion in which parts which could have been readily disjointed with the scalpel were separated with the saw, proved the murderer to have been thoroughly ignorant of the veriest rudiments of anatomical knowledge. But the practice of the public in frequently rushing to the conclusion that mutilation must of necessity be the work of the medical student, is founded upon an entire want of appreciation of the labour and nicety involved in anatomical study; whilst such a supposition can only favour the escape of a criminal, by distracting attention from the true state of matters, and by thus affording him time and opportunity for escape. In the case of the notorious Greenacre, who, in 1837, murdered a woman named Brown, in London, and scattered her remains, clumsily separated, as in the Waterloo Bridge murder, public opinion at first attributed the circumstances to the absurd and unfeeling levity of medical students; and justice was thus impeded, as it was likewise hindered for a time in the case of Dr. Parkman, by a similar supposition. In neither instance could anatomical study have been made the excuse for the appearance of the remains, and still less so in the Waterloo Bridge tragedy.

In the latter case no peculiarities of structure existed which could have been singled out with a view to the identification of their possessor; and hence, owing largely to the want of this particular kind of evidence—the kind of testimony which tells most favourably in the hands of the detective—the Waterloo Bridge tragedy, in all its ghastly details, has tacitly passed into the limbo reserved for the undiscovered horrors of our own and other ages. Not a single direct clue was forthcoming as to this mysterious crime. The articles of clothing found in the bag afforded no certain evidence of the nationality of their possessor. They were torn, and stained with blood; and a very distinct stab must have been inflicted through the double collar of an overcoat, this injury probably being of an equally fatal nature with the stab already spoken of as having been inflicted in the chest. The police inquiries appeared to point to the shifting maritime population of the Thames as the most likely source in which a clue to the mystery should be sought. A Swedish sailor was believed to have been the victim; but there were not wanting those who thought then, and think even now, that the crime was of deeper nature than that indicated by the hypothesis of a seaman's quarrel. The care shown in the disposition of the remains was said to be inconsistent with the unskilled ways of sailors, and pointed, along with the circumstances of the death, rather to the revenge of more accomplished assassins. The fate of Count Fosco in Wilkie Collins's "Woman in White" is thus believed to have been that of the victim whose remains came to rest on Waterloo Bridge in 1857. The fact of the deceased having probably been a foreigner, and possibly being in hiding in London from his enemies—on the latter theory of the crime having been one of political revenge—may account for the want of success which met the efforts of the police in tracing his identity. Of the true history of this great crime, will the world perchance hear something at some future date; or will it remain for ever buried in the oblivion of mystery? Who can tell?

The presence of peculiarities of various kinds in the bodies of persons who are lost or missing is, as has just been remarked, often of the utmost value in identifying their remains. A case in point occurred in Scotland, where a skeleton was disinterred from a sandy sea beach, an examination of the remains being duly ordered by the authorities. In the course of the investigation the medical examiners discovered that the lower portion of the spine was diseased, and from the nature of the lesion they were enabled to state that the individual in question must have walked with a marked peculiarity of gait. This clue, patiently followed up, showed that the skeleton was that of a carter, who had been deformed, and who was buried at night in the sand by his friends to avoid the chances of his body being stolen for anatomical purposes by the "resurrectionists" of his day. A similar case is related by Orfila, the celebrated continental expert, in which a man named Bonino, residing near Montpellier, suddenly disappeared in 1823. In 1826 certain suspicions attaching to the disappearance induced the authorities to examine the garden of one Dimont, with the result of discovering the bones of a human body. Bonino was well known to have laboured under a six-fingered deformity in the right hand, and to have possessed six toes on the left foot. The two smaller toes of the left foot were missing in the otherwise perfect skeleton; but on the fifth toe a surface or hollow, to which an additional toe could have been attached, was plainly discernible. In the right hand the bones of the sixth finger were absent, but the palm-bone supporting the little finger exhibited the appearance of having given support to an extra digit. The left hand and right foot were complete and entire. This evidence, supported by collateral circumstances, told against Dimont and a woman, his partner in the crime, and both suffered the extreme penalty of the law.

The list of cases in which medical science, aided by the practised and trained common sense of experts, has elucidated many of the apparently inexplicable problems and mysteries of crime, might be indefinitely prolonged. But it may be remarked that not merely in the case of the lost and missing dead does the knowledge of the expert aid the cause of justice. It may happen that in cases involving the identification of the living the final appeal is made to the medical jurist and to scientific knowledge, in deciding upon the changes of structure or appearance which may accompany and mark the varying epochs of human life. Cases have been recorded in which the examination or mere detection of a scar has settled the vexed question of identity, and has freed an innocent man from the perils of unmerited punishment. Such an instance occurred at the Old Bailey in 1834. A man, believed to possess the name of Stuart, was charged with being a returned convict, and with having escaped from transportation. Evidence was given that in 1817 a person of that name was convicted and sentenced. The governor of the gaol in which the convict Stuart was confined testified to the identity of the prisoner at the bar with the convict, and no less certain was the guard of the convict-hulk to which Stuart was consigned that the Old Bailey prisoner was his former charge. Cross-examined on behalf of the prisoner, the guard admitted that the convict Stuart in 1817 possessed a wen on his left hand, and indeed this peculiarity was duly entered in the convict-records as a distinctive mark of the person in question. In answer to the charge preferred against him, the prisoner stated that he was not the convict Stuart, and that his name was Stipler. Between 1817 and 1834, however, witnesses who might have testified to the truth of his statement had disappeared, and were not forthcoming for the defence. Already the Recorder was prepared to charge the jury, when a singular, and for the prisoner most fortunate, incident occurred. A celebrated surgeon of the day, Mr. Carpue, happened to be seated in court during the trial of the alleged Stuart. Struck with the evidence of the guard of the convict-hulk regarding the presence of a well-marked wen or tumour on the convict's hand, it occurred to Mr. Carpue that this fact could be turned to advantage in the cause of justice. Hurriedly consulting with the counsel for the defence, Mr. Carpue entered the witness-box. He testified, as a surgeon, that the removal of such a wen would entail the presence of an indelible scar as the result of the operation. If the prisoner were Stuart the convict, argued the counsel, either the wen or the scar should be found on his left hand. Both hands of the prisoner were found to be free from wens and from scars alike, whereupon the jury at once acquitted him. In this case, a chance accident and the acuteness of the surgeon may be said to have saved an innocent man from a lengthened period of incarceration as a culprit of more than ordinary nature.

The well-known case of Joseph Lesurques, whose misfortune forms the incident on which more than one melodrama and novel has been founded, has recently been brought anew under public notice through Mr. Henry Irving's performance in the "Lyons Mail," and by his assumption of the dual *rôle* of Lesurques and his villainous double. The case actually occurred in France in 1794, and its details are sufficiently well known to obviate the necessity for their repetition here. Charged with robbery and murder, the innocent Lesurques was recognised, identified, and sworn to as the real culprit by various disinterested witnesses. Notwithstanding strong exertions which were made to save his life, and, despite his previous high moral character and probity of conduct, Lesurques was sentenced to death, and executed. Soon afterwards, the real culprit, a man who bore the closest possible likeness to Lesurques, was brought to justice. It was then seen that the similarity in features, stature, build, and manner was so close as to have deceived the witnesses who gave evidence at the trial. On these grounds alone, and as a matter of common recognition and identification, the unfortunate resemblance of Lesurques to the real culprit had unwittingly led them into a "Comedy of Errors," which resulted in a legal tragedy as its *dénouement*. But more extraordinary to relate still is the incident, well-nigh unparalleled in the annals of coincidences, that *Lesurques was marked by a scar on the forehead, and by another on the hand, whilst the real criminal likewise possessed similar markings.* Surely "the grim irony of Fate" could no further go than this, in causing chance likeness to assume a form and to entail consequences so fatal and sad as in the case of Joseph Lesurques.

The *Edinburgh Medical Journal* for 1854 contains another equally curious and parallel case of mistaken identity. The body of an old man was discovered in the river Dee; the left ear being wanting, as also was the first finger of the left hand. Both injuries were clearly noted to have been of long-standing nature. There appeared to claim the body two young women, who testified that the body was that of their father; that he had suffered from the mutilations found in the drowned man's person; and that he had been in the habit of leaving home for weeks at a time. The body was duly buried as that of their father; but on the mourners returning across a ferry from the funeral, the boatman informed them that the person supposed to have been just interred, had crossed his ferry half an hour before. On arriving at home their parent was found alive and well, but the identity of the buried man, who had possessed exactly similar mutilations, was never discovered. Another curious instance of mistaken identity happened in the north of Scotland, where, in the days of the "resurrectionists," the body of a man was disinterred for anatomical purposes, but was seized by the coastguard. The body was duly claimed by a woman as that of her husband, a weaver, who had been missing for some days. Her sons also testified to the body being that of their parent. The medical student implicated in the affair, seeing that a charge of murder was impending, confessed that he had disinterred the body from a certain grave-yard, and on the locality in question being visited, the correctness of his story was confirmed by the empty coffin. The body had been duly buried, and was in turn sworn to by the relatives who had interred it. Notwithstanding this testimony, the wife and her sons maintained that it was the corpse of their relative. Popular excitement was at its height, when the missing weaver reappeared in his village safe and sound. The case in point adds another proof to the literally extraordinary difficulty which seems occasionally to attach to the identification of dead persons, even by those who may be presumed to have known them best when living.

To the questions involved in the case of persons "Lost or Missing," there may be added certain curious considerations respecting the procedure of men and women who voluntarily seek hiding and refuge from fear of the law, or from other circumstances in which no fear of legal consequences is apprehended. The story is told of a certain wily cardinal, who wishing to defeat the emissaries who were sent to discover his secret papers, placed the documents in question in an open envelope on his table, with the result that they were left unheeded and untouched from their mere position, which seemed utterly to disarm suspicion. Whether or not acting intentionally on motives allied to those of the good cardinal, it is perfectly certain that many of the "lost and missing" members of society have dwelt for months, or even years, close to the very neighbourhood from which they had fled. On this principle, more than one noted criminal has contrived to elude the grasp of the law by remaining quietly beneath the very nose of its officials, whilst the hue and cry sent abroad passed over its actual object dwelling in safety at home. A case was related to the writer in which a person of weak intellect escaped from the house of a medical man, under whose surveillance he had been placed, and caused much trouble and alarm to his friends by his mysterious disappearance. The county police—who are popularly believed to stand in the same relation to the police of cities as do the militia to the regulars—were placed on the alert; rivers and ponds were dragged, hospitals visited, and the disappearance advertised, but all to no purpose. Every trace of him appeared to have been lost; and his relatives had well-nigh given up hope of hearing of him again. Judge of their astonishment when the missing man walked into the house of his medical attendant about a fortnight afterwards, dirty, unkempt, and unshaven, and satisfying their query with the remark, "Oh, I've been hiding in the stable-loft;" the said place of temporary residence being a disused loft where he had lain concealed amidst the straw and hay, and from which he had made periodical excursions to confiscate or to purchase provisions with a small store of money with which he had provided himself.

Beyond the explicable cases of mysterious disappearances, however, there remains, as we have seen, a large proportion of instances in which the fate of numerous individuals remains apparently an impenetrable mystery. Too frequently, it may be feared, the old apothegm "Murder will out" is merely a dead letter, after all; but the course of events, and especially of criminal life, also teaches us the wholesome truth, that often in ways unlooked for, through means undreamt of, the Nemesis of crime stalks its victim down. And in such a work, equally with the diffusion of sweetness and light in more æsthetic ways, it may well prove a source of satisfaction that science is able and willing in no small degree to assist and share.

IN SOME MEDICAL BY-WAYS.

WHAT is the exact nature of the mystic halo which may be said to surround things medical, when contemplated from the popular side? Why should my doctor's caligraphy be (as a rule) thoroughly undecipherable? and why should his prescription be couched in a form, which, with its cabalistic signs and writing in an unknown tongue, savours of the occult? Why, also, does my druggist display, on those magnificent jars of coloured water in his window, signs and symbols—arcs, half-moons, and triangles—of a nature exactly fitted for the decoration of the skirts of an Arabic necromancer, and why does he puzzle the uninitiated with such legends as "Sod: Bicarb:" "Pulv: Tarax:" or other equally striking devices? Is there, after all, not a large remnant of the mystic art in modern medical affairs? and may we not also assume that perchance for our mental quietude it is just as well that the Temple of Æsculapius is an unknown territory to mankind at large? It might, for example, prove decidedly disadvantageous to the conscientious desires and labours of that worthy practitioner, Dr. Mitral Smith, F.R.C.P., were you able to construe and resolve the last prescription he left as an aid to the physical welfare of your better-half, into a mild draught composed of syrup, a little tincture of orange-peel, and water. Nor would it tend towards the clear and satisfactory relations which exist between yourself and your purveyor of drugs, Mr. Taraxacum Squills, were you to discover that the element designated in Dr. Smith's little documents as "Aqua Fontis" (and for which Mr. Squills is by pharmaceutical custom entitled to duly charge you in your bill), is obtained from the water-tap in that gentleman's back shop, and constitutes a cheap and satisfactory medium for the exhibition of many important drugs. To select another case in which ignorance of matters medical is truly bliss, and wisdom a decidedly injurious acquisition: you remember those last pills which were prescribed for your worthy self, when after a long stretch of overwork, you began to think you had the complete nosology of the College of Physicians illustrated in your humble frame. You saw the great Sir Arachnoid Membrane—called in consultation—write the prescription with the usual incantation flourish at the top thereof, and you had confidence in the great man's diagnosis, and made a good recovery from the date of his visit. How great would have been your disappointment, and how certain your relapse into those obscure and annoying symptoms over the recital of which Sir Arachnoid "humm'd" and "ah-d," could you have known that he prescribed you pills of bread-crumb, to be dexterously coated by your chemical friend, Mr. Squills, as a remedy to raze out the troubles of a worried brain which had been doing its best to disturb a healthy body. Undoubtedly, then, there is an ignorance in matters medical which in itself is highest wisdom for the non-professional mind to follow. To know the little ways and necessary subterfuges of polite physicians would be to disturb a whole army of vain cares; and best of all, there is deep security for us all in the idea that the legitimate practice of the healing art includes even a little hale and hearty deception when the harmless and everyday compound may effect the cure of the fancied ailment and of the chronic valetudinarian.

If, however, the straight and honourable course of medical practice now and then demands a slight amount of mysticism —utterly inseparable from the practice of any scientific art in uninitiated circles—no less true is it that the illegal practice of the healing art invariably relies upon such mysticism as its chief prop, and as its sole and most powerful stay and support. Suppose Doctor Cagliostro, that renowned alchemist—whose degraded descendants you behold at street corners vending cements for broken glass and tonics for incoherent digestions— had appeared in public, minus the red curtain, the flaming brazier, the ivory-tipped wand, the astrological globe, and the negro attendant, do you imagine that eminent professor's sale of the Elixir of Life or the Essential Elixir of Love would have attained the immense sale which you are aware, from accurate historical evidence, these famous preparations secured? Or, if the doctor, after the fashion of some modern survivors of the ancient alchemists, had accompanied each bottle of the Elixir with a neatly printed chemical analysis of the potion, do you think the preparation would have sold at all? Decidedly not. Mystery or nothing, was the practice of the Dr. Dulcamaras of past decades, as in another fashion it is the saving clause of modern medicine-mongers and uncertified practitioners of the healing art, concerning whose nostrums, potions and practices as related to the public welfare, we purpose to pen a very few pages.

If the proverb that "familiarity breeds contempt" be true, I think it may fairly be maintained that the corollary "Familiarity destroys wonder" is equally worthy of admission into the category of wise sayings. In the matter of medicine-manufacture the latter remark holds good. In no age more clearly than the present has a greater amount of potions, pills, elixirs and nostrums of all kinds been swallowed by the British public. The habit of swallowing by faith, and not according to knowledge or common sense, is practised in these times to an extent which few persons amongst us even dream of. Never, I believe, at any previous period of social history has the British public so energetically poured compounds of which it knows little into frames of which it knows less. And this practice of the wholesale physicking of the nations day by day proceeds without once exciting our wonder or drawing from us a comment, until we suddenly become aroused to the immensity of the traffic and to its meaning, when from some side avenue a warning cry reaches our ears.

The case in point is provable at every turn of the social wheel. You spend a weary hour at Mugby Junction, but the tedium of the waiting is relieved by the gorgeous hues of the advertisements of quack medicines and nostrums, which in every conceivable shade of colour and design appeal to human sympathy and human need. From patent this and patent that— from Mr. Bracegirdle's "patent elastic brace" for the correction of stooping habits (illustrated by a gorgeous lithograph of a young man with sloping shoulders in the act of adjusting the said brace to his manly form), to a patent "traveller's medicine chest," warranted in the compass of a cigar-box to contain remedies for well-nigh every complaint to which man's flesh is heir, the advertising tribes claim the attention and catch the eye. There is Mr. Plausible's "pills," whose virtues are in the covers of all the magazines. Close by is Mr. Tartrate's "ameliorating syrup," which will supply "tone" to enfeebled human constitutions, and to anything short of a broken fiddle or worn-out piano. You may make a note, if so disposed, that Mr. Pepsine's "pistillate powder," dispensed in bottles at one shilling and a penny halfpenny and two and nine ("larger sizes eleven shillings, specially recommended"), will effect a cure when Sir Arachnoid Membrane has shaken his head, taken a heavy fee, and left you in despair—albeit that you know, in your chemical soul, that the effervescing "pistillate powder" is but a compound of tartaric acid, citrate of magnesia, and other allied compounds familiar as "household words" to the vendors of lemon kali and other exhilarating summer beverages. It is this "powder" which is advertised all the world over. You meet Mr. Pepsine's labels on the Pyramids and in Calcutta; his advertising contractor is seen at Cairo and Jerusalem; he is as well known in New York as in London; and you may hear details, if you are curious in the way of gossip, regarding the palatial residence Mr. P. inhabits, and of the munificent schemes in the way of charitable education and otherwise he is prepared to further from the proceeds of his "powder." Everywhere your eye is met and your brain bewildered by the display of advertising sheets and placards; and your slumbers in the railway-carriage may be broken and disturbed by a horrid day-dream, in which you imagine that you have by some mistake mixed the "golden fluid for the hair" with the "pistillate powder," and that instant dissolution from the effects of the violent poison is your impending fate.

Nor is your daily newspaper free from the medicine-mongers. Here, in fact, you may revel in all the details of cures and cases by your own fireside—if so disposed. How much, you may well ask, may the "Anti-Obesity Company (Limited)" pay for these three columns which are occupied with single-line notices (in small "caps") that the stout-bodied and fatty-hearted need not despair? Either the company must be drawing very considerably on its capital thus to advertise by the column in the daily papers; or the fat and flabby portion of the community must be flocking in thousands to the *depôts* where the corrective to obesity is dispensed. Look through the columns of your newspaper, and think well over the announcements you see repeated day by day. Then you may perhaps form some adequate conception of the immense traffic in medicines which takes place outside the range of the physician's province, and for the regulation of which, be it observed, there is no legal warrant further than the stamp-duty which a paternal Government levies on the "patent medicines" and secret nostrums of the shops. Truly, a perusal of the daily broadsheet is a convincing argument of the extent of the trade; and the ingenuity with which the public is assailed, and the wares puffed and advertised, is perhaps as remarkable a feature of mercantile enterprise as any other belonging to the times we live in. But it is in the country newspapers that you may reach degrees and stages of medical practice of infinitely shadier kind than the common appeal to buy a nostrum on the faith of the virtues its proprietor warrants it to possess. Mostly in provincial journals, you will find the quack pure and simple advertising, not his nostrum, but himself. Quiet and unsuspecting persons from rural districts will send post-office orders to London, and will receive in exchange a few bottles of coloured water, advertised as a specific the production of which has cost the advertiser years of patient study and scientific toil—for such a charm does the advertisement and its claims possess in the eyes of the provincial, whose own parish doctor is certain to be a thorough counsellor, but who in such a case resembles the unhonoured prophet at home.

Thus, day by day, the public is appealed to in that most plausible of interests—its health and physical welfare—to spend its money on the potions of the unlearned, and to waste its substance on the unsatisfying pills and draughts of the quack. Who has not read, smiled at, and appreciated Wilkie Collins' sketch of Captain Wragge and his solvent condition as produced by the sale of a Pill? Let us quote the sayings of the Captain—for the sketch is not fanciful, but "an owre true tale" of the ways and manners of the age. "The founders of my fortune," says this medical and moral agriculturist, "are three in number. Their names are Aloes, Scammony, and Gamboge. In plainer words, I am now living—on a Pill. . . . I invested the whole of my capital, at one fell swoop, in advertisements—and purchased my drugs and my pill-boxes on credit. The result is now before you. . . . It's no laughing matter to the public, my dear," continues the Captain. "They can't get rid of me and my pill—they must take us. There is not a single form of appeal in the whole range of human advertisement which I am not making to the unfortunate public at this moment. Hire the last new novel—there I am, inside the boards of the book. Send for the last new song—the instant you open the leaves I drop out of it. Take a cab—I fly in at the window in red. Buy a box of tooth-powder at the chemist's—I wrap it up for you in blue. Show yourself at the theatre—I flutter down on you in yellow." Nor is the novelist less happy when he adds to his sketch the varied styles of advertising with which the successful vendor of the pill pushes his trade. "The mere titles of my advertisements," continues the Captain, "are quite inexhaustible. Let me quote a few from last week's issue. Practical title—'A Pill in Time saves Nine.' Familiar title—'Excuse me, how is your stomach?' Patriotic title—'What are the three characteristics of a true-born Englishman? His Hearth, his Home, and his Pill.' Title in the form of a nursery dialogue—'Mamma, I am not well.' 'What is the matter with you?' 'I want a little Pill.'" Thus far Wilkie Collins; and it cannot be said that our author burlesques the advertising tendencies of the patent medicine vendors, or the ways and means which these enterprising persons adopt of introducing their wares at once to the public notice and to the internal economy of the nation at large.

Treading closely on the footsteps of the patent medicine vendor, we find the proprietor of chemical wares which are destined, so run the announcements, "to add to the armamentarium of the toilet table;" and which in their nature may be often harmless, but occasionally deleterious, as every physician can attest. What is to be said of the innumerable dyes for the hair and washes for the skin which are advertised broadcast? Apart from the moral and æsthetic aspect of such "aids to beauty," there is the medical side, with its testimony to the evil effects of the lead lotions and other compounds used for changing the hue of the hair. Nor does the modern practice of fashionable æsthetics rest thus. Before me lies a ladies' newspaper, noted for its large circulation, and for the immense advertising supplement it weekly issues. Here I read of *coiffures* innumerable, of "invisible foundations for covering ladies' thin partings and bald places with hair;" of "artificial eyebrows"—these appendages being styled the beau-ideal of beauty—at twenty-one shillings the pair; of "eyebrow pencils;" of *rouge végétal*; of a "crême" for the complexion, "a new discovery for imparting a healthy (*sic*) white or pink (*sic*) tint to the complexion;" of processes for "effacing wrinkles," whereby (shade of Rachel) "the skin becomes fresh and diaphanous" (*sic*); of "an invaluable powder warranted to whiten the most discoloured teeth;" of other "crêmes" (sent by post safe from observation) warranted to give a "youthful complexion" to faces of any age; of ladies who devote their time and talents to "getting up the *face* and *eyes* in the most brilliant style"—one professor of this art confessing to having been "a lady's-maid in the highest circles of England, Paris, and Spain." All these I read with astonishment; and I begin to ask myself whether or not I live in an age when physiology is taught in schools, and in which Charles Kingsley wrote, and whether or not such contrivances for ruining health and burlesquing life are used by the fair sex to the extent that our ladies' newspaper would seem to indicate? It is certainly a marvellous age in its inventive fulness and profusion of arts wherewith an unkindly nature may be assisted and improved. But that the *morale* thus indicated is neither æsthetic, scientific, nor praiseworthy in any sense, is a conclusion in which I imagine most sensible persons will concur; whilst the general prevalence of the remark, "sent safe from observation," in the advertisements of the vendors of the toilet articles above mentioned, would seem to indicate that the knowledge of their use is a matter not for the many, but the initiated and beautified few.

Turning to the physiological and scientific aspects of medical by-ways, we may possibly find means to arrive at some conclusion respecting the probable effect of this unauthorized drugging of people, which common observation demonstrates to be of such widespread occurrence and practice. Firstly, let us glance at what, for want of a more suitable term, may be called the æsthetic aspects of those minor by-ways into which popular chemical investigators lead those whose complexions, faces, or figures, may demand amelioration at the hand of art. That the beautifying or improvement of the person under certain circumstances is a perfectly legitimate procedure when judged by the common-place rules of society, is a conclusion which demands no evidence by way of support. No one would dream for a moment of disputing the assertion, to come to personal details, that a defacing wart, mole, or wen on the face, capable of being readily removed, without danger, by surgical interference, should be so disposed of. And to take the very common and exceedingly annoying case, of a profusion of hairs attaching themselves prominently, say, to some simple skin-growth, and capable of being permanently or even temporarily removed by depilatories, the same remark holds good. Such acts of personal attention need no excuse. On the ground of common personal æsthetics, apart altogether from the freedom of annoyance from marked blemishes of face or figure, the amelioration of such deformities is a bare act of justice to the individual in question. The removal of a blemish is physiologically as defensible a proceeding as the replacement of missing teeth by the aid of the dentist, and in this latter act we find the truest warrant, since, for digestive purposes, the possession of teeth or their artificial substitutes is absolutely necessary for the preservation of health. To the replacement of a maimed limb by an artificial one, there can be still less objection. The common ground of expediency, utility, and function, presents us with an unanswerable argument in favour of the work of aiding nature, in so far as we are able, by the devices of ingenious art.

Very different, however, is the argument which would fain carry these same reasons into the domain of the peruke-maker, and into that of the manufacturer of face-paints and lotions. On what grounds, æsthetic or otherwise, could a change of colour in the hair be demanded or defended? Similarly, on what grounds could we justify the practice of face-enamelling, or the smoothing out of the wrinkles which time writes naturally enough on our brows and faces at large? It cannot be argued that a false eyebrow or curl is as justifiable as false teeth, for the purpose of the latter as aids to digestion is plain enough; whilst the only conceivable ground for the adoption of the former appendages would be " an improvement in looks "—an avowedly small-minded excuse, and one, in any sense, of doubtful correctness. To the deficiency or want of eyebrows we become accustomed, as to the whiteness of hair or other peculiarities of *physique;* but if the practice of supplying nature's defects—justifiable enough under certain conditions, as we have seen—is to be regarded as legitimate under all circumstances, the extremes of absurdity to which such a practice may and does lead are readily enough discerned. Admitting the false eyebrow, why should we exclude the "nose machine" advertised for the charitable purpose, when worn daily (in private), of altering the unbecoming natural style to that of a becoming and, it is to be presumed, fashionable olfactory organ?

Of the deleterious effects of the continued application of the fashionable lotions and varnishes for the face, medical science is not slow to testify. Few readers can forget the exposures in the famous Rachel case; or the testimony then and at other times offered, to show that such "preparations" for the toilet are made, as a rule, to sell and not to use. Let Dr. Taylor, in the name of authority, speak concerning the effects of common hair-dyes. "Cosmetics and hair-dyes," says this author, "containing preparations of lead, commonly called hair-restorers (!) may also produce dangerous effects. I have met," he continues, "with an instance in which paralysis of the muscles on one side of the neck arose from the imprudent use of a hair-dye containing litharge. These hair-dyes or 'hair-restorers,' are sometimes solutions of acetate of lead of variable strength in perfumed and coloured water. In other cases they consist of hyposulphite of lead, dissolved in an excess of hyposulphite of soda. In one instance, the continued use of such a dye is reported to have proved fatal, and lead was found in the liver, and in one of the kidneys. Mr. Lacy," adds Dr. Taylor, "has pointed out the injury to health which is likely to follow the use of white lead as a cosmetic by actors." Doubtless "preparations" do exist, in which the metal in question is absent; but in any case, the want of certainty as to the composition of the substance, should, in itself, serve as a condition inculcating caution and suspicion in regard to the use of such nostrums.

But if the case against mere outward applications to the skin is thus both strong and well founded, that against the reckless and undiscerning use of internal medicines and remedies is founded on still more plausible and efficient data. We are presented, at the outset of our inquiries in this direction, with a physiological side and a mental aspect. The physiological phase of the matter shows us that not merely a special training, but a technical education of high order is necessary before an accurate knowledge of the action of drugs in the human frame can be acquired. Even in this department of therapeutics, the dark places of inquiry are all too numerous at the present time. Nothing short of a technical training in medicine enables the practitioner to diagnose disease; and in virtue of the same training alone is he entitled to prescribe remedies to counteract the abnormal conditions. This is the physiological side of the administration of medicine, including thus, not merely a knowledge of the kind of medicine to be prescribed, but that of its effects when given at different periods of the disease, and at different ages and on varying temperaments of body. To this material side of medicine we must add, as we have said, a mental phase. The influence of mind over body is too well known to need remark. The effect of one man's natural disposition of mind may be to check disease, whilst another's psychology will predispose to it. Faith in a remedy may be the saving clause in a patient's life; a hopeless frame of mind may involve a fatal termination to an illness. Hear Dr. Carpenter on the curative power of faith. This writer, in speaking of *expectant attention* and its effects in modifying physical or bodily action, says, "The effects which are producible by this *voluntary* direction of the consciousness to the result, are doubtless no less producible by that *involuntary* fixation of the attention upon it which is consequent upon the eager expectation of benefit from some curative method in which implicit confidence is placed, or, on the other hand, upon that anticipation of unpleasant results in which some individuals are led to indulge by the morbid state of their feelings. It is to such a state that we may fairly attribute most, if not all the cures which have been worked by what is popularly termed the 'imagination.' The cures are real facts, however they may be explained; and there is scarcely a malady in which amendment has not been produced, not merely in the estimation of the patient, but in the more trustworthy opinion of medical observers, by practices which can have had no other effect than to direct the attention of the sufferer to the part, and to keep alive his confident expectation of the cure. The 'charming away' of warts by spells of the most vulgar kind, the imposition of royal hands for the cure of the 'evil' (scrofula), the pawings and strokings of Valentine Greatrakes, the manipulations practised with the metallic tractors, the invocation of Prince Hohenlohe *et hoc genus omne* . . . have all worked to the same end, and have all been alike successful. It is unquestionable that, in all such cases, the benefit derived is in direct proportion to the *faith* of the sufferer in the means employed; and thus we see that a couple of bread pills will produce copious purgation, and a dose of *red* poppy syrup will serve as a powerful narcotic (as has happened within the personal knowledge of the Author), if the patient have been led to feel a sufficiently confident expectation of the respective results of these medicaments." Dr. Carpenter adds also the important note—"It is commonly said that these effects are produced by the *imagination*; but this only serves to induce the belief that the *sham* remedy is one of *real* efficacy, and it is the state of 'expectant attention' which is the immediate operating agent, and which is necessary to the result. In whatever mode this can be induced, the effect will be the same. Thus Dr. Haygarth of Bath (in conjunction with Mr. Richard Smith of Bristol), tested the value of the 'metallic tractors' by substituting two pieces of wood painted in imitation of them, or even a pair of tenpenny nails disguised with sealing-wax, or a couple of slate pencils, which they found to possess all the virtues that were claimed for the real instruments, because the state of 'expectant attention' was equally induced by either."

Such remarks serve to explain the well-known case related, if I mistake not, of the poet Southey, who, sitting by a friend's closed plate-glass library window, in the days when the single-paned windows were first introduced, and seeing no divisions in the window, concluded that it must be open. On the strength of this latter supposition, the poet felt cold, went home and took a severe influenza, which ran through all the stages incidental to that affection—notwithstanding the fact that the window had been closed during his stay thereat. Such a case is perfectly explicable on the grounds above stated by Dr. Carpenter, and in virtue of the "expectant attention" of the subject.

The phases of faith in the cure of disease may thus be used to explain very many cases of marvellous cures, effected by agencies which have been proved to contain no ingredient possessing the slightest effect upon the diseased condition in question. With the ultimate good effect thus produced the remedy itself has nothing whatever to do; since any other, or even an inert substance would, if presented to the patient in the avowed guise of an unfailing specific, have effected the same end. Moreover, the remedy may be and often is vaunted, puffed, and advertised under conditions, expectations, and pretensions which are notoriously above its utmost power to accomplish. Add to these considerations the pregnant fact that one hears nothing of the failures of such remedies, which failures must be even more numerous than the vaunted cures, and we may find warrant enough and to spare for preferring to take our medicine as we obtain our law—from a legally recognised and duly qualified source.

It is also highly noteworthy that an element of danger to life may be very frequently represented in the injudicious use of patent and other medicines—a use which habit and custom together tend to encourage and spread. Next to the extreme folly of believing the advertiser's guarantee that this or that nostrum will eradicate from the constitution these serious constitutional diseases—such as scrofula, consumption, etc.—which pass from one generation to another with unfailing step, may be placed the absurd but common practice of using patent or unknown compounds in doses and at times utterly unsuitable or even dangerous. It is somewhat interesting, as well as surprising and important, to find Dr. Taylor, in his classical work on Medical Jurisprudence, informing us that one form of pill, advertised in well-nigh every language and sold world wide, has proved fatal, "owing to the large quantity taken in frequently repeated doses." Dr. Taylor further tells us of a trial which took place in 1836, wherein a man was convicted of homicide through the administration in large doses of the pills in question. Speaking of another and equally celebrated pill, well-nigh a household word, Dr. Taylor says that the principal ingredient therein is aloes!—surely a drug of common enough occurrence in the officinal pills of the ordinary pharmacopœia, but utterly wanting the marvellous virtues ascribed to the pills in question by the advertising proprietor. The list of nostrums is by no means exhausted with potions and pills designed to cure any and every ailment; for to these may be added the plasters and embrocations, for the use of which—judging from the advertisements once more—effects little if anything short of miraculous are claimed. That plasters and like apparatus cannot act through the medium of the skin to which they are applied, is evident from the well-known physiological fact that the skin-surface is at the best but a feeble absorbent of any matters with which it is merely brought in contact. Hence, the marvellous plasters of the quack may relieve, probably by affording heat and support to the affected parts. Certainly, there exist no facts in physiology to credit the belief in an unknown specific action exerted through topical applications to the skin. A final consideration concerning advertised nostrums and potions consists in the observation that certain substances, known to exert a natural function in the bodily processes, are duly advertised and made the subject of the usual puff medical. Such a substance is *pepsin*, the essential principle of the gastric juice, lauded for the cure of certain forms of dyspepsia. In the latter instance, there exist unquestionable grounds for the idea that pepsin may serve as a digestive stimulant; but, at the same time, its administration and the circumstances in which it is serviceable are matters to be determined by the physician alone. Considering further that all the ingredients at the command of the unscientific quack are ready on the druggist's shelves, to be compounded on the order of intelligent science for the relief of humanity, it is difficult to see wherein lies the advantage that humanity commonly supposes it may gain by taking the nostrum or potion on blind faith alone. Certainly, the advantage is not on the side of pecuniary gain or profit to the purchaser; and the less said about the purity of quality of the drugs employed the better, in the absence of any test of such purity save the advertisements, the claims and tenor of which, in other respects, are notoriously absurd. The transference of public faith—blind or intelligent—in matters medical to the educated practitioner and his work, would serve as a powerful means of limiting the injurious and unchecked sale of the tons and hogsheads of drugs which are yearly swallowed, to the good, it may be, of the few, but unquestionably to the injury of the many also. There is, in this view of matters, no wiser saw said perhaps, than that which declares that the man who is his own doctor—or, let us add, the quack he employs—has, in either case, a fool for his patient.

An incursion, however slight, into medical by-ways would be incomplete without a reference to the practice of bone-setting—a practice concerning which much misconception exists, not merely in non-professional, but it may be added in medical circles as well. The bone-setters, as a rule, flourish in provincial towns and remote districts, and include within their ranks female practitioners, known in the dialect of Northern England and of Scotland as "skilly women"—*i.e.*, skilful in their art. Prompted, presumably, by the feeling of confidence and belief in the occult and mysterious, and in the gifts of healing which, like Dogberry's writing and reading, "come by nature," the uninstructed amongst us seek this description of medical aid. For the bone-setter usually exhibits not a little of the mystic in his work. "I don't know how I got my learning of the bones," said an individual of the race to me on one occasion; "I believe it comes unbeknown to yourself. I began to feel about the bones, and I've got to know mostly what's wrong by the touch, and I learn how to put one thing right by another."

There was shrewdness in the latter part of the man's observation, namely that the experience of former cases guided him in present exigencies. Here and there one may meet with a more than usually intelligent man amongst these rough and ready practitioners. Such a man will have clear enough ideas of the number and relations of the chief bones and their joints; for it need hardly be remarked, that it is in cases of dislocations, recent and often old-standing as well, that the bone-setter's art chiefly comes to the front. But cases of the extreme of anatomical ignorance are only too frequent among the fraternity I speak of. I remember one old woman, famed for miles around her district in Scotland as a "skilly" person, who informed a friend of mine that she had, a short time previously to his visit, reduced a dislocation "of the two small bones of the elbow!" whilst I have repeatedly heard a bone-setter speak of small bones in the neighbourhood of the hip-joint—two situations in which, it is hardly needful to remark, no "small bones" exist at all.

Time was when the bone-setter's art was quietly passed over by the surgeon as simply a matter of chance success and coarse usage. Of failures he never heard aught, but the cures were naturally lauded to the skies; and hence it was not wonderful that the trained anatomist, knowing well the difficulties of reducing old dislocations and the dangers attending their treatment, should regard as impossibilities the tricks of the bone-setter and his kin. In 1871, however, appeared a highly interesting volume, entitled "On Bone-setting (so called) and its Relation to the Treatment of Joints crippled by Injury, Rheumatism, Inflammation, etc." The author, Dr. Wharton P. Hood, in a most interesting preface gives the history of his researches into the art of bone-setting. It appears that the author's father, Dr. Peter Hood, attended the late Mr. Hutton, a very famous

London bone-setter, in a long and severe illness. Dr. Hood refused to take any fees for his medical services, on the ground that Mr. Hutton had benefited many poor persons by the exercise of his art. Touched by Dr. Hood's kindness, Mr. Hutton offered to show that gentleman the details of his practice as a bone-setter, and Dr. Wharton Hood, in place of his father, went to Mr. Hutton's London residence, carefully investigated his modes of treatment, and after Mr. Hutton's death contributed to the pages of medical science a record of what he had seen and observed. "During a second illness from which Mr. Hutton suffered," says Dr. Hood, "I took absolute charge of the poorer class of patients whom he was accustomed to attend gratuitously, and found that I could easily accomplish all I had seen him do." "I found, however," adds the author, "that it (the intercourse with Mr. Hutton) had lasted long enough to give me knowledge of a kind that is not conveyed in ordinary surgical teaching, and that, *when guided by anatomy*, is of the highest practical value, as well in preventive as in curative treatment." The words which I have underlined form a most important portion of Dr. Hood's statement, and serve to show that, whilst recognising the merits of the bone-setter's art, he had also lit upon the true cause of its defects—namely, absence of anatomical knowledge.

The volume in question bears a more than usually interesting character, from its attempt to explain in detail, and in scientific fashion, the reasons for the successful practice of an art which previously had been denounced right and left by high authority in matters surgical. To its pages, I may refer those readers whose interest in the subject, and in the opening up of a curious by-way of medical science, is sufficiently strong. But I may briefly indicate here the main features of the bone-setter's treatment, and the principles to which his success is due. Dr. Hood says that Mr. Hutton "was entirely destitute of anatomical knowledge, and firmly believed the truth of his ordinary statement (repeated, I may remark, in parenthesis, by nearly all bone-setters as a kind of dogma) that 'the joint was out.' To him there was no other possible explanation of a constantly recurring sequence of events. A joint previously stiff, painful, and helpless, was almost instantly restored to freedom of action by his handling, and the change was often attended by an audible sound, which he regarded as an evidence of the return of the bone to its place. When this, to him, pleasant noise was heard, he would look in his patient's face, and say in his broad dialect, 'Did ye hear that?' The reply would be, 'Yes;' and his rejoinder, 'Now ye're all right—use your limb.' To the patient, probably as ignorant of anatomy as Mr. Hutton himself, who had hobbled to him on crutches, often after prolonged surgical treatment, and who went away 'walking and leaping,' it can be no matter for surprise that the explanation was also fully sufficient." Dr. Hood's pages abundantly prove that his definition and explanation of the bone-setter's art are correct. The art is simply that of breaking down, by dexterously applied force, the adhesions or other impediments which, as the result of accident or disease, have formed between bones or around joints. As the *Lancet* remarked, such a practice is but a "neglected corner of the domain of surgery," and when through the empirical labours of the bone-setter it is brought into the light of every-day and accurate knowledge, a new means of healing is thus placed in the hands of the educated practitioner. So that the art of bone-setting—abused as it may be in many ways, and often exhibiting its own disastrous failures—is, after all, but an illustration of the value of research into unwonted methods of practice, and of the possibility of finding wisdom in most unlikely places.

But little need be said by way of pointing the moral of the present paper, save, indeed, to indicate one very material aid towards the growth of a rational knowledge of the laws of health, in the teaching of physiology in our schools. Each year the Science and Art Department examines its thousands in physiology; government inspectors examine hundreds of schoolboys and school-girls each year in this subject; and in many ways—literary and otherwise—the knowledge how to live wisely and well grows apace amongst us as an educative, elevating, and refining influence. The best corrective to violations of the laws of health, to common abuses of foods and drinks, and to the inroads of the medicine-vendor upon civilization, is assuredly the instruction of the people, and especially of the young, in the elements of life-science and hygiene. Already the educationist's work bears good fruit, but a vast deal yet remains to be done in the way of correcting popular errors in living, and in teaching those things which make for physical salvation. One criterion of the advance of such knowledge we may possess in our daily newspaper—since the appearance of quack nostrums in its columns will be in inverse proportion to the spread of physiology among the people. We shall not see the nostrums in the stamped wrappers disappear yet awhile; but we may at least live in hope that, ere many years are past, the vendor of mystic potions will find a decreasing sale for his wares, and will light upon an evil time to find his occupation gone.

AT JAMRACH'S.

A BLOCK in Leadenhall Street—another delay, necessitating much objurgation on the part of our hansom-driver, in Whitechapel—a narrow shave and escape from a Juggernaut of a railway van in Leman Street, and at last we are deposited in St. George Street East, which is adjacent to the Docks, and which, at the same time, lies without the London that everyday people know. I suppose dwellers in the West End rarely, if ever, venture as far east even as Leman Street. I have heard, indeed, of a West End dandy who had paid a rash visit to a seafaring friend at the Docks, and whose yellow kids and shining boots interested the denizens of Smithfield so highly that he had to voluntarily imprison himself in Leman Street Police Station till the sergeant on duty called a hansom, and escorted him thereto for safe transit to Piccadilly. Even city men are hazy as to the whereabouts of St. George Street East. "Somewhere near the Docks" is the general direction; but you may take a day and a half to find the "somewhere" even after the directions just given. Hansom cab-drivers, ubiquitous and knowing as to the mazes of Pimlico, or the labyrinths of Leicester Square, Soho, Islington, or Highgate, grow cautious when closely pressed as to their topographical knowledge of the East End. "I'll ask a pal o' mine as has a wehicle in Leman Street ven I gets there," was

the promise of our Jehu when we engaged him to drive us to
St. George Street East—there and back for "'alf a dozen
shillin's," as he himself mildly put his tariff. And when we
did get to Leman Street, there was the "wehicle" and its owner
—somewhat asthmatic, elderly, and rubicund to boot. The
"wehicle" was a four-wheeled cab, looking very much like a
respectable and large-sized tea-chest—minus the lead—on
wheels, and the "pal" was the driver thereof. "What! Charley!
not know St. George Street? Why you're just agin' it," was
the "pal's" salutation to our Jehu. "Vere do the gentlemen
vish for to go?" was the next inquiry. "Jamrach's, the wild
beast——" I had begun, when the "pal" at once and emphati-
cally blowed the eyes of our driver. "Wot, not know Jammy-
racks!" said he; "not know *'im*"—with a tremendous emphasis
on the "*'im*." Disgusted with our West End hansom-driver's
ignorance, the proprietor of the "wehicle" pointed down Leman
Street; a jerk of his finger indicated Dock Street; and then,
by a mysterious movement of his arm, as if he were an ex-
temporised semaphore, the "pal" showed us that St. George
Street was nigh at hand. "Well, 'ere's yer good health, old
'un," said the hansom to the four-wheeler—who looked as though
he resented the inane and metaphorical expression of toast-
making with a public-house very near to his elbow.

A whirl round, a dash down Dock Street, a rapid run along
St. George Street, and we soon find ourselves along "Jamrach's,"
known from China to Peru, from Siberia to the Cape, from Sitka
to Patagonia, as the great buyer of "wild beasts," and purveyor
at large to all the menageries and zoological gardens of the
world. Jamrach's is not a grand place to look at. On the
contrary, it is far from genteel. You have usually to punch
the heads of some half-dozen Whitechapel "gamins" who
throng the pavement and obstruct the doorway, intent on

F

having their natural history cheap through the eminently lucid medium of Jamrach's glass door, before you can see Jamrach at all. All day long there are seafaring men looking about and strolling in to see Messrs. Jamrach, father and son, who are known and honoured for their fair dealing with Jack "all thé wide seas over." Now it is Bill from South America with a couple of fine pythons; or Jack from India with a fine boa constrictor, one of which Jamrach junior would have let me buy to-day for the small sum of three pounds sterling. "It was playful as a kitten," said he; but it was also ten feet long, and had an awkward habit of squeezing one's arm that suggested a crushing of prey unpleasant to dwell upon. Then sometimes it is "monkeys" which Tom and Harry have had a hunt after in India, or for which they have bartered a few knives and beads on the West Coast. Or bigger hauls still may often find their way to St. George Street. "I'm expecting a full-grown lion to-morrow, and a tiger the day after," said Mr. Jamrach to me to-day. "I'll get nearly two hundred for the lion, and about as much for the tiger," he added, which shows the capital required to carry on business in the practical zoological line. An elephant or two is welcomed for a week or fortnight's lodging—it is a nice speculation that of keeping elephantine bulk up to the mark—with complete placidity at Jamrach's. Whilst, if half a dozen rhinoceroses were landed to-day, and a hippopotamus and Mrs. H. and family likewise, to-morrow, Jamrach's hotel would stow them away in complete security "till called for" by some enterprising zoological proprietor. When you enter Jamrach's front shop, you may well deem yourself in the parrot house at the Zoo. There is such a crackling and chattering of scansorial birds, imitating very closely to the disinterested mind a meeting of Home Rulers or Land Agitators, with a sombre old macaw as the chairman, occasionally calling his audience to order by his gruff, hoarse "caw." There, near the door, are about a couple of hundred tortoises, to be retailed to the street hawkers, who will vocally advertise them as "tortises," and as "fine insecks for the gardin' and the 'ouse!" In a cage opposite, are some rare ducks—mandarins, and teal, and other species. Mr. Jamrach junior holds up a cage over which we have just stumbled, and lo! there dawns before our eyes visions of the Eastern Archipelago, suggested by the "fox bats" which climb on the wires, and show us their queer sharp noses peering out from between the leathery wings. "Just arrived this morning," says the proprietor, pointing in another direction; and there, basking by the dozen inside a big box, are lizards from Morocco. Near the window of the office are chameleons, of which so enamoured does my zoological henchman, Mr. Perks, become, that speedily Mr. Jamrach finds a purchaser, and is richer by a moiety of one pound and poorer by several reptiles. There are, in all, birds by the hundred at Jamrach's—siskins, grosbecks, cardinals, love-birds, paroquets, and a dozen other species, which mingle their chirp and their cry in anything but delightful harmony. A wonderful shop truly, where you may not demand your articles by the pound, but at so much a head for this elephant or that bear, so much a pair for these snakes or those birds, or so much a dozen for the lizards over yonder or the tortoises just here.

But Jamrach junior is waiting to exhibit his "showrooms." You have, as yet, been only in the "shop." The "menagerie" is a few dozen yards down street, situated within a quiet-looking entry, trod, I should say, by more queer beasts than any other thoroughfare in Europe. I wonder how the dwellers in the front street feel at the near proximity of so many beasts. What a nice situation for a nervous invalid indeed! Imagine being wakened up in the night time by an elephantine proboscis giving one a gentle salutation, or by an invasion of monkeys from the neighbouring cages! Still, I have never heard of Jamrach's beasts committing any breach of the peace. It would not pay the proprietor to have his beasts at large. Jamrach's cages are therefore strong, and well attended by a quiet-looking guardian, who is the guide of the bears, the philosopher of the tapirs, the counsellor of the antelopes, and the friend of the monkeys rolled into one. The menagerie is not large, but its contents are varied. Jamrach's is not a show place. His motto is "quick returns." I can't say anything as to the "profits," but I willingly believe they are ample. His aim is to sell quickly; he dislikes to have stock long on hand—for wild beasts, like civilized and well-behaved horses, will soon eat their heads off in victuals. Hence, if you visit Jamrach's, you need not expect to see a perfect "Zoo." On the contrary, you may think the menagerie more like a stable than a show. So it is; but the interest to the zoologist is great, notwithstanding cramped space and low roofs, and there is a good deal more to be learned at Jamrach's and from Jamrach than in many a museum, and from a long course of reading natural history lore. I say this, having personally proved the truth of the statements. Jamrach's *fidus Achates* might be an Oxfordshire farm labourer. As it is, he is a shrewd Londoner, with an intense affection for the animals whose welfare he cares for here. First and foremost, he tells us that he's "thin" at present—meaning thereby not that his personal physique requires addition, but that his stock is not by any means so varied and large as he could wish. Yet it seems to us that Jamrach's is rather full. There are two fine Russian bear cubs for instance at the door, which lick your hand, and are as gentle as kittens. You may have them —cheap—at five pounds apiece. On the other side of you are half-a-dozen different species of antelopes, gentle, timid creatures, with spiral horns, wanting the "snags" and "tynes" of the deer, with which they are so often confused. Behind, in the big cage, are two black leopards, growling and snarling like the fierce Satanic carnivores they are.

Here are vultures, and eagles, and owls, and queer turkeys close by, and upstairs you will light on other treasures. Up a flight of wooden steps, and you come to the abode of your "poor relations." A nice, warm monkey-house it is. In the top corner as you enter, on your right, is a cage with two nice Macaque monkeys from India, and another queer, black-visaged, gentle animal, called "Cetchewayo" by the *Achates*, because of a decided resemblance to a Zulu in miniature, and termed a "Sooty Monkey" by the zoologist from his black hue. "Cetchewayo" comes out of his cage, fondles his keeper, growls and purrs with delight as his woolly fur is stroked, and behaves himself much more rationally in my opinion than the Zulus at the Aquarium.* Down below are two wee baboons, or "hamadryads," one with a coat (sewed on for economical reasons), and with a visage and solemnity befitting—shall I say it?—a Free Kirk divine of the narrow kirk type. Up above, are baboons and rhesus monkeys, all fierce and snappish, and inclined to deal anything but gently with the visitors who come to see them. Here the orang-outang whom I saw on Saturday last in the Westminster Aquarium abode in peace, till he was removed to near St. Stephen's, and exhibited in all the magnificence of a corpulent frame, suited more to a Tichborne Claimant than a respectable Catarhine ape. In the corner is a South American tapir, which rubs against your legs like

* It may interest my readers to know that "Cetchewayo" was purchased by me and lived as an affectionate family pet in my household from September 1880, till May 1881, when he died. His skeleton, however, is held in affectionate remembrance in my museum.

a mastiff dog when you approach him. A lively mongoose worries the bars of his cage above, and there are some nice little Skye terriers and half a dozen lovely Persian cats, black and white, in the boxes below. Jamrach's elephant sheds and other appurtenances, as the auctioneers put it, we have no time to see to-day. Jamrach junior is eager, too, to be off to business. I rather suspect that burly man I saw enter the shop, as we came up the street, is a sea-captain, who has perchance brought "apes and peacocks" from "Tarshish," or a gorilla from the Gaboon, or, it may be, a rhinoceros from the East, or a load of broad-nosed monkeys and anacondas from Brazil. There are other customers besides waiting Jamrach junior. That lady is a well-known menagerie proprietrix; I should fancy she may give Jamrach commissions which may send telegrams round the globe. But in the corner I can also espy Antonio Metalli, of Genoa, Naples, or perhaps Turin, the organ-man—not a bad customer to Jamrach likewise. Antonio's friend, the Macaque monkey, who climbed up the lamp-posts, gathered in the coppers, and danced to the "Madame Angot" quadrilles on the top of the organ, is no more. He has gone the way of all monkeys, with phthisis, alas! and Antonio, grieved, and with a hard-won sovereign in his pocket, has come to select a successor to the late lamented Catarhine. Hansom once again; and, with a wave of the hand, Jamrach junior goes off to business, whilst the farewell screech of Jamrach's parrots and macaws sounds like a hearty *au revoir* as St. George Street East is left far behind.

JELLY-FISHES.

THERE are but few objects of the shore which to the ordinary observer appear more hopeless of evolving interest or instruction than the beings which give a title to this paper. So far, indeed, from exciting any feelings of interest, their appearance generally inspires the unscientific mind with disgust, if it does not bring to the surface a stronger and less polite trait of character in the shape of an expression of repugnance at the aspects of jelly-fish existence at large. The distrust with which the Medusæ are regarded has, it must be owned, a firm foundation in fact. As we shall see hereafter, they possess the means for making themselves intensely disagreeable to the human race and to lower organisms as well, through the possession of certain offensive organs called "stinging cells." And it is not at all an improbable idea that, handicapped thus in public opinion, the more æsthetic aspects of jelly-fish life and structure have not received that amount of justice which the unprejudiced scientist, with an eye for the ethereal, may fairly maintain they possess. But as in many other departments of human knowledge, so in the history of jelly-fishes, a one-sided philosophy neither does justice to the objects it investigates, nor brings profit to its students and devotees. Although "philosophy" may seem a high-sounding term to apply to a study of beings which, like the Scotch minister's sermon (described by an ancient lady-member of his congregation), may well-nigh be said to have "nae vitals," it may nevertheless be shown that a large modicum of interest is bound up with the story of their life and existence. It might be fairly enough maintained that, from a zoological point of view, there are few animal forms which possess a more curious history that those masses of living jelly that pulsate through the summer sea, and occasionally strew the coast for miles, when the fury of contending winds and waves has wreaked itself upon the hopeless race. The natural history of these beings has ere now enjoyed the earnest attention of more than one eminent observer,—witness, in proof of this statement, the researches of Edward Forbes, the charming studies of Professor and Mrs. Alexander Agassiz, and the recent work of Mr. G. J. Romanes. At any rate, in the structure and life-actions of these organisms, we are certain to find some material even for wonderment; and if only as a sea-side study, when the summer days and smooth waters lure us seawards, the history of a very "common object of the shore" may perchance awaken wholesome thought concerning many other and higher objects, even in the nearer circle of human interests themselves.

Perhaps the biography of the jelly-fishes, or *medusidæ*, as they are scientifically named, may, as a primary recital, serve to elucidate certain important matters connected with their structure and life. Going back some twenty or thirty years in the history of zoology, we find that those arrangements of animals we term "classifications" presented a widely different aspect from those of the more modern lecture-room. Classifications of any and every kind, really represent the presumed relationships of the beings we classify. Hence when, of old, the jelly-fishes were arranged along with the star-fishes, sea-urchins, and their neighbours, in a large division named the *Radiata*, such a classification indicated that, in one respect at least—that of the circular form of their bodies—these animals exhibited a close likeness. But Cuvier's *Radiate* animals, and the *Radiata* of later days as well—when the lowest forms had been deleted from that group to constitute a new division of the animal kingdom—soon underwent revision. The sea-anemones, corals, zoophytes, and jelly-fishes, were in due time separated from the star-fishes and their neighbours, and were banded together to form a division known still as that of the *Cœlenterate* animals. At the present day, when biological revolution reigns everywhere paramount, the jelly-fishes are still spoken of as cœlenterate animals. They are, in other words, near relations of the sea-anemones and corals, and possess those plant-like animals, the zoophytes, as their nearest kith and kin. If, however, the broad place and position of the jelly-fishes has been amicably and easily settled in the ordinary run and progress of zoological history, the changes which have taken place within the circle of their own family-group have been more numerous and important. Thus, for instance, we find that a division termed *Acalephæ*—a name given by the Greeks to these beings in allusion to their nettle-like or stinging powers—was constituted to receive all and sundry in the way of jelly-fishes. There are jelly-fishes and jelly-fishes however. A "Portuguese man-of-war," the *Physalia* of the naturalist, met with in the tropical seas and notorious for its nettle-like properties in the way of stinging, and the little "Sallee man," or *Velella*, with its diagonal sail, also an inhabitant of warm seas, but occasionally drifted on our southern coasts, would, according to the old and very general arrangement, be named "jelly-fishes." If the softness of body proper to these—

> "Gay creatures of the element
> That in the colours of the rainbow live,"

as Milton has it, be regarded as a warrantable feature for

classing them with the objects of our study, such an arrangement might be permissible enough. But mere softness of body counts for nothing in scientific arrangement; because, as common sense itself would urge, such a character indicates nothing regarding the structure of the beings we are classifying. Hence, we find that in due time, the division of the "nettle-stingers" was disbanded, and its members rearranged. First in the field with a new and better arrangement was Edward Forbes, who divided the jelly-fishes proper into the "naked-eyed medusæ," and "hidden-eyed" forms. Forbes likewise cast out the "Portuguese man-of-war" and allied beings from amongst the jelly-fishes proper, and thus in a satisfactory form represented the progress of science in his day. But since the days of the witty and learned Edinburgh Professor, the pet objects of his study have been arranged anew. Fresh facts of exceeding interest concerning their development came to light after his time, and brought their influence to bear upon the arrangement of the jelly-fishes in the animal series. These newer facts we mean to glance at in our brief study of the jelly-fish race, but enough has been said in the present case to answer the first great question—asked by the naturalist of every living being from monad to man—"What is it?" And to this inquiry, referring to the jelly-fishes, we reply that they are cœlenterate animals; near relations of sea-anemones and corals, and more nearly related still to the zoophytes which, in the guise of sea-weeds, deck the oyster-shells we obtain in the dredge, or litter the shore after ground-swells and gales.

There is but little need to describe in anything like minute detail the general form of a jelly-fish. If we capture a few specimens by aid of a muslin tow-net, dragged after a boat in which we lazily paddle over the calm surface of the summer sea, and convey our booty homewards to a jar of sea-water or place them in a convenient rock-pool, we may study their principal features in ready fashion. A jelly-fish is then seen to resemble a bell in shape; and the resemblance to that object is further increased by the presence of a central organ depending from the roof of the body and corresponding to the clapper or tongue. Although, as will be hereafter noted, the term "jelly-fish" may even now include forms of widely different kind and of varied nature, the structure here described is common to all of those forms which belong to the medusoid kith and kin. So close is the resemblance first alluded to, that the domelike body of the jelly-fish is spoken of by naturalists as the "swimming-bell;" whilst it may be useful to bear in mind that the clapper of the bell is named the "polypite."

The delicacy of jelly-fish substance is tacitly implied in the name itself. So unresisting is the bodily fabric of these beings that they seem to drain away into a shapeless pulp if we attempt, even carefully and gently, to lift them from their native waters. And their delicacy of structure is fully paralleled by the ethereal beauty of their tints, and by the iridescent hues that play throughout the glassy dome as it pulsates through the sea, with a regularity of rhythm that speaks volumes for the stable ordering of its nervous arrangements. Agassiz, amid his severer studies of jelly-fish form, has not neglected to adorn the tale whilst pointing the moral of their history. Says this author: "There is a deep scientific interest connected with the study of medusæ. Notwithstanding their slight consistency and their extraordinary transparency, a highly organised structure has been observed in many of them; and though the most opposite opinions still prevail among observers respecting the signification of the facts thus ascertained, it is not less evident that their structure deserves to fix the attention of physiologists in the highest degree. It is, in reality, one of the most wonderful sights which the philosophic naturalist can behold, to see animals scarcely more dense than the water in which they play, and almost as limpid, perform in that medium movements as varied as those of the eagle which soars in the air, or of the butterfly dancing from flower to flower, testifying, by their activity, their sensitiveness and their volition. Their mode of living, so far as it is known; their periodical appearance, like annual or biennial plants; their rapid growth; the short duration of their life; the brightness or softness of the light which they emit during night, and which illuminates even the deep ocean; the wonderful facts which have been ascertained respecting their mode of reproduction: all this is of a character to strike, in the highest degree, the curiosity even of the most careless." Nor is it wonderful to find that Crabbe, with his predilections in favour of the poesy of sea-objects, should have noted in his measured rhyme the same points of jelly-fish history:—

> "Awhile to wait upon the firm fair sand,
> When all is calm at sea, all still at land;
> And there the ocean's produce to explore,
> As floating by, or rolling on the shore
> Those living jellies which the flesh inflame,
> Fierce as a nettle, and from that its name;
> Some in huge masses, some that you may bring
> In the small compass of a lady's ring;
> Figured by hand Divine—there's not a gem
> Wrought by man's art to be compared to them;
> Soft, brilliant, tender, through the wave they glow,
> And make the moonbeam brighter where they flow."

Poet and naturalist have alike noted the delicacy of jelly-fish structure. It is true that their bodies are of exceptionally delicate structure, but this fact does not appear to have interfered with the practical ideas of a Scottish farmer, who carted load after load of the medusæ which strewed the sea-coast in his neighbourhood, from the shore to his fields, to serve as manure. The chagrin of the agriculturist over his lost labour may be imagined when he was informed that he had in reality been merely watering his fields, instead of adding fertilising matter thereto. Owen calculates that in a jelly-fish of two pounds weight, the solids amount to about thirty grains. Every ton of jelly-fishes would therefore contain about four pounds of solid matter. The large proportion of water in jelly-fish structure is not unparalleled, even in the human economy; for two-thirds of the body consist of water. Thus, in a body weighing 165 pounds, there exist 110 pounds of water.

Notwithstanding the delicacy in question, the regular and active movements of these beings may strike us as of somewhat peculiar nature. The bell and the clapper are both formed of a jelly-like tissue which is not contractile, and is of tolerably firm consistence. When, however, the surface of the clapper, or "polypite," is examined, and when we investigate the nature of the tissue that lines the inside of the bell, we at once discover the seat of the jelly-fish movements. Both clapper and bell are covered with a thin layer of a tissue, which, without straining any analogy, may be termed "muscle." No doubt there is little apparent resemblance between jelly-fish muscle and human biceps; but there are to be seen in the former the incipient stages of the latter; whilst physiologically both agree, in that they contract at once and forcibly under appropriate stimulation. How and why these rudimentary muscle-fibres act, are matters which do not call for notice here, and which the interested reader will find fully described in the papers of Mr. G. J. Romanes in *Nature*, and in the *Fortnightly Review* (October, 1878). Suffice it to say, at present, that, like man's muscles, those of the jelly-fish are stimulated by nerves, which, in the shape of the merest rudiments, appear to present us with the beginnings in the animal world of a defined sensory and motor apparatus. But when we consider the regularity of the graceful movements whereby the jelly-fish swims through the water, we may well be inclined to agree that such regularity speaks volumes for the accurate and stable nature of the ruling power seated in its tissues. Thus the animal pulsates through the water through the action of a veritable hydraulic engine. As the bell expands, water passes into its interior; as the bell contracts, this water is expelled with force from its mouth, and by its reaction on the surrounding water drives the jelly-fish forwards. Thus contraction and expansion proceed with stable regularity. Only when unduly alarmed does jelly-fish existence seem to bestir itself. If we touch a jelly-fish whilst, in the full play of its vigour, the being is pumping its way through the sea, we may note that we thereby increase the activity of its pulsations, and accelerate its movements. The bell-shaped disc contracts and expands under the stimulation of our touch at an increased rate, and jelly-fish alarm thus carries the organism to lower depths and to safer regions of sea. As has been well remarked, there is the most patent correspondence and likeness between the regular rhythm of the heart and that of the jelly-fish body. Essentially similar movements of contraction and expansion operate in both; unusual stimulation presents us, in both, with the same increase of play; and if we further reflect that the heart, like the jelly-fish body, possesses within its tissues its own and peculiar nerve-centres, we may perceive a further and most interesting analogy between the physiology of the medusa and that of the central organ of our own circulation.

The further structure of the jelly-fish bell or body, however, awaits our consideration. One distinctive point of jelly-fish structure consists in the fact that the mouth of the bell is partially closed by a membrane named the "veil," through an opening in the centre of which the water flows in, and is ejected from the cavity of the bell in the act of swimming. The clapper of the bell—or, as we have already named it, the "polypite"—may readily be discovered to form a highly important part of jelly-fish personality. At the free extremity of this tongue which hangs from the roof of the bell, we discover the mouth bounded by prominent "lips." This mouth leads into the hollow of the polypite; and the cavity of this structure—albeit that a naturalist would regard it as strictly corresponding with the inside of the body—serves the medusa for a digestive sac, or stomach. Hither are brought the morsels in the shape of the marine water-fleas and the allied small fry upon which jelly-fish existence is maintained, and in the hollow of the tongue, or polypite, they may be regarded as being assimilated and converted into the substance of the medusa. From the base or attached end of the polypite, certain canals are readily seen to be distributed through the soft jelly-like body. Thus usually four canals pass away from the base, in diverging fashion, towards the circumference of the bell; these being named accordingly the "radial canals." At the margin of the body, these canals join another vessel which runs completely round the edge of the jelly-fish body, and which is termed, appropriately enough, the "marginal canal." The purport and use of this system of canals are clearly nutritive. Through these vessels flows the blood which jelly-fish digestion has elaborated and prepared from jelly-fish food. They represent, along with the central polypite, the commissariat department of the organism, whereby nourishment is distributed to the body, and whereby the losses of tissue and the wear and tear, which beset jelly-fish activity as inevitably as they follow human action, are repaired and renewed. Considering the activity of movement in the medusa, such loss of substance must be considerable; and even if existence be of short duration in the jelly-fish race, it is clearly maintained only at the expense of some considerable amount of energy displayed in the work of bodily repair.

The margin of the bell, however, may claim further attention, as in reality the most important region of the body when the innervation or nervous regulation of the organism is taken into account. Here appears to be specially localised those powers and properties which, diffused through the bell itself, and propagated to the muscular tissue already noticed as lining its interior, produce those movements and manifestations of action that in one form or other are invariable concomitants of life itself. What, then, are the structures to be perceived at the boundary or margin of the medusa's body? First in order, we may perceive the tentacles, or feelers, varying in number and disposition in different species. Secondly, the "eyes" of the jelly-fish, in the form of spots of pigment, are readily observed; and thirdly, a more careful examination of the rim of the bell reveals the presence of "ears" as well as "eyes." Each of these organs constitutes so distinct and typical a portion of medusa structure, that a few words concerning their nature and functions are demanded as an aid to the elucidation of the history of their possessions.

The tentacles are unquestionably organs of touch, but their functions in the capture of prey appear to be equally, if not more important. Here are specially localised those means of offence for which jelly-fish nature, despite the beauty of form and the ethereal elegance of its frame, has attained a somewhat evil reputation. The "living jellies which the flesh inflame" form an important feature in Crabbe's description of the beauties of the shore; although, indeed, his impartial mention of their urticating powers, whilst perfectly true to nature, may be held to somewhat vitiate the otherwise pleasant picture of medusoid loveliness, and illustrate anew the axiom that beauty may not merely be vain, but deceitful likewise. Stinging powers are not limited to the jelly-fishes, but are possessed in greater or less perfection by every member of the great division of the animal series to which these forms belong. From the *Hydra* of the ditches to the corals and anemones of the ocean, stinging powers form a natural heritage of the race of "cœlenterate animals," as we have named them. The nature of the offensive apparatus is not difficult to discover. If we take a hydra from its pool, place it under our microscope, and greatly press its body, we may discern numberless little threads shooting out from the tissues, and we may likewise see imbedded within these tissues little cells, each containing a thread-like filament, similar to those which have been protruded. The little cells, or capsules, are "thread-cells," and a thread-cell is simply a minute bag, filled with fluid, and having coiled up within it a thread-like filament, which is attached to one extremity of the cell. Under pressure, or even under the mere stimulus of touch, this cell ruptures, and thread and fluid are discharged upon the offending body. The threads are often armed with barbs or hooks, adapted probably to effect their adherence to the body in question. There seems no reason to doubt that the thread is simply a dart, and the fluid a poison—in short, we are presented in each "thread-cell" with a miniature poison-apparatus. Such is the armature of our sea-anemones and jelly-fishes and their zoological relations. By aid of these thread-cells, acting upon tissues of the requisite degree of delicacy, the prey is paralysed or killed outright. By these thread-cells the larger jelly-fishes "sting" the incautious bather, and capture the nutritious objects which come in contact with tentacles or polypite. One species of jelly-fish, indeed, seems to have developed special nervous powers, and through these powers to have inaugurated special movements for the purpose of seizing and killing prey by aid of the mouth and central tongue or polypite. *Tiaropsis indicans*, for instance, will unerringly move the central mouth and polypite towards any point in its body which has been touched. Such an act follows the stimulus of touch as unerringly as the needle of a telegraph-instrument obeys and reflects the touch of the handle. At the mouth in this species we find a special armature of thread-cells; hence the necessity for special sensory powers enabling the animal to localise the seat of contact with prey. Many of the jelly-fishes are enabled to sting severely by aid of the thread-cells and their contained darts. The smaller species do not affect the human organisation, owing to the inability of the lassoes of the thread-cells to pierce the epidermis; but if applied to a more delicate region, such as the mucous membrane of the lips, the effect of the thread-cells' virus may then be practically illustrated. The tentacles of a sea-anemone, which do not affect the hands, will cause a smarting sensation if applied to the more tender lip. The Abbe Dicquemare, an enthusiastic observer of the jelly-fishes and their relations, somewhere remarks that the sting of certain species of *Oceania* was felt only when they were brought in contact with sensitive portions of the body, such as the eyes—an observation which called forth from Edward Forbes the remark that most sensible people would prefer to keep "their eyes intact to poking medusæ into them." Forbes has left on record an amusing account of the virulence of *Cyanœa*, one of the species of jelly-fishes common on our southern shores. "Once tangled in its trailing 'hair,'" says Forbes, "the unfortunate who has recklessly ventured across the graceful monster's path too soon writhes in prickly torture. Every struggle but binds the poisonous threads more firmly round his body, and then there is no escape; for when the winder of the fatal net finds his course impeded by the terrified human wrestling in its coils, he, seeking no combat with the mightier biped, casts loose his envenomed arms and swims away. The amputated weapons, severed from their parent-body, vent vengeance on the cause of their destruction, and sting as fiercely as if their original proprietor gave the word of attack." After this graphic description of the stinging propensities of the jelly-fishes, the appellation of "medusæ" bestowed upon these forms, in allusion to the snake-locks of the mythological personage, is seen to be by no means of far-fetched nature.

Jelly-fish existence is thus seen to be accompanied by powers of offence of no mean order. Those near neighbours of the medusæ, already alluded to—the Portuguese men-of-war—possess, of all members of the race, the most powerful thread-cells. Not merely are the thread-cells in these elegant creatures of large size, but the body is provided with what have been named by Carl Vogt *fils pecheurs*, or "fishing-lines," these latter organs being long filaments, provided with thread-cells, and capable of being projected like armed lassoes against any body floating at a distance. The sting of a "Portuguese man-of-war" appears to be no light matter, judging from the accounts of its severity furnished by more than one trustworthy observer. Symptoms resembling those of severe acute inflammation persist for days in some cases, and pain may be experienced in the injured part for a lengthened period after the physalia's attack.

Turning to the remaining organs borne by the margin of the jelly-fish body, we find eyes and ears to await our survey. The "eyes" in question are represented by specks of colour, on the surface of which a little clear refractile body, probably of the nature of a lens, is found. In the determination of the nature of organs of sense in the lower confines of the animal world, the zoologist is naturally led to associate the beginnings of the sense of sight with the appearance of pigment-spots. Even in infusorian animalcules there occur pigment-masses, often of bright hue, which, for want of any better explanation of their function or use, we may consider to represent eyes, because pigment is invariably associated with organs of sight of a well-developed nature. There would seem to be little doubt, therefore, that the pigment-specks of the jelly-fish are rudimentary "eyes" —organs of vision these, not capable of discernment in the sense in which we speak of "seeing" in higher life, but probably highly sensitive to alternations of light and darkness, and thus serving to guide their possessors to the surface or to the depths below, when sweetness and light prevail in the upper world, and when darkness reigns supreme, respectively. Closely associated with the "eyes" are the reputed "ears" of the medusa. As the elementary eye is merely a sensitive pigment-spot, so the rudimentary ear presents itself to view in the form of a sac, or bag, containing fluid, suspended amidst which are particles of lime. Such an apparatus dimly foreshadows ears of a more perfect type; but even in jelly-fish existence it is not difficult to understand how waves of sound falling upon these sacs will cause disturbance of their contained fluid and its lime-particles, and how such disturbance, propagated along nerves and affecting nerve-centres, will produce actions and movements of corresponding kind in the organism at large.

One pregnant fact connected with the sense organs of jelly-fishes, and testifying to the extreme probability of the body margin and its belongings being the seat and sources of "sense," is found in the discovery that this region of the jelly-fish is that which reigns paramount in the direction and regulation of the creature's movements. When Mr. Romanes removed the margin of the swimming-bell, "immediate, total, and permanent paralysis of the entire organ" followed the operation; or, as that experimenter remarks, "that is to say, if, with a pair of scissors, I cut off the whole marginal rim of the bell, carrying the cut round just above the insertion of the tentacles, the moment the last atom of the margin was removed, the pulsations of the bell instantly and for ever ceased." No less remarkable were the acts of the detached portion. On this head Mr. Romanes remarks, "On the other hand, the severed margin continued its pulsations with vigour and pertinacity, notwithstanding its severance from the main organism. For hours, and even for days after its removal, the severed margin would continue its rhythmical contractions; so that the contrast between the death-like quiescence of the mutilated bell, and the active movements of the thread-like portion which had just been removed from its margin, was as striking as it is possible to conceive." Such facts are absolutely conclusive in their affirmation that in the margin of the jelly-fish bell we must locate the active and controlling centres and parts of its nervous system. Hence, as an additional conclusion, we may safely enough maintain that it is but natural to find, in this nervous area of the animal's body, the organs of sense just described. The details of jelly-fish structure may be fitly concluded by a passing reference to the modern position of the jelly-fishes in the zoological scale, as compared with their previous relationships indicated in the classifications of days gone by. Allusion has already been made to the divisions which Forbes instituted in classifying these creatures, and which were named the "naked-eyed" and "hidden-eyed" medusæ, respectively. We are now in a position to appreciate the meaning of Forbes's terms and arrangement. The "hidden-eyed" medusæ of Forbes are now represented by animals which are truly "jelly-fishes," but which exhibit certain important differences from the common medusæ of our coasts. One such difference consists in the fact that the organs of sense in the "hidden-eyed" group are covered by a kind of hood; whereas in the common jelly-fishes the eyes and ears are not so protected. At the same time, the differences between the two classes tend to disappear when we discover the similarity in organisation which certain species in one division bear to species in the other; and, in truth, so far as the popular name "jelly-fishes" is concerned, the "hidden-eyed" medusæ are even more typical representatives of the term than the "naked-eyed" species.

Leaving zoological taxonomists to dispute the correctness of their systems and arrangements, we find yet awaiting us, in our study of the jelly-fishes, phenomena which certainly far excel in interest even the personal history and individual structure of the race. The history of any animal or plant is not fully answered when we have replied to the query "What is it?" and when its structure has been fully investigated. To fully answer this question, we must understand its early history. The query "What is it?" really includes a knowledge of the past life of a living being in its reply; and since the adult stages of existence form only a part of the term of life, it follows that the "development" of the living being presents us with subject-matter for study of essential nature to a full and complete knowledge of the organisms around. These remarks apply with double force and meaning to jelly-fish history. It can readily be shown that the exact answer to the inquiry "What is a jelly-fish?" can only be supplied by a study of the medusa in the days of its infancy and youth. Much of the mystery of jelly-fish nature really springs from our ignorance of their early history, coupled with the curious relationships to other diverse organisms disclosed by the recital of their development. On all grounds, therefore, that development demands notice; and even its cursory investigation may be found to reveal much that is startling, not merely in jelly-fish affairs, but in the philosophy which regulates living nature at large.

Reference has been made to the fact that the "zoophytes" are near relations of the medusæ. Now, the name "zoophyte" happens to be a very generalised term for a plant-like animal; and as employed here, it is certainly not misapplied, seeing that the zoophytes which claim the jelly-fishes as near kith and kin, are so plant-like that, when picked up on the beach by ingenuous collectors of seaweeds, their plant nature seems unquestionable. Growing on oyster-shells, such zoophytes as the "sea-firs" or Sertularians are seen to mimic in perfection the forms of miniature fir-trees; and a visit to any museum of note, will fully convince the observer who glances into the zoophyte-case, that the animal form may mimic in exactitude not merely the appearance, but the fixation and manner of growth of the plant. We have little concern at present with the structure of the zoophytes, beyond indicating that each of these plant-like beings is in reality a colony of little animals. Each member of this colony is connected through the hollow stem and branches —on which the individuals are borne—with every other citizen of this plant-like republic. Through the hollow stem and branches flows a continual stream of nutriment, which is continually being elaborated by the mouths and digestive sacs of the members of the colony. So that as each member draws its own nourishment from the stream it has helped to manufacture, the principle of perfect and harmonious co-operation seems to be realised in zoophyte existence with a unanimity and peace from the bliss of which the most perfectly organised of human societies appear to be, as yet, far removed. Zoophyte life thus speeds its commonplace round. The individuals which die and fall off like the ripe blossoms of the plant, are replaced, as losses of plant existence are repaired, by new buds which grow into new individuals. But the parallel between a zoophyte colony and a plant, ends not thus. The latter will, in due time, make provision for the future of its race by the production of seeds—seeing that the budding of one individual affects not the increase of the species at large. Each seed is capable of giving origin to a new plant, and of thus perpetuating the race in time. In the zoophyte, similarly, there exists provision for the maintenance of the species, and for repairing the loss which death inflicts thereupon—just as the local and partial death in the individual is arrested and opposed by the development of new buds.

At this stage of our inquiries, the interests of the zoophytes would seem in a marvellous fashion to join issue with those of the jelly-fishes. In the ordinary course of zoophyte existence, the little eggs which have been produced by the zoophyte colony at first swim freely through the sea. Ultimately each egg settles down to develop, first one little individual of the colony, by way of a founder of the community; and then, by budding, produces a whole connected series of beings. That is to say, from a zoophyte's egg, a zoophyte, as the ordinary course of nature directs, is seen to spring. But zoophyte development is more frequently extraordinary than commonplace in its methods. From very many zoophytes, "buds" of a shape not in the least resembling the ordinary members of the colony are produced in large numbers. As these buds develop, they assume the exact likeness of jelly-fishes, or medusæ. Sooner or later, these jelly-fish buds are seen to detach themselves from the zoophyte-stock which produced them, and not merely to swim freely in the sea, after the fashion of medusæ—pulsating through the water with rhythmical stroke—but to exhibit the central mouth, the radiating canals, and the sense organs, which, as we have noted, are the natural belongings of jelly-fish existence. So that, in short, from a fixed and rooted zoophyte-stock, a free-swimming medusa is thus produced.

But the history of the zoophyte's jelly-fish progeny includes a further stage of development, since the cycle of its life is not completed with its detachment from the plant-like parent. For a lengthened period, in some cases, this jelly-fish progeny will swim in the sea, indistinguishable, save through the knowledge of its origin, from the ordinary or true medusæ. Sooner or later, however, the jelly-fish bud of the zoophyte will produce "eggs;" and when this work has been completed, the clear glassy dome will decay and become dissolved amidst the waters to which in the delicacy of its structure it was so near akin. But the "eggs" will undergo the regular development proper to their race. They will at first swim freely in the sea. Next they will settle down, attach themselves, and develop each a little stalked organism, in which we can have no difficulty in recognising the first beginnings and lineaments of the zoophyte. This first seedling of the zoophyte-tree will then exhibit the process of budding; the primary bud produces a second; these buds in turn develop others, which, remaining to form a single and connected organism, in due time reproduce before us the zoophyte-stock. From this stock, when the proper period arrives, the jelly-fish buds will once again be produced; and thus the circle of development and the perpetuation of the race will be illustrated anew.

In the consideration of these marvellous relationships betwixt zoophyte and jelly-fish, it is not wonderful to find that the older naturalists should have applied the name "alternation of generations" to the included phenomena. One generation (of zoophytes) was seen to reproduce another generation of animals (the jelly-fishes); and this latter in turn reproduced the zoophyte-stock; generation alternating with generation in a curious and apparently inexplicable relationship. Nor was the problem of such relationship rendered anywise clearer by the discovery that in certain cases jelly-fishes produced jelly-fishes without any apparent zoophyte stage or interpolation of plant-like forms whatever. Forbes remarks such an anomaly, and Sars of Christiania, at the same period, confirmed the observation of his English neighbour. Chamisso, the versatile and talented author of "Peter Schlemil," making similar observations regarding certain curious species of sea-squirts, summed up the alternations by saying that the offspring never resembled the parent, but reproduced the likeness of the grandparent. And applying such a remark to the case in point, the likeness of the zoophyte-parent might be held to be reproduced in the grandchildren; the children of the zoophyte being, of course, represented by the dissimilar medusæ.

As zoological science advanced, however, the true nature of this so-called "alternations of generations" became apparent. This latter term was applied to the development we have been studying, because two distinct animals—zoophyte and jelly-fish—were found to apparently reproduce each other. A better acquaintance with zoophyte history reveals the interesting fact, that between the ordinary buds of these forms—buds which never leave the zoophyte branch and which give origin to eggs that develop directly into zoophytes—and the jelly-fish buds, there is a gradual and well-marked series of transitions. Further, it is noted that the jelly-fish bud corresponds in its type of structure with the ordinary fixed bud of the zoophyte. And best of all, the study of the comparative physiology of buds and zoophyte brings clearly to view the important fact, that the jelly-fish is not a distinct animal in any sense, but merely a detached part of the colony, specially developed and organised for a free life, during which it is intended to mature the "eggs" or clements which otherwise would have been developed in a fixed part of the zoophyte-stem. The roving jelly-fish is physiologically a part of the mother colony, even although separated by leagues of sea from its parent stock. It is simply an emigrant member of that colony, connected by every tie of blood, and still more by the results of its life history, with the rooted colony of the coast or sea-depths. Hence the applicability of the term "alternations of generations" was first questioned and then denied. It no longer finds a place in the phraseology of philosophic natural history, when the true relation of the jelly-fish bud to the zoophyte-stock is comprehended and made plain.

But the question may be asked, How does this discovery that zoophyte-buds mimic the jelly-fishes affect, firstly, our recognition of a true jelly-fish when we see it, and secondly, the origin of the connection between jelly-fishes and zoophytes—or in other words the causes which have evolved jelly-fishes and zoophytes respectively? To reply to such important queries requires a little further acquaintance with the jelly-fish race. It may, however, be remarked, that it was formerly, and still is, a highly difficult question, apart from a knowledge of their exact origin, to say whether a given jelly-fish was a true medusa, possessing a personality and existence entirely independent of the zoophyte-stock, or merely the detached reproductive bud of some zoophyte colony. The ranks of the true medusa have been sadly thinned of late years through the discoveries that many of the so-called "jelly-fishes" were the offspring of the zoophytes, and that their proper place in zoology was amongst their plant-like parentage. Indeed, being merely "buds," and not individual animals in any sense, they had as animals no classification at all—any more than a leaf or a flower possesses a classification apart from the plant of which it forms part. It may be asserted that by far the greater proportion of jelly-fishes—especially the smaller species that exist by the hundred or thousand in the summer seas—found around our coasts, are the free "buds". of zoophytes, and that only a small remnant of the *Medusidæ* of past zoology represents a true and distinct class of animals. Thus, at present, we limit the term "jelly-fish," popularly applied and scientifically used, to those organisms which consist of a single mouth or polypite (to quote the zoological definition) suspended from the roof of a single swimming-bell, and whose eggs develop directly into forms resembling themselves. It must be confessed that the jelly-fishes thus defined form a very limited class. Still such beings do exist, and remain as the representative "jelly-fishes" of modern zoology.

Such a typical and zoologically familiar form as *Pelagia*, for instance, fully accords with the definition just given. A new phase of the difficulty, however, arises when the history of certain other members of the jelly-fish group is made known. Amongst the "hidden-eyed" medusæ (or *Lucernaridans*, as we now name them) there are many jelly-fishes which appear in the most aggravating fashion to turn the tables upon their zoophytic relations. Here in the course of true jelly-fish development the likeness of the zoophyte may be temporarily assumed; just as, in zoophyte development, the form of the jelly-fish is for a time developed.

One of the most notable cases of this curious development amongst the jelly-fishes is illustrated by the history of one of the commonest members of the race—the *Aurelia aurita*, whose title to be called the "common jelly-fish" can hardly be disputed. From the egg of this organism, at first, is developed a little oval free-swimming speck, named the *planula*. Attaching itself to some fixed object, the planula assumes a pear-shaped form; and as a depression at its free end deepens to form a mouth, little tentacles bud out around the opening. In such a guise—exactly resembling the hydra of our freshwater pools, or the primitive bud of a zoophyte—does the progeny of the Aurelian jelly-fish appear; and when the tentacles have become numerous, it receives the name of *Hydra tuba*—a term applied, under the belief that it was a distinct form of animal life, by Sir J. G. Dalzell, the once-famous authority on zoophyte life and structure. In length the hydra-tuba organism measures about half an inch, and it has been known to continue in this stage of development for years. It moreover possesses a power of producing other *Hydræ tubæ* by a process of budding, and thus comes to imitate perfectly the conditions of zoophyte existence. Its further history begins when the body elongates, and when it becomes marked across by grooves or indentations, which gradually deepen, whilst their edges become notched. In this stage, Sars named the organism *scyphistoma*, believing it to be a new and mature animal. As the *Hydra tuba* becomes further divided crosswise, it assumes the appearance aptly described as that of a pile of saucers with notched edges, placed one within the other, their hollows being turned upwards. Now it is known as the *strobila*. Sooner or later this pile of saucer-like bodies—each called an *ephyra*—falls to pieces. The saucers each swim freely in the water; they assume a more concave form; and soon appear before the observer as veritable jelly-fishes, or *Aureliæ*, which pulsate through the sea, and which exhibit all the characters of their species and race. Not the least surprising fact in connection with this curious life-history, is that which informs us of the extreme disparity between the size of the hydra-tuba and of the beings to which it thus gives origin. A hydra-tuba, measuring about half an inch long, breaks up into saucer-like *ephyræ*, or jelly-fishes, each of which latter, when fully developed, may measure seven feet in diameter, and may possess tentacles fifty feet long. Huge oceanic jelly-fishes, occurring in tropic seas, and measuring from six to eight feet across, may thus spring from a fixed organism whose diminutive size would seem to preclude the possibility of its containing, potentially, the energies requisite for the development of even an ordinary-sized jelly-fish. Such facts are not unparalleled in higher histories. The germ of the huge sperm whale is a mere microscopic speck in its earlier phases; and the red kangaroo, which in its full growth attains a height of seven feet and a half, measures at birth about an inch in length.

Summing up this brief recital of the history of jelly-fishes, the question now awaits us as to the deliverance which modern natural history may make respecting the origin of the jelly-fishes themselves, and of their relations with the fixed and rooted zoophyte-stocks. The explanation which modern zoology is prepared to make respecting these matters is founded necessarily upon the perfectly rational dictum, *that the history of an animal's development furnishes us with the means for tracing its origin and descent.* Regarding the varied universe of life as having been evolved from originally simple forms—just as to-day we see from the shapeless and uniform germ or seed, the complex and intricate animal or plant arise—we should find small difficulty in discovering, in the history of the jelly-fishes, a clue to the origin of their race, and possibly to that of the zoophyte-stock likewise. If one stage in the common development of zoophytes and jelly-fishes may be credited with representing, more typically than other, the elementary form of the race, one might reasonably lean towards the hydra-tuba as illustrating this primitive type. Not merely is the hydra-tuba the initial stage in the development of the special forms of jelly-fishes already mentioned. It also represents the permanent form of the common hydra of our pools, and it recalls the first beginnings of the zoophyte, ere the process of budding has produced the compound and connected colony. In both cases the jelly-fish type arises from the fixed zoophyte-stock, and this latter originates, in turn, from the simpler type of the hydra-tuba. If, therefore, speculation is content to be guided by the light of facts as they stand, such theorising will accept some primitive hydra-like animal as the root-stock of the jelly-fish race. The free jelly-fishes, like pelagia, which pulsate in all their independence of zoophytes, and in whose development no hydra-tuba stage is found, represent, on this theory, the most specialised and highly developed forms of the group. In their development, the panoramic display of the stages in their past history has been modified, and here and there obliterated, through the operation of causes beyond our ken. Their independence has been attained possibly through better adaptation to the free life of the ocean, but their former connection with the rooted zoophytes, and with past and gone types of zoophyte life, cannot be doubted. Otherwise, the fact that, before our waiting eyes to-day, zoophytes produce medusæ, and true jelly-fishes in turn exhibit a zoophyte stage in development, has no meaning, and must prove, as hard facts do to the prepossessed understanding, but stumbling-blocks and causes of offence. Bound up in the history of a jelly-fish, we thus find problems which directly concern the origin of the whole universe of life. And it may well be maintained that it is in these mental pathways, which, from a study of commonplace things, lead outwards to the great questions of organic existence, that the highest aims and greatest triumphs of science are to be sought and found.

THREADS AND THRUMS IN LOWER LIFE.

DESPITE the polite attentions of the housemaid's broom and the avenging duster wielded by that enemy to dust and cobwebs, an indefatigable member of the spider fraternity has been busily engaged in a snug corner of my room for some days past. Day by day some new phase or feature has been apparent in the work whereon Madame Arachne has been employing her energies and time. The ruthless duster has more than once despoiled the fabric which took two days' hard labour to rear; and to my certain knowledge the broom on one occasion has annihilated a structure the manufacture of which cost probably as much labour and ingenuity to devise, as did the production of that æsthetic coloured print in which the goddess of the duster is arrayed. But the household deities possess their own peculiar views concerning the selection of a legitimate site for a spider's dwelling-place. It is, in truth, questionable whether Arachne and her web would be accorded any place whatever on the face of the earth, were the notions and proclivities of our practical Lares and Penates consulted in the matter. Purpose, design, and use are paramount ideas in

the mind accustomed to "set things straight" in our homes
and by our hearths; and flies in the matter of provisions and
edibles, or spiders in the matter of cobwebs, naturally meet
with scant ceremony from practical hands and hearts of non-
zoological type. Even admitting that purposive design and a
plain use of the Arachne-family, as well as a moral for the
infant mind, are embodied in the well-known nursery rhyme
detailing the results of a spider's invitation to a frivolous and
unsuspecting fly, the web-makers are not regarded as well-
favoured creatures on account of their rapacious propensities,
and from their enmity to the buzzing nuisance of the household.
But both insect and Arachnidan are assailed and assaulted by
aid of the lethal broom and duster and by the seductive *papier-
mouche*; and captor and captured thus meet with the stern and
uncompromising fate which ofttimes environs the footsteps of
lower as well as of higher existence.

Gazing at Madam Arachne's handiwork in the corner of
the room, one's thoughts run off, if not exactly at a tangent,
at least into by-ways which lead to the shallows of philosophy,
and occasionally into the depths of profound reflection likewise.
Speculation becomes rife regarding the source, origin, and
growth of the constructive powers and of the trained faculties
which decide the site and build the house of Arachne and Co.,
spinners and fabricators, of Britain and the South, East, and
West generally—although, be it remarked, the branches of the
firm which flourish in the South are more notable even than
the representatives which carry on the business within the
limits of "the adjacent islands of Great Britain and Ireland,"
as the Free Kirk minister in the Hebrides denominated these
realms. Then to such sage reflections, succeed others not less
profound perhaps, regarding the spiders' place in nature, and
the nearest relatives of such "mechanical persons," as Rob Roy,

to Bailie Nicol Jarvie's extreme disgust, termed the spinners and weavers of his day. And again one's thoughts speed sidewise to consider other makers of threads and fabrics, dwelling some by land and some by sea. Finally comes the determination to afford some light, if not sweetness, in the matter of the spinners of lower life. And so, here ends this rambling introduction to a brief chronicle of spiders and spinners, of cobwebs and silken frabrics, and other materials, known as a rule only to the cunning and industrious few.

Once upon a time a Lydian purple-dyer had a beauteous daughter, Arachne by name, and she, so runs the legend, was a spinner of no mean powers. But vanity of her deft art was the fair Arachne's weakness, and she was led to challenge Minerva to a trial of skill in spinning. Such a challenge, coming even from a demi-goddess, not to speak of a humble mortal, would have been rudeness enough; and, resenting the liberty, Minerva is said to have changed the purple-dyer's daughter into a spider, in which guise, it is to be presumed, she would have scope and use for her weaving powers. Thus much for mythology, and by way of accounting for the zoologist's reasons for including the spider tribes and their near relatives the mites and scorpions under the common term *Arachnida*. In the popular zoology which grows with us from our earliest days, a spider is, of course, an "insect." Zoologically, Arachne and her neighbours claim a rank of higher nature than that assigned to the bulk of the insect class; and it may be well, as facilitating our recognition of the personal history of the spinners in question, to glance at the head-marks of their race. A spider's head, to begin with an important region of its body, does not exist as a separate and distinct portion of its body, as in an insect, but is amalgamated with its chest. Like the insects, the spider and her neighbours possess legs which are attached to the chest region alone, and which do not belong to the tail as in the nearly related lobsters and their relations. The tail or "abdomen" of the spider is moreover unjointed, and in this latter respect differs from the tails of the insect tribe; and whilst the latter possesses a pair of "feelers"—technically termed "antennæ"—springing from the head, the spider exhibits a total want of such appendages, although persons skilled in the science of comparisons (which the learned name "homology") are prone to consider that the big jaws of a spider, carrying the poison-fangs, are in reality the altered "feelers" of the Arachnidan fraternity. Be this as it may, feelers are plainly wanting in the spinners and weavers; and another point of difference between the insects and the latter is found in the total absence of wings; although it is noteworthy that certain insects, by no means of lowly grade, in addition to those of plebeian and parasitic habits, want wings entirely. Nor must we neglect to note that the Arachnidans are the gainers in respect of legs, which invariably number eight. The veriest aristocrat of an insect never possesses more than six legs, at least when fully grown; for it is permissible neither from an æsthetic nor from a scientific point of view to take into account the fleshy stumps with which some insects, in the days of their infancy, and when appearing as the Epicurean caterpillars, are provided. In the matter of breathing as well, the Arachnidans bear off the palm in respect of their possessing certain peculiar bags placed in the sides of their bodies, filled with delicate folds or leaves, and named pulmonary sacs or lung sacs. The insect breathes by a curious arrangement of air-tubes, branching everywhere throughout its body; so that the spider possesses a more localised and a better-defined breathing apparatus—although a close likeness to the features of the insect in this latter respect, that of breathing, may exist amongst Arachnidans themselves. Last of all, amongst characters in insects which spiders lack, we may place the compound eyes of the former. Our Arachnidans have simple eyes, consisting of a few—usually some half-dozen, or at most eight—specks scattered over the front part of the body; but they never possess the great masses of visual organs we familiarly see distending the sides of the head in the fly and other insects, and which constitute veritable wonders, upon which the entomologically-minded amongst us are never weary of expatiating in learned discourse.

So much for the *personnel* and distinguishing features of Arachne and her neighbours. A similar inquiry into the disposition and private character of the Arachnidan species would reveal much that was puzzling, and not a little that might prove inexplicable, even in these days of ready theorising and explanatory speculation. Take as an example the domestic life of Madame *Tegenaria domestica*, as the lady-person domiciled in the corner of the room is named. There can exist no reasonable doubt—indeed, there are no grounds whatever for doubting the statement—that Madame is thoroughly paramount, and that Mr. *Tegenaria domestica*, like not a few male animals inhabiting the highest spheres of society, is practically a nonentity, and might, without very great loss to Arachnidan society, be regarded as practically non-existent. The gentleman in question, like erratic humans too much given to club-life, is rarely, if ever, seen within his domestic circle; and the difficulty connected with his movements and existence is not merely when, but where he takes his walks abroad. The ladyspiders are, indeed, a race of viragoes pure and simple. The most enthusiastic students of Arachnidan ways have never described those of the female sex as bland; and it is by no means a mythical or supposititious statement that the henpecked husbands are not merely frequently mauled in unmerciful fashion, but are actually devoured by their mates.* This is truly a horrible state of matters, but it is nevertheless true; and Arachnidan society appears tacitly to justify the extreme procedure last mentioned, and to regard the mysterious disappearance of a husband as an event which the lady most interested is entitled to regard with equanimity, if not as an utterly uninteresting proceeding.

But if Madame Tegenaria and her blood relations are thus given to husband-slaughter in a wholesale way, it must not be imagined that the social feelings or affections are wholly unrepresented in Arachnidan society. There is a tacit agreement among the best friends and biographers of the race, that in the matter of affection for their progeny Mesdames Tegenariæ and friends are models of parents. The young appear to be tended and fed with scrupulous care, and the race before us presents thus a certain marked contrast to such cruel mothers as the queen bees which kill their daughters, and to the workers which kill the drones. The male spiders by all accounts are peripatetic and erratic in their ways, and wander about from nest to nest in a thoroughly Bohemian fashion. Statisticians inform us that the males as a rule preponderate in the Arachnidan race—an apparently wise provision, considering the frequency with which they are slaughtered by their mates. In one or two families, however, the female sex appears to predominate as in higher life; and Thorell, of Upsala, has left it on record that in his opinion the lady-spiders on the whole exceed their mates in numbers. Blackwall, in his work on the spiders, indicates that the males are darker-coloured, as a rule, than the females; but there are cases where the male and female appear as exact counterparts one of another.

* De Geer, as quoted by Kirby and Spence, tells us that he has witnessed an unfortunate husband "seized by the object of his attentions, enveloped by her in a web, and then devoured; a sight which," he adds, "filled him with horror and indignation."

A chapter of high interest might be written on the courtship of the Arachnidan race, involving, as do the matrimonial intents of the race, many curious features. In one or two species of spiders, the gentlemen possess the power of emitting a curious chirping sound, the ladies being, wonderful to relate, voiceless: a quality upon which Anacreon, as will be remembered, congratulated the insect-Cicadas, since their wives—as is really the case—are dumb. There is no doubt that such a musical apparatus, consisting of a roughened patch on the tail against which the chest is rubbed, is intended as a species of loving blandishment to captivate Mesdames. And Monsieur Theridion, approaching the domicile of Mademoiselle Theridion, softly twangs his guitar, and thus announces at once, and through the appropriate medium of the divine art, his intentions and emotions. Such a procedure reaches, it is true, in the insect group, a higher stage of culture than in the Arachnidan fraternity; but its occurrence anywhere in lower life affords a foundation for the belief, that courtship by serenade and the blandishments of Orpheus had plain precedents ages ago, in the loves of the insects and their allied kith and kin. So also, it has been alleged by high authority that spiders have been attracted by music. If this latter assertion be correct, it places the idea of a defined purpose underlying the sounds of Theridion on a basis of more than ordinary probability and reasonableness. Thus, in the matter of woman's rights alone, the Arachnidans are all that, and perhaps a good deal more than, our own lady-liberationists could wish for; whilst there is no doubt that in attention to domestic duties, and in the ordering of household ways and domestic life—as occasionally proved by the experiences of mankind—the shrew may take precedence of some more amiable and milder-tempered wives.

The ways of spider-existence can only be fully comprehended when we dip into the general anatomy of the group. Even the nature of the threads and thrums with the mention of which this rambling chronicle was begun, may be understood solely by the light thrown on the spinning-apparatus by a popular and short lecture on comparative anatomy. Let us thus firstly examine the mouth and its belongings, by way of satisfying a normal curiosity regarding the well-known sting and poison of the race. The jaws of a spider, like those of a beetle, number four—a large and a small pair. The large pair —technically the "mandibles"—are hooked at their tips; the hooks being the poison-"fangs," in each of which the duct or tube, leading from the poison-gland in the head, terminates. When I discern Madame Tegenaria in her web, busily engaged in mastering the struggles of the fly which has just become entangled in the deceitful snare, I can predict that there will be both scant mercy and "Jeddart justice" shown to the hapless victim. Soon the poison-fang will be plunged into its body; the deadly secretion will pass rapidly to mingle with the vital fluid, and *Musca domestica's* struggles will speedily cease. The bite of any known species of spider is certainly neither fatal nor dangerous to human life. At the very most, a spider's wound might produce an inflamed puncture; but the virus is not potent enough to affect human muscles, nerves, or tissues at large. Even the famed Tarantula itself, is a delusion and a snare. The Tarantula spider is the *Lycosa tarantula* of Italy and Spain, whose bite was long believed to produce a species of dancing madness—imitated, of course, in the fashionable *Tarantelles* wherewith young aspirants in pianoforte practice torture at once their own fingers, the instrument in question, and the ears and minds of their hearers. The Tarantula is one of the wandering or peripatetic members of its race. Making no web, it hides beneath stones, and like a lurking bandit pounces upon its prey when occasion offers. "Tarantism," as the condition alluded to is named, unquestionably does exist as a species of uncontrollable muscular spasm; but the association of the affection with the bite of the spider in question is simply mythical, and rests on no certain or demonstrable basis. Arachnidans, however, are well provided with means of defence and offence suiting their life. The large tropical species can sting small birds to their death; and, in any case, the spider is a superior creature in this respect to its clumsy scorpion neighbour, which wanders hither and thither with its tail curled over its back by way of protecting its sting from injury: whilst a somewhat foolish trait of scorpion character is also known, wherein, when made to sting itself, the animal succumbs to its own injury.

But we are veering round gradually towards the threads and thrums, to the spinners and spun; and the inquiry, "Where is the loom, and how does it work?" may now be said to await us. Let authority in the guise of the zoologist reply. Looking at the tail-extremity of a spider, we can readily perceive by aid of a strong lens from two to four pairs of conical projections. These are named the *spinnerets*. Each is but a much altered limb, and indeed, were proof of this latter statement required, we might point to one group of Arachnidans (*Hersilla*), in which the three pairs of spinnerets are seen to present a thoroughly leg-like nature. What, then, is the function of these spinnerets, which exist to the number of three pairs in Madame Tegenaria in the corner? The reply is, that they are used to reel off the silk wherewith the domicile is woven and built. Microscopically examined, you would find that each spinneret is in reality composed of a multitude of very fine tubes, which open at its tip. Next let us inquire as to the mode of production of the thread. Our spiders are by no means the only weavers in nature. Those lazy gourmands the caterpillars, which cause the gardener's heart to grow faint when he contemplates their Sybaritic ravages on the choicest of his leaves, spin a thread likewise, and afford us "floss" silk when the fabrication happens to be an infant moth belonging to one or other of the silk-producing species. And removed from the insect class altogether, and passing into the depths of the sea, we may still find spinners enough and to spare. The mussels of our own coasts, and the Pinnas of the Mediterranean Sea, present us with instances of animal weavers in plenty, and with examples of the manufacture of threads sometimes of a nature durable in the extreme.

But in insect or mollusc, in Arachnidan or caterpillar, there is a striking similarity in the manner of production of threads and fabrics. The material wherewith Madame Tegenaria spins is secreted or manufactured from her blood, like every other product of the animal economy, by special organs which receive the name of "glands." These silk-glands manufacture a dense semi-fluid matter, which, so long as it remains within the gland, retains its fluid nature. When, however, it is exposed to the air, it becomes more tenacious, and is then capable of being pressed out through the infinitesimally fine tubes we have seen to compose the spinnerets. The conversion of a glutinous fluid into a thread is strictly paralleled by the familiar illustration of glue in a glue-pot. So long as the glue is kept heated on the fire, it is fluid. But if, when the process of liquefaction has proceeded to a certain stage, we lift the glue on the brush, we may draw out the semi-fluid mass in the form of threads into which it has rapidly cooled by exposure to the air. And so with the threads of Arachnidans. But if the spinnerets are perforated with numerous tubes through which the fluid silk is drawn to form threads, why do we not perceive the numerous threads in question? The zoologist replies that the many threads are united to form the single strand with which the web is formed and other operations of spider-life carried on. Think for a moment of the extreme fineness of this apparently single, but in reality compound, rope of Madame Tegenaria, for instance, and then try to imagine, if you can, the delicacy of the four hundred odd strands of which it is composed; or hie you to Madame *Epeira* in the garden, and try to conceive how infinitesimally slim must be the thousand or so threads which make up her single strand—itself a mere gossamer string with which the summer breeze plays at will, and which even a gentle gust of wind mocks to its destruction. Scientific imagining has its limits, like the thoughts which run at will on mountains of vanity in common life; but in the face of the fineness of spiders' threads, we may well think of a boundary, not to the indivisibility of matter, but to our powers of following matter into its lesser and microscopic phases.

As Arachne spins her fabric, so insects spin their threads, and molluscs weave their thrums, as we shall see. But the manner in which this raw material—the thread—is wound and woven to form the domiciles of the spider tribe, awaits our further thought. Out in the garden exist plenty of spinners belonging to a very notable family—the Epeiras—whose web-spinning habits you may watch, provided you can extricate yourself sufficiently early from the toils of Morpheus, and sally forth in the early summer morning bent on a zoological study. You will then see *Epeira diademata* hard at work house-building and repairing, like a busy contractor with his hands full. Engaged on a new venture in the way of domicile, Epeira may be seen bustling hither and thither over the twigs and branches of the shrub whereto the web is to be attached, and, having fixed upon a site, may be seen suddenly to drop from the twig, and as suddenly to be arrested in some mysterious fashion in mid air. This is no mere acrobatic exhibition, but a preliminary measure probably having for its object the drawing of a mass of silken threads from the spinnerets. Soon the morning breezes waft the threads towards the projecting tips of neighbouring branches, to which they adhere; and when the threads have become fixed, you will see Epeira hauling at the threads with her fore-legs like some deft sailor, by way of testing their strength. Selecting her special thread, Epeira will now probably cut adrift the remainder, and will turn her attention towards the stability of her line. This first thread runs across the centre or thereabouts of the future web—for you remember that Epeira spins a geometric house—and from the point of attachment of this first thread, Epeira will pass to fix the line, spun as she runs to point after point, and thus to mark out the circumference of her habitation. Next are formed diagonal lines across the outer circle already made; and soon a series of radiating threads is formed, and the outline or skeleton of the edifice is completed. In her journeys you will see, and I hope admire, how cleverly Epeira, like a skilful rope-walker, travels back to the centre of the web, along the line she has spun, and you will notice also how her feet, or rather her toes, serve as most admirable tools and combs in arranging the threads and in fixing them as well.

The next portion of Epeira's task consists in the formation of the series of circular threads which pass from each of the spokes or radii of her wheel-like outline, and which convert the spaces between the spokes into veritable ladders. Proceeding to the centre, Epeira begins to spin a spiral thread, the whorls of which grow larger and larger as she approaches the circumference of her net. Round and round she weaves, crossing the radii in her spiral track, and deftly fastening the thread to each spoke as she crosses it, with a minute globule of some glutinous fluid. The larger the spider, the greater will be the space between the spirals of the web; and on approaching the circumference of her domicile, a second spiral thread seems to replace the first which began in the centre. This outer thread, as you may see by inspecting a web, is perfectly bedizened with globules of a gummy fluid, which, like the sundew's glittering secretion, will fast bind the unwary insect that comes in contact with the snare.* And thus Epeira makes her web, and lays a snare which Nature perfectly approves of, and authorises as one way of gaining an easy livelihood, and of placing the operator and builder well forward in the inevitable "struggle for existence."

But showers of rain and dust-storms sadly annoy our Epeira. Often a single shower will materially damage a web, and set the owner to work biting through the inner threads, which she rolls into a ball and then drops to the ground, and thereafter makes new spirals as before. Or dust-laden and wet, the domicile may be useless as a snare, and Epeira, deserting a ruined home, constructs a new dwelling-place, and appears in

* Speaking of these globules, Mr. Blackwall writes: "An estimate of the number of viscid globules distributed on the elastic spiral line in a net of *Epeira apodisa* of a medium size will convey some idea of the elaborate operations performed by the Geometric Spiders in the construction of their snares. The mean distance between two contiguous radii is about seven-tenths of an inch; if, therefore, the number 7 be multiplied by 20, the mean number of viscid globules which occur on one-tenth of an inch of the elastic spiral line at the ordinary degree of tension, the product will be 140, the mean number of globules deposited on seven-tenths of an inch of the elastic spiral line; this product multiplied by 24, the mean number of circumvolutions formed by the elastic spiral line, 3,360, (as) the mean number of globules contained between two radii; which multiplied by 26, the mean number of radii, produces 87,360, the total number of viscid globules in a finished net of average dimensions."

the genuine excitement of work to forget the troubles of the past.*

Watch Epeira, as she lies in wait for prey, realising Sir John Davies' apt description of her attitude :—

> A subtle spider, which doth sit
> In middle of her web which spreadeth wide ;
> If aught do touch the utmost thread of it,
> She feels it instantly on every side.

Firm poised sits Madame in the centre of her geometric spiral, usually head downwards, but listening intently—albeit that we know nothing of her ears, which, perchance, like those of the lobster, may exist somewhere in or near the belongings or appendages of her head. With that sense of touch praised by him of Twickenham as so "exquisitely fine," and with each foot firmly set on a radius or spoke of her web, Epeira waits for the coming fly. Soon the insect comes. A vibration passes along the cords from the sticky circumference where Musca is entangled in extreme perplexity of mind. At once, Epeira is on the alert. Seizing several radiating threads, she sharply jerks them; and if the subsequent struggles of the captured one convince her that she has landed her prey, she will rapidly traverse the web towards the outside edge, seize the prey in her jaws, and instil her potent venom. Thereafter she will enclose her victim in a silken shroud, and dispose of him in some quiet corner, whither in due time she may retire to feast upon the juices and fluids of his frame. You will have witnessed in such a

---

* Judging, indeed, from the rapidity with which Epeira works, there should exist much leisure time and breathing space for the race, if the effects of work and the dissipation of energy in the Arachnidan bear any relation to those seen in the human species. Mr. Blackwall says an *Epeira apodisa* will complete its web in about forty minutes, provided it meets with no interruption; and the rapidity with which spinnerets and legs move, and the work of thread-production proceeds, may best be proved by interviewing the artisans at home.

study, how greatly Epeira and, indeed, all Arachnidans depend on their sense of touch for information regarding the outer world. We know little or nothing of the seeing powers of those insignificant eye-specks scattered over the back of her head and chest, but we may readily conceive that the acute sense of touch, resident not merely in the palpi or feelers of the mouth, but in the legs as well, and which responds to every vibration, will very fully supply to the spider race the place of the visual and other sensory organs of higher existence. Not a movement appears to be made by the ordinary Arachnidan without the accompanying work of spinning a thread. From place to place Epeira moves, quickly and deftly too, but ever accompanied by the thread which she who runs, spins. A friendly call—a practice which, by the way, is not much in vogue in Arachnidan society—would be performed by aid of the thread, the one extremity of which is secured at home, whilst the other end merges into the as yet unformed strands of the spinneret. Along this thread the return journey is made. From a height Epeira drops safely and securely by means of the well-nigh invisible strand, and up this thread she clambers with agility when danger looms or necessity drives. Thus does the Arachnidan literally live "along the line," and it is perhaps hard to conceive of any exactly similar mode of progression in the animal world. Imagine an aerial humanity proceeding, on business or pleasure bent, by means of clothes-lines. Or think of the announcement made by a polite attendant that Madame Tegenaria's "line" was at the door, and waiting to take her home; whilst, instead of the complaint that "Madame Epeira's carriage stops the way," it would be said that the lady's "line" had got entangled with the threads of other members of society, and that the owner would oblige by speedily attending to its due arrangement.

The phases of Arachnidan society might, if pursued and described in detail, lead us very far from our room and our garden; but there remain for notice several features connected, firstly, with the varying habits of spinning and weaving seen in the class, and secondly, with the nature of the instincts which the race of Epeiras, Tegenarias, and their friends, regarded as a whole, exhibit. Place for utilitarian considerations, and for the domestic economy of spiders' webs. During last century Le Bon of Languedoc wove spiders' silk into various articles, such as gloves and stockings. Bermuda ladies use spiders' silk for sewing, such strands being thick and strong. But spider-nature is by no means docile, and the domestication and civilization of the errant race to become respectable fabricators of silk for the use of man is simply a dream of the future, which may or may not be realised. Only this much may be said, that Dr. B. G. Wilder of America asserts that the *Nephila plumipes* of the Southern States of America affords a silk which, could it be procured in sufficient quantities, would be a perfectly marketable commodity. It is the above-named species of *Nephila* which in tropic forests constructs nets of strength sufficient to capture small birds, and from this genus the Bermuda dames obtain sewing thread. The lady Nephilas are the workers; Messieurs the Nephilas are minute as compared with their spouses; and from what we already know of the degraded state of male society in the Arachnidan race, it would be too much to expect these wretched creatures to emulate the ways and industry of their literally giant partners.

A ramble through pastures Arachnidan, calls up in imagination not a few curious and interesting forms to which a walk through the nearest museum of large dimensions, and a glance at the Arachnidan cases, will serve as a practical commentary and illustration. A summer day and a green meadow, with its waterpool by the clump of osiers, rises to mental view as we recall to mind the *Argyroneta* we saw there—this last being a spider which takes to water as its natural habitat, and which builds a nest and cocoon beneath the surface in the shape of a veritable diving-bell. Here this amphibian lady lives and thrives, ascending periodically to the surface of the pool to entangle a bubble of air in the hairs with which her body is covered, and to descend with this atmospheric supply to her nest. Then, also, we are reminded of the " Wanderers," which, making no web or nest, lurk beneath stones and rush out to seize their prey, like the Tarantula of evil fame. And we remember the Leaping Spiders (*Salticus*); so named because they progress with a leaping gait, and recall to mind certain insect-brethren of the hearth and meadow. Nor must we neglect to mention the *Mygale* tribe or Mason Spiders, which construct the trap-door abodes so familiar in Southern Europe; excavating a deep pit which is lined with the silken material, and closed by a cunningly contrived and cleverly concealed lid. Whilst, lastly, may be mentioned Madame *Clotho*, well named after the Fate, since of the spinners and weavers she might well represent the chief, or an embodiment of Arachne herself. Here you will find a weaver which constructs a tent of a fine taffeta, secures it to the ground with silken cords, and stains the outside so as to mimic accurately the hue of the surrounding objects. Herein the Clotho family lives; herein the young are reared; and herein are exercised those instincts which puzzle us the more as we continue to dwell upon the variety and perfection of their work.

So we bid farewell to the spinners and weavers, *en famille*, and approach at least part of the philosophy of their being. The spider may, in one sense, be well compared to a headless insect; the organs and parts constituting the insect head—

always a well-defined part of the economy in question—are but imperfectly developed in the spider race. But on all grounds, our spider is an animal of much higher instincts than the average insect. Wary to a fault, strategic in the highest degree, cunning in every detail of life, active and mechanically minded—such qualities, I repeat, would naturally be regarded as the outcome and work of a nervous system higher than that of the careless insect the current of whose existence, as a rule, flows evenly along. Now, in nature, there exists such principles as type and likeness, whereby each animal belonging to any given group, preserves, beneath variations in form, the typical or primary disposition of parts seen in the least modified members of its class. Worms, insects, centipedes, crabs, lobsters, and a host of other and allied creatures, thus fall into one and the same group. In the worm and insect, the nervous system exists typically as a double chain of nerves and nerve-knots lying along the floor of the body. Now, Arachnidan society, in virtue of its relations to the insect type, is bound to possess a nervous system of like character; and so we find the guiding apparatus of the spider to be situated below. But when we scan the form of that nervous system we seem to lose sight of the double or single chain arrangement just mentioned as characteristic of the insect-class and its allies, for we notice the spider's nerves to form a great mass in the floor of its head and chest. How and why has this altered arrangement been produced? The answer is clear. To produce a nervous system of higher type than that of the insect, two courses were open to Dame Nature. She might have supplied Arachne with additional nerves and nerve-knots; but such a procedure, as we have just observed, is against the rules, which forbid any great departure from a given type. Or, secondly, Nature might, by *concentrating* otherwise scattered nerve-centres, give

I

increased nerve-power. And this latter alternative has been duly pursued in the case of our spiders. Increased centralisation of nerves has afforded increased nerve-power, and hence we perceive a natural basis for replying to the query concerning the origin of the higher powers of Arachne as compared with the average insect. That spiders and insects may have had a common origin is by no means a far-fetched supposition. Insects, as they are entitled to claim by reason of their older fossil history, may take the first place; but it is not difficult to conceive that from some primitive insect-like stock the tribe of spinners and weavers descended in the far-back ages. Whilst here and there, as in the spinning insect-caterpillars, or in that poor relation of the centipedes named *Peripatus*—which spins threads when alarmed, by way, presumably, of showing its fear and disgust—we also meet with traces of a development of spinning powers, imitating, in feeble degree only, the more perfect workmanship of the beings which claim the purple-dyer's daughter as their patron and mythological heroine.

But little space remains wherein the spinners of threads and thrums amongst the shell-fish may receive a just meed of attention. Still, to pass over these molluscan fabricators in silence would seem to cast a slur on their handiwork, although their labours may seem but dull and commonplace after the lively land-weavers of nets and webs. Perhaps the best-known spinner of threads on our own coasts is the common mussel, which one may pick up by the dozen on rocky coasts, having bound to itself, by means of its strong threads, stones and shells, often making up a mass many times its own weight and bulk. Try to detach a mussel from a secure crevice in a rock, where it lies hidden along with numerous neighbours, and your weary fingers will attest the strength of the mussel's "beard," as its collection of threads is popularly named—the "*byssus*" of those whose business it is to lecture upon big and little fish alike. Whence does the "beard" come, and how is it formed? Open your mussel—for the more familiar oyster has no beard, at least when adult, and prefers to fix itself in its "bed" directly, by implanting its shell in its native mud. You will then see a prominent organ of conical shape, and deeply grooved in appearance. This is the "foot" of your mollusc, an organ more familiarly seen in the broad walking-disc of that retiring mollusc the snail or slug. And it is a "foot" identical in nature with that of the mussel by means of which the familiar cockle leaps over its sandy habitation, and by aid of which the Solen or razor-shell burrows swiftly and deeply into the obscurity of the sand.

From the base of the foot hangs the bundle of stout threads which this foot moulds and forms. The "foot" is thus the weaver of the mussel's beard, and the manner of secretion of the threads takes place in a fashion quite analogous to that in which the spider makes its thread. From special glands forming part of the mussel's belongings, comes the same semi-fluid material, which, run into the groove in the foot, sets therein as a firm thread. This thread is drawn out of the foot by the retraction of that organ, and another thread is rapidly formed, until the "beard" grows apace, and the mussel has tied itself to something, or has tied something to itself, as we have seen.

The "beard" of the mussel as a zoological curiosity is interesting enough, no doubt, but that it could by any stretch of the imagination be regarded as subserving an important function in defending man's structures against the ravages of time and tide, is altogether an unlikely supposition. Listen, however, to a curious recital, quoted by Mr. Gosse in his manual of the "Mollusca":—"At the town of Bideford in Devonshire, there is a long bridge of twenty-four arches across the Torridge river, near its junction with the Taw. At this bridge the tide flows so rapidly that it cannot be kept in repair by mortar. The corporation, therefore, keep boats in employ to bring mussels to it, and the interstices of the bridge are filled by hand with these mussels. It is supported from being driven away by the tide entirely by the strong threads these mussels fix to the stonework; and by an Act or grant, it is a crime liable to transportation for any person to remove these mussels, unless in the presence and by the consent of the corporation trustees." Such a history is both curious and interesting, and in the absence of any contradiction—Mr. Gosse's "Manual" bears date 1854—the correctness of the narrative may be assumed, if only from an inductive inference concerning the strength of the byssus of the mussels on the beach. The story, besides, presents but another and perhaps novel illustration of the old axiom, *L'union fait la force.*

Utilitarianism may again claim us when we find that a near neighbour of the mussel—the Mediterranean Pinna—manufactures a silky byssus in sufficient quantity to enable the Sicilians to weave it into gloves and stockings. These latter are rather *articles de luxe,* however, than garments of wear, and are costly withal; the latter fact depending on the nature of their origin and the trouble of manufacture. Pope Benedict XV. received in 1754 from certain of his subjects a pair of stockings of Pinna's "beard," and the event was regarded as testifying to the worth of the present and to the dexterity of the manufacturers—a dexterity which was certainly equalled in respect of its ingenuity by Dame Nature herself in the production of the raw material.

This history of threads and thrums draws to a close. Madame Tegenaria is busy in her corner still. It was she who inspired this subject and its title, and I think of bestirring myself, in common gratitude, to capture that buzzing insect, whose disturbing hum must reach Arachnidan society in the corner, and fill it with vain hopes of a goodly banquet. I shall, at any rate, say farewell to the history of Tegenaria and her race for the nonce. Some other day Arachnidan ways and customs may engage an hour of leisure-time. In her corner Tegenaria may live and prosper, it is true; but the inevitable duster looms in the distance, and of the fate which may possibly await our deft spinner—who can tell?

WHALES AND THEIR NEIGHBOURS.

The medical student who, in answer to an examiner anxious to ascertain the exact amount of the lad's knowledge concerning fishes, replied, that "he knew them all from the limpet to the whale," must indeed be credited with a larger share of candour than of zoological science. The limpet is a shell "fish" by courtesy at the best, but the whale, public opinion notwithstanding, is not a fish in any sense of the term. The most that can be said of the whale in this respect is that it is fish-like; and, admitting that appearances in zoological society are as deceptive as in ordinary existence, it behoves us to be cautious in accepting outward resemblances as indicative of real and veritable affinity. A popular lesson in natural history, then, teaches us that a whale is a mammal or quadruped—that is, apart from the mere etymology of the word, it belongs to the quadruped-class. It possesses but two legs, or rather "arms," it is true, and these members do not resemble limbs. But it is a quadruped notwithstanding its deficiencies in this respect; and it agrees in all the characters which are found to distinguish the class to which man himself belongs—that of the mammalia. These characters it may be advantageous very briefly to detail, by way of preliminary to the general study of whales and their nearest relations. Thus, firstly, they are warm-blooded animals, a statement which must be taken as meaning that their blood is of a temperature considerably higher than that of the medium in which they live. The fish, on the other hand, is a cold-blooded creature. Its temperature is only slightly higher than that of the surrounding water, and in this respect it agrees with all invertebrate animals and with the frogs and reptiles of its own sub-kingdom. Next in order, may be noticed the agreement of the whale with the quadruped in the matter of body-covering. The covering of the latter consists of hairs. Although the body of the whale cannot be described, by any stretch of the imagination, as having hair, the presence of a few bristles around the mouth-extremity sufficiently indicates the nature of its outer garment; whilst, before birth, the body-covering in some whales is tolerably plentiful, but is soon shed, leaving the hide thick, shining, and hairless. The microscopist might inform us that the blood of the whale presents the same characters as that of other mammals, and possesses red corpuscles or coloured bodies, which, unlike those of the fish, reptile, and bird, have no central particle or "nucleus." And whilst the heart of the fish is a comparatively simple engine of propulsion, consisting of two contractile chambers or cavities, the whale's heart will be found like that of man and other quadrupeds in all essential details of its structure. It is thus a four-chambered organ doing double duty, in that it sends blood not only through the system, but also to the lungs for purification.

The mention of lungs, as the breathing organs of whales, at once introduces us to a new field of inquiry concerning the habits and life of the aquatic monsters. A popular notion exists that of necessity a water-living animal must be a *water-breather*. The idea of fish-existence and of the manner in which fishes breathe evidently reigns paramount in the present case. That an animal may be completely aquatic in its habits, and yet breathe air directly from the atmosphere, and after a like procedure to that witnessed in human respiration, is a notable fact. A water-newt, despite its aquatic habits, ascends periodically to the surface of the water to breathe, and seals, walruses, and whales agree in that they are truly lung-breathers, and possess gills at no period of their existence. True, a gill differs from a lung only in that it is capable of exposing the blood circulating through it to the air which is entangled or mechanically suspended in the water. Atmospheric air, containing the vitalising oxygen for the renewal and purification of the blood, is the great *desideratum* on the part of all animals, high and low alike. And the gill and lung, therefore, differ simply in the manner and method in which the blood in each is brought in contact with the air, and not in the essential details of their work. The whales are known to "blow," and the act of "blowing" is simply the act of breathing—to be more particularly noticed hereafter. Thus a whale or seal would be drowned, as certainly as an ordinary quadruped would be asphyxiated, were its periodical access to the atmosphere prevented; and the curious fact may here be mentioned that there are also certain abnormal living fishes—notably the climbing perch and *Ophiocephali* in India—which, to use the words of a writer, are as easily drowned as dogs when denied access to the air. There is little need to particularise any of the remaining characters which demonstrate the whale's relationship to mammals, and its difference in structural points from the fishes. The young whale is thus not merely born alive, but is nourished by means of the milk-secretion of the parent, and this last evidence of direct connection with higher animals might of itself be deemed a crucial test of the place and rank of the whales in the animal series.

But, granting that in the whales we meet with true quadrupeds, it may be well to indicate the chief points in which they differ from their mammalian brethren at large. It may be admitted, at the outset, that they present us with a very distinct modification of the quadruped type. Their adaptation to a water life is so complete, in truth, that it has destroyed to a large extent the outward and visible signs of their relationship with mammals. The body is thoroughly fish-like and tapers towards the tail, where we meet with a tail-fin, which, however, is set right across the body, and not vertically as in the fishes. This latter difference, indeed, is a very prominent feature in whale-structure. The limbs, as already remarked, are represented by the two fore-limbs alone. No trace of hinder-extremities is to be perceived externally, and the anatomical investigation of the skeleton reveals at the best the merest rudiments of haunch-bones and of hind limbs in certain whales, of which the well-known Greenland whale may be cited as an example. A distinct character of the whales has been found by naturalists of all periods in the "blowholes," or apertures through which the whale is popularly supposed to "spout." Thus we find on the upper surface of the head of a Greenland whale a couple of these "blowholes," or "spiracles," as they are also called. These apertures exist on the front of the snout in the sperm whales, whilst in the porpoises, dolphins, and their neighbours the blowhole is single, of crescentic shape, and, placed on the top of the head. It requires but little exercise of anatomical skill to indentify the "blowholes" of the whales with the nostrils of other animals; and it becomes an interesting matter to trace the adaptation of the nostrils to the aquatic life and breathing habits of these animals.

There are natural-history text-books still extant in which a very familiar error regarding the "blowing" of the whales is propagated—an error which, like many other delusions of popular kind, has become so fossilised, so to speak, that it is difficult to convince believers of its falsity. A manual of natural history, of no ancient date, lies before me as I write, and when I turn to the section which treats of the whales, I find an illustration of a Greenland whale, which is represented as lying high and dry on the beach, but which, despite its stranded state, appears in the act of vigorously puffing streams of water from the blowholes on the top of its head. To say the least of it, such an illustration is simply fictitious, and might safely be discarded as of purely inventive kind, were it only from the fact of its supposing a whale to be provided with some mysterious reservoir of water from which it could eject copious streams, even when removed from the sea. The common notion regarding the "blowing" of the whale appears to be that which credits the animal with inhaling large quantities of water into its mouth, presumably in the act of nutrition. This water was then said to escape into the nostrils, and to be ejected therefrom in the act of blowing. The behaviour of a whale in the open sea, at first sight favours this apparently simple explanation. Careering along in the full exercise of its mighty powers, the huge body is seen to dive and to reappear some distance off at the surface, discharging from its nostrils a shower of water and spray. The observation is correct enough as it stands, but the interpretation of the phenomena is erroneous. Apart from the anatomical difficulties in the way of explaining how water from the mouth could escape in such large quantities, and so persistently, into the nostrils, there is not merely an utter want of purpose in this view of the act of "spouting," but we have also to consider that this act would materially interfere with the breathing of the animal. Hence a more rational explanation of what is implied in the "blowing" of the whales rests on the simple assertion that the water and spray do not in reality proceed from the blowhole, but consist of water forced upwards into the air by the expiratory effort of the animal. The whale begins the expiratory or "breathing-out" action of its lungs just before reaching the surface of the water, and the warm expired air therefore carries up with it the water lying above the head and blowholes of the ascending animal. That this view is correct is rendered highly probable, not merely by the observation of the breathing of young whales and porpoises kept in confinement, but also by the fact that the last portion of the "blow" consists of a white silvery spray or vapour, formed by the rapid condensation of the warm air from the lungs as it comes in contact with the colder atmosphere. The water received into the mouth escapes at the sides of the mouth, and does not enter the nostrils at all.

The furnishings of the mouth of the whales include sundry remarkable structures peculiar to a certain family circle of these animals. Such are the "whalebone"-plates, furnishing a substance familiarly spoken of by everybody, but exemplifying at the same time a kind of material regarding the origin of which a tacit ignorance, sanctioned by the stolid indifference of many years' standing, commonly prevails. Whalebone, or "baleen," is a commodity occurring in one group of these animals only, this group being that of the whalebone whales (*Balænidæ*), of which the Greenland or right whale (*Balæna mysticetus*) is the most noteworthy example. From this whale the whalebone of commerce is derived; other and nearly related species—such as the rorquals and furrowed whales—possessing the whalebone plates in a comparatively rudimentary state. The baleen occurs in the mouth of these whales, and is disposed in a curious fashion. It exists in the form of flat plates of triangular shape, each plate being fixed by its base in the palate. The inner side, or that next the centre of the mouth, is strongly fringed by frayed-out whalebone fibres, the outer edge of each plate being straight. A double row of these triangular plates of baleen depends in the form of two great fringes from the palate of the whale; and it would appear that each baleen-plate is in reality a compound structure, being composed of several smaller plates closely united. The largest plates lie to the outer side of the series, and in a full-grown whale may measure from eight to fourteen feet in length, and as many as 250 or 300 plates may exist on each side of the palate.

The nature of these curious organs forms an appropriate subject of inquiry. It is exceedingly rare in nature to find an animal provided with organs or structures which have no affinity with organs in other and related animals. On the contrary, the principle of likeness or "homology" teaches us that the most unwonted and curious structures in animal existence are for the most part modifications of common organs, or at any rate of parts which are represented under varying forms and guises in other animals. By aid of such a principle we discover that the fore-limb of a horse, the wing of a bird, and the paddle of a whale, are essentially similar in fundamental structure, and in turn agree in all necessary details with the arm of man. Through the deductions of this science of tracing likenesses and correspondences between the organs of different animals, the zoologist has been taught that the "air-bladder" or "sound" of the fish is the forerunner of the lung of higher animals—an inference proved by the fact that in some fishes, such as the curious lepidosirens, or "mud-fishes" of Africa and South America, the air-bladder actually becomes lung-like, not merely in form but in function also. By means of this useful guide to the mysteries of animal structure we note that the bony box in which the body of the tortoise or turtle is contained, is formed by no new elements or parts, but consists chiefly of the greatly modified backbone, and of the ribs and scales of these animals. To what conclusion, then, does this same principle lead us respecting the nature of the baleen-plates in the mouth of the Greenland whale and its allies? To a sufficiently certain, but at the same time startling thought, is the reply of the comparative anatomist.

If we examine the structure of the human mouth, or that of animals allied to man, we find that cavity to be lined by a delicate layer named *epithelium*. This epithelium consists really of a modification of the upper layer of the skin, and we see this modification familiarly in the difference between the skin of the face and the layer which is infolded to form the covering of the lips and the lining membrane of the mouth. No tissue is more familiar to the student of physiology than epithelium, composed, as it is, of *epithelial cells* or microscopic elements, which in one form or another are found in almost every important tissue of the body. The epithelium is a delicate tissue, as usually seen in man and vertebrate animals; but in some instances it becomes hardened by the development of horny matter, and may then appear as a tissue of tolerably solid consistence. In the mouth of a cow or sheep, the epithelium of part of the upper jaw is found hardened and callous, and there forms a horny pad against which the front teeth of the lower jaw may bite in the act of mastication. It is exactly this epithelial layer, then, which becomes enormously developed in the whalebone whales to form the baleen-plates just described. That this is actually the case is ascertained by the development of the baleen-plates, as well as by their situation and relations to the gum and palate. And the recital becomes the more astonishing when we consider that from cells of microscopic size in other animals, structures of enormous extent may be developed in the whales. The baleen-plates possess a highly important office. They constitute a kind of huge strainer or sieve, the possession of which enables the whale to obtain its food in a convenient fashion. Whether or not biblical scholars and commentators agree in regarding the "great fish" which wrought calamity to the Prophet Jonah as a special creation, and as an entirely different animal from the whale of to-day, the plain fact remains that a whale has a gullet of relatively small size when compared with the bulk of the animal. Fortunately, however, the faith of rational mankind is not pinned to literal interpretation of the untoward incident chronicled in Jonah; and, whale or no whale, it is curious to learn that the largest of animals may in a manner be said to feed on some of the most diminutive of its fellows. In the far north, and in the surface-waters of the Arctic seas, myriads of minute organisms, closely allied to our whelks, and like molluscs, are found. Such are the "sea-butterflies," or *Pteropoda* of the naturalist; little delicate creatures which paddle their way through the yielding waters by aid of the wing-like appendages springing from the sides of the head and neck. These organisms are drawn into the mouth of the Greenland whale in veritable shoals, and as the literal flood of waters streams out at the sides of the mouth, the "sea-butterflies" are strained off therefrom, the savoury morsels being retained by the fringed edges of the baleen-plates, and thereafter duly swallowed as food.

An interesting speculation yet remains, however, regarding the origin and first development of these peculiar whalebone structures. Advocates of the doctrine which assumes that animal forms and their belongings arise by gradual modifications of pre-existent animals, may be reasonably asked to explain the origin of the baleen-plates of the whales. Let us briefly hear what Mr. Darwin, as the spokesman of the party, has to say in reply to such an inquiry. Quoting a remark of an opponent regarding the whalebone, Mr. Darwin says, if the baleen "'had once attained such a size and development as to be at all useful, then its preservation and augmentation within serviceable limits would be promoted by selection alone. But how to obtain the beginning of such useful development?' In answer," continues Mr. Darwin (in his own words), "it may be asked, why should not the early progenitors of the whales with baleen have possessed a mouth constructed something like the lamellated beak of a duck. Ducks, like whales, subsist by sifting the mud and water; and the family (of ducks) has sometimes been called *Criblatores*, or sifters." Mr. Darwin's reference to the duck's bill is peculiarly happy. The edges of the beak in these birds are fringed with a beautiful series of horny plates named *lamellæ*, which serve as a straining apparatus as the birds grope for their food amidst the mud of ponds and rivers. These plates are richly supplied with nervous filaments, and, doubtless, also some as organs of touch. Mr. Darwin is careful to add that he hopes he may not "be misconstrued into saying that the progenitors of whales did actually possess mouths lamellated like the beak of a duck. I only wish to show," he continues, "that this is not incredible, and that the immense plates of baleen in the Greenland whale might have been developed from such lamellæ by finely graduated steps, *each of service to its possessor.*"

In these last words, which we have italicised, lies the strength of Mr. Darwin's hypothesis. Nature will preserve and develop useful structures alone, and will leave the useless and unneeded to perish and decay. This, indeed, is the keynote of Natural Selection. Mr. Darwin next proceeds to examine in detail the plates and lamellæ in the bill of a shoveller duck. He describes the horny plates, 188 in number, which "arise from the palate, and are attached by a flexible membrane to the sides of the mandible." He further notes that these plates "in several respects resemble the plates of baleen in the mouth of a whale." If the head of a shoveller duck were made as long as the head of a species of whale in which the baleen-plates are only nine inches long, the duck's lamellæ would be six inches in length. The head of the shoveller is about one-eighteenth of the length of the head of such a whale, so that the difference in size between the duck's lamellæ and the imperfect baleen-plates of this whale is not markedly disproportionate after all. After the examination of the beaks of various species of swimming-birds, Mr. Darwin arrives at the conclusion that "a member of the duck family with a beak constructed like that of the common goose, and adapted solely for grazing, or even a member with a beak having less well-developed lamellæ, might be converted by small changes into a species like the Egyptian goose (which partly grazes and partly sifts mud)—this into one like the common duck,—and lastly, into one like the shoveller, provided with a beak almost exclusively adapted for sifting the water; for this bird could hardly use any part of its beak, except the hooked tip for seizing or tearing solid food. The beak of a goose, as I may add," says Mr. Darwin, "might also be converted by small changes into one provided with prominent recurved teeth, like those of the Merganser (a member of the same family), serving for the widely different purpose of securing live fish."

Mr. Darwin next endeavours to apply the moral of this interesting sketch of probable modification of the bills of ducks to the case of the whales. If the stages of modification in these animals are hypothetically so clear, may not the case of the whalebone-bearing whales be susceptible of like explanation? A certain whale (*Hyperoödon*) belonging to a small group known popularly as the "beaked whales," from the possession of a prominent beak or snout, has no true teeth, but bears rough, unequal knobs of horny nature in its palate. Here, therefore, is a beginning for the work of selection and development. Granted that these horny processes were useful to the animal in the prehension and tearing of food, then their subsequent development into more efficient organs is a warrantable inference if the order of living nature teaches us aright. From rudimentary knobs, a further stage of development would lead to an increase in which they may have attained the size of the lamellæ of an Egyptian goose, which, as already remarked, are adapted both for sifting mud and for seizing food. A stage beyond, and we reach the shoveller's condition ("in which the lamellæ would be two-thirds of the length of the plates of baleen"), in a species of whalebone whale (*Balænoptera*) possessing a slight development of these organs. And from this point, the further gradations leading onwards to the enormous developments seen in the Greenland whale itself, are easily enough traced. Hypothetically, therefore, the path of development is clear enough. Even if it be remarked that the matter is entirely one of theory, not likely to be ever partly verified, far less proved at all, we may retort that any other explanation of the development of the organs of living beings, and of living beings themselves, must also be theoretical in its nature and as insusceptible of direct proof as are Mr. Darwin's ideas. But the thoughtful mind must select a side, and choose between probabilities; and it is not too much to say that towards the side of the idea which advocates gradual modification and selection as the rule of life and nature, every unbiassed student of natural science will by sheer force of circumstances be led to turn.

The whalebone whales have no teeth, although the sperm

whale possesses teeth in the lower jaw; but thereby—that is, as regards the teeth of whales at large—hangs a tale of some importance, and to which our attention may be briefly directed. Amongst the paradoxes of living nature, no circumstances present more curious features than those relating to the so-called "rudimentary organs" of animals and plants. Now, the whales furnish several notable examples of the anomalies which apparently beset the pathways of development in animals. The adult whalebone whale is toothless, as has just been remarked; and this fact becomes more than usually interesting when taken in connection with another, namely, that the young whale before birth possesses teeth, which are shed or absorbed, and in consequence disappear before it is born. These teeth never "cut the gum," and the upper jaw of the sperm whale presents us with a like phenomenon for consideration. Nor are the whales peculiar in this respect. The upper jaw of ruminant animals has no front teeth—as may be seen by looking at the mouth of a cow or sheep,—yet the calf may possess rudimentary teeth in this situation, these teeth also disappearing before birth. Now, what meaning, it may be asked, are we to attach to such phases of development? Will any considerations regarding the necessity for preserving the "symmetry," or "type," of the animal form aid us here? or will the old and over-strained argument from design enable us to comprehend why nature should provide a whale or a calf with teeth for which there is no conceivable use? The only satisfying explanation which may be given of such anomalies may be couched in Darwin's own words. The embryonic teeth of the whales have a reference "to a former state of things." They have been retained by the power of inheritance. They are the ignoble remnants and descendants of teeth which once were powerful enough, and of organs with which the mighty tenants of the seas and oceans of the past may have waged war on their neighbours. Again, the laws and ideas of development stand out in bold relief as supplying the key to the enigma. Adopt the theory that "things are now just as they always were," and what can we say of rudimentary teeth, save that Nature is a blunderer at best, and that she exhibits a lavish waste of power in supplying animals with useless structures? But choose the hypothesis of development, and we may see in the embryo-teeth the representatives of teeth which in the ancestors of our whales served all the purposes of such organs. Admit that through disuse they have become abortive and useless; and we may then, with some degree of satisfaction, explain their true nature. To use Darwin's simile, such rudiments are like letters in a word (*e.g.*, "debt" and "alms") which have become obsolete in pronunciation, but which are retained in the spelling, and serve as a clue to the derivation of the word.

In the course of these remarks allusion has been made to more than one species of whale, and it may therefore form a study of some interest if we endeavour shortly to gain an idea of the general relationship and degrees of affinity of the various members of this curious family-circle. The whale order includes several of the divisions to which the zoologist applies the name of "families," indicating by this latter term a close affinity in form, structure, and habits between the members of each group. First in importance amongst these families comes that of the whalebone whales (*Balænidæ*). Here we find family characters in a head disproportionately large when compared with the body as a whole, whilst the muzzle is sloping, and of rounded conformation. Teeth are absent, as we have seen; whalebone-plates fringe the palate; and the "blowhole" is single, and exists on the top of the head. Such are the family characters in which the Greenland or right whale, and the still larger rorqual participate, along with the "finner" whales and "humpbacked" whales. There is no back fin in the Greenland whale, but the rorquals and their neighbours possess this appendage. It need hardly be said that, commercially, the former animal is of most importance; whilst the rorquals are famed as the largest of the whales. Specimens of the rorqual have been captured exceeding 100 feet in length. One specimen, measuring 95 feet in length, weighed 245 tons.

Next in importance to the Greenland whale and its relatives may be mentioned the family (*Physeteridæ*), of which the sperm whale is the representative form. Here, the head reaches literally enormous proportions, and may make up fully one-third of the body. A blunt, square muzzle; a lower jaw armed with teeth; an absence of baleen-plates, and a front blowhole —such are the characters of the sperm whale, which gives sperm oil to the merchant, and spermaceti and ambergris to the man of drugs. A whole host of "small fry" present themselves as near relations of the whales in the shape of the dolphins, porpoises, grampus, "bottle-noses," and other animals, including the famous narwhal, or sea-unicorn, possessing the longest tooth in the world, in the shape of a spiral ivory pole of some eight or ten feet in length. Here also the *Beluga catodon*, or "white whale," finds a zoological home, this latter form being the species of which more than one specimen has been recently exhibited in London. The beluga, being a member of the dolphin family, is a "whale" by courtesy only. Like the other members of this group, its blowhole is single and crescentic in shape, and both jaws are well provided with teeth. But the beluga, unlike the dolphins and porpoises, has no back fin, and its muzzle is blunt. This animal, however, is still certainly "very like a whale" in its general shape and aspect. Its creamy white skin is certainly a peculiar feature; but the broad, horizontal tail-fin is well exemplified in this northern stranger, whilst the breathing habits of its group may also be studied superficially but satisfactorily on the specimen in question. The beluga inhabits the North American coast, at the mouths of the rivers on the Labrador and Hudson's Bay coasts, whilst it is known to penetrate even to the Arctic regions. These whales are plentiful in the Gulf of St. Lawrence in spring and summer, and appear to migrate to the west coast of Greenland in October and November. The Esquimaux regard the beluga as their special prize, and contrive, with the aptitude for design which the necessities of savage existence teach, to utilise well-nigh every portion of its frame, even to the manufacture of a kind of animal-glass from its dried and transparent internal membranes.

But little space remains in which to treat of certain near relations and somewhat interesting allies of the whales. Such are the *Manatees*, or "sea-cows," and the dugongs, collectively named *Sirenia*, in the category of zoologists. The origin of this latter name is attended with some degree of interest. It has been bestowed on these animals from their habit of assuming an upright or semi-erect posture in the water; their appearance in this position, and especially when viewed from a distance by the imaginative nautical mind, having doubtless laid a foundation, in fact, for the tales of "sirens" and "mermaids" anxious to lure sailors to destruction by their amatory numbers. Any one who has watched the countenance of a seal from a short distance must have been struck with the close resemblance to the human face which the countenance of these animals presents. Such a likeness is seen even to a greater degree in the sea-cows, which also possess the habit of folding their "flippers," or swimming paddles, across their chests, and, it is said, of holding the young to the breast in the act of nutrition by aid of the paddle-like fore limbs. If I mistake not, Captain Sowerby mentions, in an account of his voyages, that the surgeon of the ship on one occasion came to him in a state of excitement to announce that he had seen a man swimming in the water close at hand; the supposed human being proving to be a manatee, which had been, doubtless, merely exercising a natural curiosity regarding the ship and its tenants.

These animals are near relatives of the whales, but differ from them, not merely in habits, but in bodily structure and conformation. They live an estuarine existence, rarely venturing out to sea. The manatees occur in the shallow waters and at the mouths of the great rivers of the Atlantic coasts of America and Africa. The dugongs inhabit the shores of the Indian Ocean, and are common on certain parts of the Australian coasts. There are only two living genera—the manatees and dugongs—of these animals; a third, the *Rhytina Stelleri*, having, like the famous dodo, become extinct through its wholesale slaughter by man in 1768—just twenty-seven years after it was first discovered by the voyager Behring on a small island lying off the Kamtschatkan coast. The rhytina was a great unwieldy animal of some twenty-seven feet in length, and about twenty feet in circumference. It fell a ready prey to Behring and his crew, who were located on the island for several months, the work of extermination being duly completed by subsequent voyagers who visited the island. The manatees are no strangers to London, since in 1875 one of these animals was to be seen disporting itself in the seal-tank in the gardens of the Zoological Society at Regent's Park. This specimen—a female of immature age—was brought from the Demerara coast, and was the first living specimen which had been brought to England, although attempts had been made in 1866 to procure these animals for the gardens at Regent's Park, one specimen, indeed, dying just before reaching Southampton. A member of the manatee group, obtained from Trinidad, was recently exhibited in London, and the public, interested in the curious in zoology were thus enabled to interview a living member of the siren group—whilst comparative anatomists, in their turn, have been afforded a rich treat from the fate which awaits rare and common specimens alike, having overtaken the illustrious visitor in question.

The manatees and dugongs possess bodies which, as regards their shape, may be described each as a great barrel "long drawn out." No hinder limbs are developed, this latter peculiarity distinguishing them from the seals, and relating them to the whales. The hide is very tough, sparsely covered with hair, and most nearly resembles that of the hippopotamus. The "flippers," or paddle-like limbs, are placed far forward on the body, and on the edge of the paddle rudimentary nails are developed; whilst concealed beneath the skin of the paddle we find the complete skeleton of an arm or fore-limb. The tail is broad, horizontally flattened, like that of the whales, and forms an effective propeller. These animals are vegetable feeders, the Zoological Society's specimen having exhibited a strong partiality for lettuce and vegetable-marrow. In a state of nature, the sea-cows crop the marine vegetation which fringes their native shores. The remaining outward features of interest in these creatures may be summed up by saying that no back fins are developed; that the eyes are very small and inconspicuous; and that although the anterior nostrils are never used as "blow-holes," they can be closed at will like the nostrils of the seals—a faculty of needful kind in aquatic animals. To the technical anatomist, the sea-cows present strong points of resemblance to some of the hoofed quadrupeds. The anatomical examination of these animals has shown that their peculiarities are not limited to their outward appearance and habits. It is not generally known, for example, that the neck of the vast majority of mammals consists of seven vertebræ or segments of the spine. Man thus possesses this number in common with the giraffe, the elongation of whose neck is produced not by introduction of new vertebræ, but by the great development of the normal number, seven. The manatees, however, present a very remarkable exception to this most general of rules, in that they possess only six vertebræ in their necks. The only other exceptions to the rule of seven as the normal number of neck-vertebræ in quadrupeds, are found in one species of sloth which has six vertebræ like the manatee, and in another kind of sloth which possesses nine. Then, also, the dugongs possess a heart of very curious conformation, its apex or tip being widely cleft or divided—a feature much more plainly marked in these animals than in the elephants and seals, whose hearts, anatomically speaking, are also divided. The manatees possess well-developed molars or grinding teeth, but have no front teeth in the adult state. Like the whalebone whale, however, the young manatee has front teeth, these, again, disappearing before birth, and presenting us once more with examples of rudimentary organs which possess a reference " to a former state of things."

What evidence is at hand respecting the remote ancestors of the whales and their neighbours? is a question which may form a fitting conclusion to these brief details of the family history of the group. The geological evidence shows us that the whales are comparatively "recent" forms, speaking geologically, and dealing—notwithstanding the word "recent"—with very remote and immense periods of time. Amongst the oldest fossil whales we find one form in particular (*Zeuglodon*) which had teeth of larger kind than are possessed by any living whale, this creature being by some authorities regarded as linking the whales with the seals. The fossil remains of zeuglodon and its neighbours first occur in Eocene rocks—that is, in the oldest formations of the Tertiary series, and in rocks of relatively "recent" nature. These remarkable creatures were as gigantic as their living representatives. One species is known to have attained a length of seventy feet. Their remains are of such frequent occurrence in the "Jackson Beds" of the United States, that Professor Dana remarks, "The large vertebræ, some of them a foot and a half long and a foot in diameter, were formerly so abundant over the country in Alabama, that they were used for making walls, or were burned to rid the fields of them." The teeth of this curious monster of the vasty Eocene deep were of two kinds, and included front teeth of conical shape, and grinders or molars; the latter exhibiting a striking peculiarity in that they were formed each of two halves, or teeth united by their crowns, but separated at their roots. Zeuglodon, as already noted, appears to connect the whales and their neighbours with the seals and walruses, and thus in one sense may be said to constitute, if not a "missing link," at least an intermediate form of anomalous kind, when viewed relatively to the existing cetaceans. According to the geological evidence at hand, we may assume that the modifications which have produced the existing whales and their neighbours are of comparatively recent date, and that their adaptation to an aquatic life is a thing but of yesterday, when compared with the duration of previous æons in the history of our globe.

FOOD AND FASTING.

THE recent experiment of Dr. Tanner, in proving the possibility of sustaining life during a long fast upon air and water alone, affords a text whereon some interesting particulars concerning food and starvation at large may be hung. Apart from their notoriety, such experiments can have little interest. They can certainly never overthrow established physiological ideas regarding the necessity not merely for solid food, but for that due and natural mixture of food-principles which we can easily show Nature insists upon our receiving day by day. Unless we could rationally indulge in the wild supposition that man's constitution is susceptible of fundamental alteration and sweeping change, the idea of living for any length of time on water and air alone must be viewed as a dream, worse by many degrees than Utopian. These may be strongly expressed opinions, but they can be more than justified by the most elementary study in physiology.

Why do we require to take food? or, in plainer terms, why do we eat our dinner? are questions demanding no great exercise of knowledge for their clear solution. It constitutes a great fact of Nature that every action we perform entails a corresponding amount of waste on our physical frame. Work means waste, equally to a human body and a locomotive engine. "More work, more waste," is a motto alike true of the mechanic's apparatus and of the mechanic himself. Not an action, we repeat, is performed by us which is not accompanied by an expenditure of force derived from and accompanied by a proportional waste of substance. The movements of muscles, the beating of the heart, the winking of an eyelid, the thinking a thought, entail wear and tear upon the muscles that work and upon the brain-cells that think. Every action necessitates bodily waste and corresponding physical repair. Waste, however, cannot of necessity be a single and final process in a living body —unless, indeed, we were born with a full complement of matter, and were permitted in the order of Nature to live on the principal with which we had been provided, instead of wisely using that principal as a means of gaining a livelihood through the interest it acquired. That we are not so constituted, is an evident fact; hence our bodies demand pretty constant repair as a companion action to that of work, labour, and duty. This process of repair consists in the reception of matter from the outer world, in the transformation of this matter into ourselves, and in its utilisation in the work and repair of the frame. Such matter we shortly name *food*, and the processes whereby it is converted into our own bodily substance we term *digestion*.

One of the plainest rules for taking food is that which insists that we must find in our nourishment the substances of which the body itself is composed. If we think of it, such a rule is in strict conformity with the dictates of common sense. We are bound to obtain from our food the matter the body lacks; and any food, however pleasant to the palate, but which does not contain elements naturally found in the frame, may be unhesitatingly rejected from the lists of our dietaries. It follows, therefore, that to know what foods are required for our sustenance, we must investigate the chemical composition of our frame. In this way we discover, for instance, that we are largely composed of *water*. Two-thirds of a human body by weight are composed of water. A body weighing one hundred and sixty-five pounds, will include in its belongings one hundred and ten pounds of water. Water further permeates or enters into the composition of every tissue; hence the reason why thirst is so much more painful than hunger, and that whilst the latter is a comparatively local condition, the former affects the entire frame. And we also thus see the importance of water as an article of diet—a phase in which we are not usually accustomed to regard it. If we take even the most cursory survey of our bodily composition, we find that our chemical structure is of the most motley and varied description. Thus we shall find a large selection of minerals in our tissues; lime, magnesia, etc., in our bones; common salt in our stomachs and elsewhere; iron in our blood; and phosphorus in brain and nerve. Then coming to our soft parts, we find that these may be divided into what physiologists call the *nitrogenous* and *non-nitrogenous* compounds. Of these, the former contain the element *nitrogen* in addition to other elements, whilst the latter want this element. Thus the "albuminous" or white-of-egg-like substances existing in our frames, contain nitrogen; whilst the fats of the body, and the sugars and starches, do not. To these latter, we may add water and minerals, as also non-nitrogenous in their nature.

Now in such a simple study of what we are made of, we have already made some important discoveries as to the kinds of food on which we are intended to subsist. If these matters compose our frames, and if further the substances just enumerated waste and wear and disappear in the work of life, it must follow that we shall require to find new matters of like kind in our food. And it is in accordance with such plain information afforded by chemistry, that we find physiologists dividing foods into two classes—the "nitrogenous" and "non-nitrogenous" groups just alluded to. When, for example, we eat a piece of beef, we are receiving "nitrogenous" food in its juice and in its fibres; and we are also obtaining the other variety of foods from its water, its fats, and its mineral matters which are not nitrogenous in their composition. If we eat an egg, we are presented with a more perfect compound and union of the two classes of foods; for in an egg, water, fats, and minerals are present, in addition to the white and other parts which consist largely of albumen or nitrogenous matter. It is perfectly clear, therefore, that for health we require a mixture of the two kinds of foods just mentioned. We cannot live either on a diet solely nitrogenous, or solely lacking nitrogen. And this great truth as to foods can be proved very directly by an appeal to Nature herself. On what food, let us ask, does Nature intend and cause us to subsist during the earliest or infantile period of life, when bones, muscles, sinews, nerve, and brain are all growing rapidly, and laying the foundations of their future? The reply bears that *milk* is the fluid-food upon which Nature relies for the perfect support of man in his early life. Hence it is but proper to acquire a knowledge of the component parts of milk. In one thousand parts of cow's milk, for example, there are eight hundred and fifty-eight parts of water and one hundred and forty-two parts of solids. Here, again, we find a proof of the importance of water, even in Nature's typical food. The solids of cow's milk are distributed as follows: of casein there are sixty-eight parts, this substance representing the nitrogenous element in milk; of butter or fat there are thirty-eight parts; of sugar thirty parts; and of mineral matters six parts. Thus milk, then, is purely and simply a mixture of nitrogenous and non-nitrogenous foods. Nature teaches us through the composition of her own fluid food, that on both classes of nutriment we must rely for support; and experiment shows us that one kind of food alone, however nutrient it may be, will not nourish the body or maintain it in a normal state. In an egg, too, we find much the same composition. From this body which forms the young animal and which affords all the nourishment necessary for growth, we obtain a combination of the nitrogen-bearing substances with the non-nitrogenous, such as milk itself contains. We are not at present concerned with discussing the merits of a vegetable or a mixed dietary. From plants alone, or from animal matter alone for that matter, both kinds of foods can be obtained. All that is required in any dietary is to insure that a due mixture of nitrogenous and non-nitrogenous parts should enter; and we obtain such a mixture more readily from a mixed, that is, an animal and plant diet combined, than from a purely vegetable or a purely animal dietary alone.

Bearing these facts in mind, the folly of attempting to sustain life, without having recourse to those substances which can give heat and restore waste, is plainly apparent. Water and air alone, cannot support life adequately. The water will, of course, enter into combination with the tissues, and will in that sense prove itself a necessary condition for normal and healthy existence. The oxygen of the air entering the blood in the lungs into which it has been breathed, will give heat, but only through entering into chemical union with the carbon found in the body, and most notably in the fats. Hence mere atmospheric air itself is relatively useless, unless we can supply it with substances with which it can combine; and these substances it need hardly be said are daily renewed from the solid foods we eat.

So much for the foods we require. It may interest our

readers to learn that even plants require something more than air and water to support them. True, a plant is a more wonderful organism than an animal in one sense, because it can live upon inorganic or lifeless matter, and also because it has the power of converting that matter into a living plant. Plants live upon water, minerals, ammonia, and carbonic acid—the latter being the gas which is exhaled from the breathing organs of animals. From these matters, the life-forces build up the living plant. On the other hand, an animal demands living matter for its support. It could not live on the water, carbonic acid, and other matters with which the plant is perfectly contented. And we accordingly find animals requiring the matter of other animals or plants for their food. There are some plants—such as the fungi and lower plants at large—which resemble animals in that they demand living matter for their support. A mushroom, for instance, can only thrive where there is decaying living or organic matter. It likewise breathes oxygen as if it were an animal, and utterly rejects the carbonic acid gas which the green leaves of its plant-neighbours are greedily drinking in. So that the boundary lines between plants and animals are but faintly drawn in the matter of foods; and we also learn that even the plants which we are accustomed to regard as lower than animals in their feeding and dietary, may in reality approach very near to the animal world in the essential characters of their nutrition.

When the human body suffers from a lack of food, it practically feeds upon itself and absorbs its own substance as food. Every one knows that certain animals normally exhibit this process of feeding upon themselves under certain conditions. The humps of the camel or those of the Indian cattle visibly decrease and may disappear altogether, if the animals are starved. A superfluous store of fat, in other words, is made use of under the exigency of hunger. So is it also with the bears and other animals which hibernate or sleep through the winter's cold. The bear, which in autumn retires to winter-quarters in a well-favoured condition, comes forth in spring lean and meagre. His fats have been absorbed in his nutrition, and the succeeding summer will lay the foundation of new stores of stable food to be utilised during the next winter. With man, we repeat, the phenomena of starvation are essentially similar. In the starving man, the fats of the body are the first substances to disappear. The fats lose weight to the extent of ninety-three per cent.; next in order the blood suffers; then the internal organs, such as liver and spleen, suffer; the muscles, bones, and nervous system being the last to lose weight. In due time, also, the heat of the body decreases to such an extent that ultimately death in a case of starvation is really a case of death from loss of heat. When the temperature falls to about thirty degrees Fahrenheit, death ensues. This decrease arises from want of bodily fuel or food; but the immediate cause of the fatal ending of such a case is decrease of temperature. It is likewise a curious fact that the application of external warmth is even more effectual in reviving animals dying of starvation than a supply of food. In exhausting diseases in man, in which the phenomena are strikingly alike, and indeed thoroughly analogous to those of starvation, the same facts are observed.

A highly interesting and important observation in reference to starvation is, that life may be prolonged well-nigh indefinitely by fluid nourishment alone, and for long periods simply on water. Life will continue surprisingly long if water be within reach; but, as a rule, it terminates in from six to ten days with a total deprivation of food and water together; though much depends upon the state of health, condition, and weight of body. As can readily be understood, the stout will last longer than the lean, and the healthy and strong will possess a plain advantage in starvation over the diseased or weak.

Many interesting cases are on record, in which the phenomena of starvation have been practically even if painfully illustrated. As illustrating the fact of the prolongation of life when small quantities of water have been at hand, we may cite a case quoted by Foderé, who mentions that some workmen who had been accidentally buried in a damp vault by the fall of a ruin, were extricated alive after fourteen days' entombment. The dampness of the atmosphere doubtless materially aided their preservation through retarding the exhalation from the skin. It is on the same grounds that shipwrecked sailors assuage the pangs of thirst by soaking their clothes in sea-water. It was formerly believed that the water was inhaled by the skin. It is not any longer matter of doubt, however, that the skin is but a poor absorptive medium, and that therefore the wet clothes of the sailors merely act through lessening the skin-evaporation which in its turn causes thirst.

Cases of extreme prolongation of life under a dietary consisting of fluid alone are familiar to every physician. In exhausting diseases, life may be sustained, as already noted, on small quantities of fluid nourishment for lengthened periods of time. Dr. Willan records a case in which a gentleman, the subject of religious melancholia, and who abstained from solid food, lived for sixty days on a little orange juice. Dr. Carpenter quotes a case in which a young French lady who was insane, ate nothing during a period of fifteen days; whilst in hysterical states, as Carpenter remarks, "there is frequently a very remarkable disposition for abstinence and power of sustaining it. In a case of this kind," continues Dr. Carpenter, "a young lady who had just before suffered severely from the tetanic form of hysteria, was unable to take food for three weeks. The slightest attempt to introduce a morsel of solid matter into the stomach occasioned violent efforts at vomiting; and the only nourishment taken during the period mentioned was a cup of tea once or twice a day."

By way of showing how much depends on the weight of body prior to starvation, we may by way of conclusion mention the case of a fat pig weighing one hundred and sixty pounds, and which, by the fall of a Dover chalk cliff, was buried beneath a mass of *debris* for one hundred and sixty days. At the end of that period it was dug out lean and meagre, and weighing only forty pounds. Here the heat of the body had been preserved by the utilisation of the fat, and to this circumstance the preservation of life must be chiefly attributed. A case equally in point appeared some time ago in the newspapers. This was an instance of a Syke terrier belonging to a gentleman in Devonshire, which went a-missing about the time of its master's departure on a series of visits. On his return home, after an absence of one month and five days, he unlocked the library, the doors and windows of which had been bolted and barred during his absence. To his astonishment the missing dog crept out into the light, a living skeleton, and totally blind. Being well cared for, he quite recovered his health and sight. During this period of cruel imprisonment he had neither food nor water, and had not gnawed the books or obtained sustenance from any source whatever, but had subsisted by the absorption of the fatty parts of his own body.

To sum up our inquiries, we thus learn, firstly, that in the healthy adult the requirements of Nature demand daily a due supply of food, liquid and solid, equal in amount to the wear and tear of the body. About eight and one-third pounds of matter are thus on an average daily given off and daily received by the healthy adult frame; or about three thousand pounds of matter are excreted and received in the year. Secondly, we learn that the food must give to the body the substances of which the body consists, and that mere air and water are in nowise sufficient to sustain life beyond a varying period of days. Whilst, lastly, we may form the opinion that experimentation on foods to be of practical value should lie within the lines which physiology has clearly enough marked out.

SCIENTIFIC GHOSTS.

MODERN science has made us aware that the old belief in apparitions rested on nothing more than illusive fancies caused by some kind of physical derangement of the person so affected. It is important that young persons should be made thoroughly aware of the fact, that there never was and never will be any such fancy which is not capable of being explained upon natural grounds. A person in weak health, though in perfect possession of all his faculties, begins to be troubled by waking visions of persons with whom he may be familiar, or who may have been long dead, or who sometimes may appear as perfect strangers to him. The spectres who flit before him, "come like shadows" and "so depart." They represent, in the most perfect manner, the reproductions of things that are or were—utterly intangible creations. The subject of these visitations may hear the spectres converse, and they may even talk in turn to him. He is perfectly aware of their visionary nature, and is as convinced of their unreality as is the friend who sees them not, and to whom the phantoms are described. No suspicions of insane delusion as to these visitations can be entertained for a moment, and the question may therefore naturally be put to the man of science, "How can these illusions be accounted for?" The answer is to be found in one of the simplest studies in the physiology of nerves and of mind, and shows us that these illusions have a material basis, or that, in the words of the poet, the "shadow proves the substance true."

To thoroughly elucidate the subject of illusions within a brief space, we may begin by selecting one or two illustrations of illusive vision, such as have been recorded for instruction and edification in the pages of the physiologist. One of the best known cases—deriving its interest from the fact that the subject of the visitations in question himself narrates the facts —is that of Nicolai, a well-known citizen and bookseller of Berlin, who read an account of his case before the Berlin Academy of Sciences. We shall give the account in his own words. "During the few latter months of the year 1790," says Nicolai, "I had experienced several melancholy incidents, which deeply affected me, particularly in September, from which time I suffered an almost uninterrupted series of misfortunes, that affected me with the most poignant grief. I was accustomed to be bled twice a year, and this had been done once on the 9th of July, but was omitted to be repeated at the end of the year 1790. . . . I had, in January and February of the year 1791, the additional misfortune to experience several extremely unpleasant circumstances, which were followed on the 24th of February by a most violent altercation. My wife and another person came into my apartment in the morning in order to console me; but I was too much agitated by a series of incidents which had most powerfully affected my moral feeling, to be capable of attending to them. On a sudden, I perceived, at about the distance of ten steps, a form like that of a deceased person. I pointed at it, asking my wife if she did not see it. It was but natural that she should not see anything; my question therefore alarmed her very much, and she sent immediately for a physician. The phantasm continued for some minutes. I grew at length more calm, and being extremely exhausted, fell into a restless sleep, which lasted about half an hour. The physician ascribed the vision to violent mental emotion, and hoped there would be no return; but the violent agitation of my mind had in some way disordered my nerves, and produced further consequences, which deserve a more minute description.

"At four in the afternoon, the form which I had seen in the morning reappeared. I was by myself when this happened, and being rather uneasy at the incident, went to my wife's apartment; but there likewise I was persecuted by the form, which, however, at intervals disappeared, and always presented itself in a standing posture. About six o'clock there appeared also several walking figures, which had no connection with the first. After the first day, the form of the deceased person no more appeared; but its place was supplied with many other phantasms, sometimes representing acquaintances, but mostly strangers: those whom I knew were composed of living and deceased persons, but the number of the latter was comparatively small. . . . When I shut my eyes these forms would sometimes vanish entirely, though there were instances when I beheld them with my eyes closed; yet, when they disappeared on such occasions, they generally returned when I opened my eyes. . . . They all appeared to me in their natural size, and as distinct as if alive, exhibiting different shades of carnation in the uncovered parts, as well as different colours and fashions in their dresses, though the colours seemed somewhat paler than in real nature; none of the figures appeared particularly terrible, comical, or disgusting, most of them being of an indifferent shape, and some presenting a pleasing aspect. The longer these persons continued to visit me, the more frequently did they return, while at the same time they increased in number about four weeks after they had first appeared. I also began to hear them talk; sometimes among themselves, but more frequently they addressed their discourse to me; their speeches being uncommonly short and never of an unpleasant turn. At different times there appeared to me both dear and sensible friends of both sexes, whose addresses tended to appease my grief, which had not yet wholly subsided; their consolatory speeches were in general addressed to me when I was alone. Sometimes, however, I was accosted by these consoling friends while I was engaged in company, and not unfrequently while real persons were speaking to me. The consolatory addresses consisted sometimes of abrupt phrases, and at other times they were regularly executed."

Such was Nicolai's account of the phantom-visitors who addressed and consoled him in his domestic affliction. It is interesting to pursue still further his account of their disappearance. The reader will recollect that Nicolai had neglected to repeat at the end of 1790 the blood-letting in which it was customary in the days we speak of for our forefathers to indulge. It was at last decided that leeches should be used, and on April 20, 1791, at eleven o'clock in the morning, Nicolai informs us the operation was performed. "No person," he continues, "was with me besides the surgeon; but during the operation my chamber was crowded with human visions of all descriptions. This continued uninterruptedly till about half an hour after four o'clock, just when my digestion commenced. I then perceived that they began to move more slowly. Soon after, their colour began to fade, and at seven o'clock they were entirely white. But they moved very little, though the forms were as distinct as before; growing, however, by degrees more obscure, yet not fewer in number, as had generally been the case. . . . They now seemed to dissolve in the air, while fragments of some of them continued visible for a considerable time. About eight o'clock, the room was entirely cleared of my fantastic visitors. Since that time," adds Nicolai, "I have felt twice or three times a sensation as if they were going to reappear, without, however, actually seeing anything. The same sensation surprised me just before I drew up this account, while I was examining some papers relative to these phenomena, which I had drawn up in the year 1791."

Such is an historical account of what may appear to the senses of a sane and reasonable individual. Before entering on their scientific explanation, it will be advisable to give one or two further examples of the phenomena in question. On the occasion of the fire which destroyed part of the Crystal Palace in the winter of 1866-67, part of the menagerie had been sacrificed to the flames. The chimpanzee, however, was believed to have escaped from his cage, and was presently seen on the roof endeavouring to save himself by clutching in wild despair one of the iron beams which the fire had spared. The struggles of the animal were watched with an intense curiosity mingled with horror and sympathy for the supposed fate which awaited the unfortunate monkey. What was the surprise of the spectators of an imminent tragedy, to find that the object which in the guise of a terrified ape, had excited their fears, resolved itself into a piece of canvas blind, so tattered, that to the eye of the imagination and when moved by the wind, it presented the exact counterpart of a struggling animal!

Such an example is of especial interest, because it proves to us that not one person alone, but a large number of spectators may be deceived by an object imperfectly seen—and aided, in the illusion by a vivid imagination—into fancying all the details of a spectacle of which the chief actor is entirely a myth.

A singular case has been given on strict medical authority

of a lady, who, walking from Penrhyn to Falmouth—her mind being occupied with the subject of drinking-fountains—was certain she saw in the road a newly erected fountain, bearing the inscription, " If any man thirst, let him come unto me and drink." As a matter of course she mentioned her interest in seeing such an erection to the daughters of the gentleman who was supposed to have placed the fountain in its position. They assured her that no such fountain was in existence; but convinced of the reality of her senses on the ground that " seeing is believing," she repaired to the spot where she had seen the fountain, only to find, however, a few scattered stones in place of the expected erection.

We may now turn to consider the scientific explanation of such curious phenomena in human existence. The causes of these illusions are not difficult to understand, since they in reality depend upon a slight derangement of the powers whereby we see and hear in an ordinary and normal method. To make our meaning clear, let us briefly consider what takes place in ordinary sensation, when we see or hear the objects and sounds of every-day existence. The eye alighting on an object transfers an impression of that object to the brain through the special (optic) nerve of sight, which leads from the eye to the part of the brain exercising the sense of sight. We in reality do not see with the eye. That organ is merely an arrangement of lenses adapted to receive, focus, and otherwise adjust rays of light streaming from the objects we see. The function of the eye is simply that of adjusting and correlating the conditions necessary for the production of an impression. This impression is carried in due course to a special part of the brain, where it becomes transformed into a special sensation—that of sight. We thus truly see not with the eye, but with the brain, *or rather with that portion of the brain which lies in direct relation with the nerves of sight.* The eye represents the lenses of the photographer's camera; but the brain corresponds to the sensitive plate which receives the image of the sitter, and on which all subsequent alterations of the image are effected. Of the other senses, the same prominent feature may also be expressed —namely, that in the brain and not in the mere organ of sense must be allocated the true seat of knowledge. The ear modifies waves of sound; but it is the brain which distinguishes, appreciates, and acts upon the information conveyed by the organ of hearing. The finger touches an object; but the seat of knowledge does not exist at the extremity of the hand. The impression of touch is duly conveyed to the brain as before, there to be analysed, commented upon, and, if necessary, acted upon as well.

On the appreciation of the simple fact that the brain is the true seat of the senses, rests the whole explanation of the ghosts and apparitions which occasionally attend the footsteps and meet the eyes of humanity. When we are conscious of looking at a real object, a sensation of sight is formed in the brain, as we have seen. Such a sensation we call an "objective" one, because it is derived from a veritable object. So also, when we hear a tune played by a person whom we see, or of whose existence, even when unseen, we entertain no doubt, the sensation of sound is then called "objective." But there are many familiar instances in which the power of the mind to reproduce the sensations, sights, and sounds we have received, is demonstrated. The day-dreamer can sometimes bring the scenes in which he has once taken part so vividly before his mental gaze, that his reverie may actually be broken by the words which unconsciously flow from his lips as his imagination starts into bodily action. Such a power of fancy and imagination is the beginning or faint imitation of a still more powerful means which we possess of bringing before ourselves the forms and scenes which have once been objectively present with us. In the dream, this power is illustrated typically enough. From the background of consciousness, so to speak, we project forwards, in our sleep, the pictures which a busy brain is reproducing, or it may be piecing together the odds and ends of its fancy to form the ludicrous combinations we are familiar with in the "land of Nod." And if we carry the idea of this same power being exercised in our waking moments, to form the ghosts of science, the explanation of the otherwise curious and mysterious subject of illusive visions will be complete.

We know then, that the brain has the ordinary power of forming images which may be projected outwards in the form of the fancies of every-day life. But these projected fancies may grow into plain and apparent sensations or images under the requisite conditions. When we hear a "ringing in the ears," we know perfectly well that no objective sound exists, and scientifically we say that the sensation of hearing in such a case is an internal or *subjective* one. When we see flashes of light which have no existence in the outside world on which we happen to be gazing, we explain their occurrence in the same way. Now, on such a basis, the ghosts of science are both raised and laid. The images and phantoms of Nicolai, like the sparks or flashes of light, are *subjective sensations*. They arise, in other words, from some irritation of that part of the brain, which would have received the impression of sight had the objects in question had an actual existence. But the subject also involves a reference to bodily condition and to memory itself. Primarily, it will be found that illusive visions appear only when the health of the subject of these visitations is in a weakly state. The derangement of the health is the primary cause of these curious states.

It is, however, equally worthy of remark that many of the

phantoms of Nicolai were persons whom he knew. Such visions then may be supposed to simply represent the effects of very recent images which had been received and stored in the brain, and which were evolved by the exercise of unconscious memory. Of the deceased persons whose images appeared to him, the same remark may be made—memory again reproducing, by the subjective impressions of the brain, the forms of dead friends. But what, it may be asked, of the strange visions whom Nicolai did not recognise? The reply which science offers, is that these also were images or conceptions of persons whom Nicolai must have seen at some time, but whom he could not remember; mysterious reproductions, by the brain, of events that had been impressed thereon, but which had escaped remembrance by ordinary memory. Even the characters whom Nicolai may have simply heard described, could be thus produced, and could present apparently the images of persons with whom he was not, as a matter of conscious memory, familiar. The brain, in other words, registers and remembers more than memory can evolve; and it is reasonable to conceive that forgotten images of things or persons once seen formed the mysterious strangers of Nicolai's waking dreams.

It is noteworthy that only after a long period of visitation from his fantastic friends, did Nicolai begin to hear them speak. Thus, the sense of hearing had also come in time to lend its aid in propagating the illusions; and the fact that the visions addressed Nicolai concerning his own immediate affairs and his personal griefs and sorrows, clearly shows the unconscious action of a mind which was brooding over its own trials, and which was evolving from within itself the comfort and consolation of kindly friends. Last of all, that the material basis of these visionary friends resided in the weakly body of their host, is proved by their disappearance on the resumption of the customary blood-letting and the improvement of the health—an additional fact showing the relation of the healthy body to the sound mind.

One of the most interesting cases of vision-seeing by a person of culture and intelligence is that related in the *Athenæum* of January 10, 1880, by the Rev. Dr. Jessopp, who, in Lord Orford's library, when engaged in copying some literary notes, saw a large white hand, and then, as he tells us, perceived "the figure of a somewhat large man, with his back to the fire, bending slightly over the table, and apparently examining the pile of books I had been at work upon." The figure was dressed in some antique ecclesiastical garb. The figure vanished when Dr. Jessopp made a movement with his arm, but reappeared, and again vanished when the reverend narrator threw down a book with which he had been engaged. Dr. Jessopp's recital called forth considerable comment, and amongst others a letter from the present writer, detailing the familiar theory based on the principles of subjective sensations, treated of in the present paper. After noticing the fashion in which subjective sensations become projected forwards, the author says (*Athenæum*, January 17, 1880): "The only point concerning which any dubiety exists, concerns the exact *origin* of the specific images which appear as the result of subjective sensory action. My own idea is that almost invariably the projected image is that of a person we have seen and read about. . . . In Dr. Jessopp's case there is one fact which seems to weigh materially in favour of the idea that the vision which appeared to him in Lord Orford's library was an unconscious reproduction of some mental image or figure about which the Doctor may very likely have concerned himself in the way of antiquarian study." It is most interesting to observe that in the succeeding number of the *Athenæum*, Mr. Walter Rye writes: "Dr. A. Wilson's solution 'that the "spectre"... was an unconscious reproduction of some mental image or figure about which Dr. Jessopp may very likely have concerned himself in the way of antiquarian study,' seems the right one, and I think I can identify the 'ghost.' The ecclesiastically dressed large man, with closely cut reddish-brown hair, and shaved cheek, appears to me the Doctor's remembrance of the portrait of Parsons, the Jesuit Father, whom he calls in his 'One Generation of a Norfolk House,' 'the manager and moving spirit' of the Jesuit mission in England.... Dr. Jessopp when he thought he saw the figure, was alone in an old library, belonging to a Walpole, and Father Parsons was the leader of Henry Walpole, the hero of his just-cited book. Small wonder, therefore, if the association of ideas made him think of Parsons."

All such illusive visions are thus readily explained as the creatures of an imagination which, through some brain-disturbance, is enabled to project its visions forward, on the seats of sense, as the "ringing" in our ears is produced by some irritation of the hearing-centre of the brain. The known vision is a reproduction of a present memory, and the unknown vision is the reproduction of a forgotten figure which has nevertheless been stored away in some nook or cranny of the memory-chamber.

We may thus dispel the illusion by its free explanation; and science has no higher function or nobler use than when, by its aid, a subject like the present is rescued from the domain of the mysterious, and brought within the sphere of ordinary knowledge.

THE EARLIEST KNOWN LIFE-RELIC.

ABOUT twenty-five years ago, the attention of Canadian geologists was called to a curious mineral, or rather combination of minerals, which was chiefly notable from the fact that layers of a dark-green colour were found alternating with white or limy layers in a fashion till then unnoticed by science. These specimens were collected at Burgess in Ontario by a Dr. Wilson, who forwarded them to Sir William Logan, the Director of the Canadian Geological Survey, as examples of a new or rare mineral. Analysed, in due course, the dark-green layers were found to consist of a new form of the familiar mineral named "serpentine;" the name "loganite" being given to the new substance in honour of the eminent geologist just mentioned.

Some years after the first discovery, which seemed thus to end with the naming of a new mineral, other specimens, presenting variations in their composition, were obtained by a Mr. M'Mullin from the limestones of the Grand Calumet on the Ottawa River. In these latter specimens, ordinary serpentine was the chief mineral represented. Of the age of those curious products no doubt was entertained. They occurred in rocks named Laurentian from their great development near the St.

Lawrence; these rocks forming the great water-shed which lies betwixt the St. Lawrence valley on the one hand, and the plateaux which stretch away to the north and to Hudson's Bay on the other.

When the second find was made on the Ottawa River, the appearance of the minerals suggested to Sir William Logan that possibly the structures might represent traces of once living matter—that, in other words, he might be dealing with no mere collection of mineral particles, but with matter that had replaced living structures, and that had preserved these structures more or less completely as a "fossil." After various investigations made by Dr. Sterry Hunt of Montreal, the matter was settled by Dr. Dawson and Dr. Carpenter, who showed, by microscopic examination, that the limy material represented the shell, whilst the serpentine had replaced the living matter. Branching out within the limy layers, minute tubes were discovered; and thus, whatever the nature of the fossil, it was proved that its limy parts were to be regarded as the actual representatives of the original shell or structure, and the serpentine or loganite as the matter which had filled up the shell and replaced the living matter in Nature's process of fossil-making. The opinion has thus been formed that in these Canadian limestones we find not merely a curious fossil, but actually the oldest known traces of living things. Hence the objects we are considering have received the not inappropriate name of the *Eozoon Canadense* —or, in plain English, the "Dawn of Life Animalcule" from Canadian rocks.

In these latter features alone, the "Dawn of Life Animalcule" —or Eozoon, as we may term it for shortness—merits our interest. Popularly, it has been described as the "first created" thing; but for such a title there is no justification whatever. What the first created organism was we do not know, and in

Eozoon's age is that it is older than any other known fossil. It is the oldest recognised fossil—the first preserved trace—*so far as we at present know*—of life on the earth. Nor was the interest attaching to the discovery of Eozoon limited to the popular mind. When it is learned that prior to the investigation of the dark-green and white layers, the Laurentian rocks were regarded as simply representing a remote period of time in which no living thing existed, it can readily be imagined that the discovery of a fossil organism threw a new light upon the condition of the earth in the days of its youth. These rocks are spoken of by geologists as "metamorphosed"—that is, their original nature has been changed by forces acting upon them subsequent to their formation as rocks. Whilst, before Eozoon had been brought to light, the more sanguine of geologists had ventured to think of the Laurentian age as not wholly lifeless and its seas as having been tenanted by lower forms of life, there were others who not merely regarded the discovery of fossils therein as an utterly hopeless idea, but included these rocks under the name "azoic," a term meaning "without life."

To understand fully, then, the revolution in scientific ideas which the discovery of this singular fossil brought about, it is necessary to think of the geological position of the rocks in which it occurs. By way of rendering this latter subject clear, let us select a well-known group of rocks, as a kind of geological landmark, and test the age and position of the Laurentian rocks by a comparison with the familiar series. Such a well-known series of rocks we find in the Old Red Sandstone beds, which in turn are overlaid, in their natural order of formation, by the Coal or Carboniferous series. Most readers are aware that the Old Red Sandstone rocks belong to the oldest of the periods into which, for geological purposes, we divide time past. They are infinitely older rocks, for instance, than the familiar Chalk.

As, therefore, the Old Red Sandstone is older than the Chalk, and in its natural position in the earth's crust lies so much lower, so the Laurentian rocks in their turn exceed the Old Red Sandstone in point of age. They lie at the very base and root of the rocks which contain fossils. The Laurentian formations thus appear before us as the oldest of the stratified rocks, and probably represent the solidified ocean-beds which held the primitive waters that for many early ages surrounded and covered the solid earth as it was then represented. But it must be also noted that rocks of similar age, and of like or allied mineral composition, occur in other regions of the world. Near ourselves, these rocks are found in the Isle of Skye, in the Hebrides, and in Sutherland. In the Malvern Hills and in South Wales, the Laurentian rocks are represented; the north of Ireland possesses them; and Bohemia and Bavaria recognise them as part and parcel of their respective geological constitutions.

Having thus described the home of the Eozoon, we may now turn to consider the "Dawn of Life Animalcule" itself. And first as to its structure. What does the microscope reveal concerning the nature of the so-called "shell," the fossil remains of which are presented to view in the limy layers which vary the monotony of the serpentine of the Laurentian limestones? If we slice a portion of our Laurentian rocks to the degree of thinness requisite for microscopic examination, we may soon discover therein very plain evidence of the nature of the organism which boasts to be the oldest known fossil. The limy layers are arranged in tiers like the seats in a theatre, and enclose between them a space which we may discern has been divided into chambers—once occupied by living matter, but now filled with the green serpentine of the rock. Imagine a series of chambers placed in a line, like a set of rooms *en suite*; and further suppose that many such sets of chambers were placed tier upon tier, and we may form a correct idea of the manner in which the parts of Eozoon are arranged. But it may also be noted that each set of chambers was not wholly shut off from the tier above and the tier below. Definite passages which might accurately be compared to the staircases connecting the flats of a house, appear to have existed between one tier of chambers and another; and even in the partition walls separating one tier from its neighbours, delicate tubes are seen to branch out. The walls of the chambers were apparently perforated by numerous minute holes, the purport of this arrangement being apparent when a comparison is made between Eozoon and its nearest neighbours amongst living beings.

Such are the appearances presented by a vertical section of the "Dawn of Life Animalcule." Other methods of investigating its nature have not been neglected by geologists; and the writer has had the pleasure and advantage of personally inspecting specimens of this fossil, prepared in various ingenious ways and by various methods under the direction of Dr. Carpenter of London, one of the highest authorities on the Eozoon and its nearest living allies to be presently mentioned. Thus we may "decalcify" specimens—or, in other words, remove the limy layers by means of an acid, and leave the serpentine unaffected, in the form of a solid cast of the interior of the shell, representing the living matter which once filled it, and which built up the shell from the lime of the primitive ocean in which Eozoon dwelt. Curiously enough, this process of removing the lime of a shell and leaving the mineral matter which filled its interior, is known to occur in Nature and around us to-day. Internal casts of shells, the living matter of which has been replaced by the green mineral named "glauconite," and whose limy substance has been dissolved away, are familiar to geologists; and it is noteworthy that some of the shell-casts thus preserved are nearly related to Eozoon itself.

The next point for discussion concerns the nature of this the oldest relic of life. Its identification is not a difficult matter, since there exists only one typical group of animals possessed of an outer limy skeleton perforated, as we have noted the shell of Eozoon to be, with holes. The name "Foraminifera" is by no means unfamiliar to ordinary readers who have interested themselves in the accounts of deep-sea dredging expeditions. But even if the organisms in question be quite unknown, their nature may be readily enough comprehended. Imagine a little speck of living jelly—the "protoplasm" of the naturalist—to be possessed of the power of taking lime from the water of the ocean, and of building this lime up to form a "shell" for the protection of its body. Let us further suppose that through minute holes in this shell, the little living speck could protrude its substance to form delicate filaments adapted for movement and for the seizure of food, and we shall then have formed a plain but strictly correct idea of a Foraminifer. The shell of our animalcule, as thus figured, consists of but a single chamber. Suppose further that it begins to throw out buds or processes of its substance, and that the buds remain connected to the parent shell, and develop in time into new chambers, each containing its speck of living matter, and we may conceive of our little animalcule duly increasing in various ways. It may bud in a spiral fashion, and thus produce a spiral shell ; or it may grow into a straight rod-like structure ; the form of the shell thus depending on the direction and extent of the process of budding by which new chambers are produced.

Such a description is paralleled by the actual life of the little animalcules which exist in myriads in our existing seas, as in the oceans of bygone days, and whose shells are forming a thick layer of limy matter in the bed of the present seas, as in the past, when the Chalk rocks of to-day were thus being formed. For the white cliffs of Dover simply represent the shell-*débris* of these animalcules consolidated to form the well-known formation in question. With these animalcules, then, we readily identify the Eozoon of the Laurentian rocks, despite obvious differences in size and manner of growth. But the differences between the "Dawn of Life Animalcule" and its modern representatives, the Foraminifera, are not incapable of being reconciled. An appeal to certain odd and still living forms of these animalcules serves to narrow the gulf between the Laurentian shell-former and its existing relatives. Take as an example of such connecting links the living *Polytrema* of the zoologist, a member of the Foraminifera; but which differs from its neighbours in that it grows in a branching form, and then comes to somewhat resemble a coral. The many chambers of which this organism's shell consists grow in an irregular fashion, and communicate as freely as do the chambers in one tier of Eozoon. Nor must we neglect to remark that in the shell-wall of Polytrema a curious set of tubes is found, analogous to those we see in Eozoon, and which are also represented in many other living species of Foraminifera. Allied likewise to the "Dawn of Life Animalcule" is the living *Calcarina*, which also grows in patches, as if imitating the higher corals; and a curious extinct coin-like shell, that of the Nummulite, also deserves mention, in respect that the structure of its shell-wall exhibits a close relationship to that of the oldest fossil.

We may now briefly glance at the probable condition under which the life of this "oldest fossil" was carried on. In such a survey, we picture to ourselves the bed of the Laurentian ocean occupied by vast colonies of the Eozoon-shells, containing—as do the living Foraminiferous shells—the soft living substance, which radiated through the shell-apertures in the form of the delicate threads and processes whereby food-particles were seized and drawn into the organism. A low form of life this: hovering, as it were, on the very twilight of existence, but still exhibiting in its own fashion many of the acts which characterise life of the highest grade. Year by year these colonies extended their growth; and as the colonies of one generation died off, to be replaced by others, the shells of the defunct races would be imbedded in the sea-deposits, there to become the fossils of the future. We can also form some idea of the subsequent changes to which these old Laurentian rocks were subjected as the ages passed; their structure being altered so that their original nature was disguised, and the Eozoon-remains becoming also largely transformed in certain localities. Finally, we see the modern disposition of this world's order wrought out as the ages passed; and in time we find the discovery of life-traces to connect us once again with the days when the world was young.

Such is an outline sketch of the progress of events which geological history is prepared to chronicle. It would be idle to speculate on the probabilities of the Laurentian age having harboured other forms of life in addition to Eozoon. But it is only fair to remark that recent research supports such a suggestion. Of the soft-bodied organisms which may have existed in the waters of these early ages, no traces could be preserved, any more than the jelly-fishes and soft-animals of our own seas can be regarded as destined to hand down their lineaments to the future of the earth—although, indeed, traces of fossil jelly-fishes are not unknown to geologists. In this latter view, the Laurentian ocean may possibly have been the scene of a great life-development, which must, however, have been of the lowest grades, represented typically enough by Eozoon itself.

The balance of evidence in favour of the truly animal nature of Eozoon is thus very apparent. From every consideration of its structure, from the resemblances it presents to existing shell-animalcules, as well as from collateral proofs drawn from mineralogy itself, there remains little doubt that Eozoon really represents what its name implies—the most ancient record of life which, so far as we know, has been preserved in the rock-formations of the globe.

SKATES AND RAYS.

"Not by any means an inviting subject for even a popular dissertation," may possibly be the verdict of more than one reader upon the subject and title of the present paper. The fishes in question are undeniably commonplace. Indeed, their appearance may be regarded as by no means interesting in any sense, and even to minds of a scientific bent the group may not seem at first sight inviting by way of intellectual repast, as their substance may be regarded but poor fare in an actual sense. But in science, as in ordinary existence, appearances frequently count for nothing. The phrase *omne ignotum pro magnifico*, may be paralleled by the expression of our belief that much of the truly "unknown" exists in the commonest objects of the world around us, and that a wealth of information awaits the search of every patient observer in even the tracts of knowledge which are most beaten and most hardly worn.

The skates and rays figure, of course, as important items in our list of food-fishes—albeit, as already mentioned, that their flavour is somewhat peculiar, and apt soon to pall on the taste of those accustomed to fresh fish of superior kind, such as the tasteful haddock or whiting, or the still more delicious sole or flounder, not to speak of more lordly fare. Zoologically regarded, the skate or ray is a prince among the fish kind. From every limb and feature of its economy, the professor of natural history —using the word in its modern sense, and not as indicating an acquaintance with all the known as well as certain occult and unknown "'ologies"—may extract tomes of information not merely concerning fish-life at large, but regarding other and very varied groups of animals. Our scientific observer would sorely miss the skates and rays, since they form cheap, accessible, and handy "subjects" for zoological investigation—notwithstanding that the fish, at an advanced stage of such scientific research, whilst becoming "small by degrees and beautifully less," increases in an inverse ratio as regards olfactory prominence of a kind the reverse of agreeable to unscientific bystanders.

Whoever has watched a skate or ray in an aquarium must have been struck by the somewhat human expression assumed by the front portion of the under surface of the body, which portion, for want of a better term, we may call the face. By the same rule that in the faces of dogs, cats, and horses we may occasionally detect a most marked resemblance to some human physiognomy, so it may be noted that in the skates and rays there is a rough but discernible likeness to be seen to the human countenance. In a lively mood the skate is quite a graceful fish. He may be seen to swim elegantly enough by the wavy movements of those great side or breast fins, which really form a very large part of his broad back and body. For our fishes rank amongst the few members of their class that are truly "flat," in the sense of possessing a broad back. The flounders, soles, turbot, and their allies, are flat, it is true, but their flatness is that of the sides of the body and not of the back. A sole or flounder swims and lies on one peculiarly modified side; its other and upper side bearing the eyes, which have thus come to be transferred to one side of the body by the twisting of the bones of the head. This latter process takes place in these fishes owing to an acquired habit of their ancestors in resting and lying on one side shortly after leaving the egg, at which period the eyes are normally placed, one on each side of the body. This much, however, by way of showing that the skate and ray are really flat-bodied. Their back is a great broad surface, which, as already remarked, owes something of its extent to the fact that the breast fins, instead of being free and separate from the body, as in other fishes, are united to it, and are thus incorporated into and add to its breadth.

Scattered here and there over the body of the skate or ray we perceive numerous bony granules of small size. These are the "scales" of the fish, and are of the variety named "placoid" by the naturalist. Occasionally the rays may develop formidable spines in connection with their scales. The thornback skate (*Raia clavata*) thus presents a perfect array of such spines along the middle line of its back and tail. Each spine has a broad base, and is of curved shape and pointed form. And the thornback in a passion is no mean foe. Bending its body like a bow, until the tip of the tail well-nigh touches its pointed nose, this ray will suddenly lash out the tail with great force, and more than one unwary fisherman has had good and sufficient cause to remember the ray's attack for weeks together. Provided in an equally formidable manner we find the sting ray (*Trygon pastinaca*) of our southern coasts. Here the tail reminds one of a lithe, supple whip. About its middle extent the tail bears a prominent spine, which is not merely sharp-pointed, but is serrated or cut into sharp, back-edged teeth along its sides. Using the thinned out tail as a lasso, the bayonet-like spine can be worked against an offending body to the utmost advantage, and is likely to inflict a very severe and ugly wound. Armed in similar fashion is the eagle ray—so named from the prominent and projecting nature of the breast fins, which appear in the form of miniature wings.

Respecting their internal structure, there is much in the build of the skate and ray bodies to stamp these fishes as in some respects of very high organisation. They claim the sharks and dogfishes as first cousins, and resemble the latter forms in many characteristic and peculiar points of their anatomy. Their skeleton—to begin with their bodily framework—is perhaps the least perfect part of their structure; that is, when compared with the better developed support of commoner fishes. Our skate like the shark possesses a skeleton composed in greater part of "gristle," or cartilage. Bony elements are few and far between in these fishes. The skull, which is perhaps the most complicated part of the anatomy of an ordinary fish, is a mere gristly box, exhibiting in its composition no distinct bony regions or separate divisions, but serves, as in other fishes and vertebrates, to enclose the brain. This latter structure, in strange contradistinction to the inferiority of its investment, is of very high type, and the senses of the skates and rays are also well represented. That of smell is well developed, judging not merely from the large size of the parts of the brain which afford the nervous supply to the nose, but also from the keen scent which these fishes evince for their food or prey. The eyes are equally perfect, and the ears—internal ears, as in all lower vertebrata, being alone represented in the rays—exhibit a complexity of structure surprising in animals of such a grade.

No part of the anatomy of these fishes, however, is more noteworthy than the mouth and its furnishings. Perhaps one of the most extraordinary developments in this latter respect is presented by the eagle rays already mentioned. Looking at the jaws of one of these fishes, the observer is reminded by the arrangement of the teeth of nothing so much as a thickly paved street. In the middle part of the jaw, the teeth are long and narrow, and are arranged so as actually to cross the line of union of the two jaws. At the sides of the jaws, the teeth become smaller and six-sided, and present the appearance of a mosaic-like pattern. Altogether such an armature is highly characteristic, and is perfectly adapted, as one may readily conceive, for serving as a veritable crushing-mill in bruising whatever tough bits happen to form items in the bill of fare of its possessor. Nor are the skates and rays simply provided with a single set or series of teeth. One of the peculiarities of fish life in general is the continual succession and renewal of the teeth. New teeth are supplied as fast as the old are worn away, and, indeed, new rows are developed long before those teeth which are being used are at all ready for replacement. The skates and rays in general are exceedingly well supplied among their fish-congeners in the matter of teeth, and exhibit not a few peculiarities in their dental arrangement when compared with their nearest neighbours, the sharks and dogfishes.

Persons not professing an intimate acquaintance with zoology, nevertheless know the "gills" or breathing organs of ordinary fishes. These gills exist in the neck-region of the fish, and beneath the horny flap known as the gill cover. Each gill in a haddock, cod, or other familiar fish, resembles a comb in shape. It consists of an arched piece corresponding to the back of the comb, and of numerous delicate red threads or filaments corresponding to the teeth of that familiar object. Each thread of the gill is really a network of minute blood-vessels, within which the impure blood is subjected to the action of the vivifying oxygen of the surrounding water, which, as any one who has watched a gold fish knows, is constantly being taken in by the mouth so as to bathe the gills, and is then ejected from behind the gill-cover. Such is the structure of the gills in an ordinary fish. Our skates and rays differ materially—as also do the sharks and dogfishes—from common fishes in the arrangement of their breathing organs. Looking at our skate we fail to perceive any gill-cover. But in the region in which we should have found such a structure, that is, on the under surface of the body, and on either side, we may perceive a series of slits. In the living skate we may see these slits expand every now and then as currents of the water which has been used in breathing are ejected by the sharp contraction of the gills. These slits are the outer openings of the gills. Each slit, in fact, leads from a curious little pouch, which also opens into the mouth by a distinct aperture of its own. Thus we find that water is taken into the mouth in the act of breathing, passes into the gill-like pockets—in the walls of which the impure blood, driven there by the heart, is circulating—and is finally rejected by the outer slits. In the possession of pouch-like gills, then, skates, rays, sharks, and dogfishes present a marked peculiarity; and they also differ from all other, save a very few fishes, in possessing two openings called "spiracles," on the upper surface of the head. These openings lead into two tubes, which in turn open into the hinder portion of the mouth; and water for the gills is also admitted by these spiracles, which may be seen to open and close in the living fish in regular sequence. Thus the skate or ray is comparatively independent of the mouth as an entrance for its breathing-water; and, doubtless, such a provision has a distinct reference to the readier capture of prey and seizure of food.

Space would fail us were we to trace the personal history of these fishes farther, but there remain three points in their biography which may be simply alluded to by way of suggestion as to the interest which awaits the reader and observer who may make the better acquaintance of the skates and rays. Thus, firstly, we know of huge developments of certain species of these fishes, whereby they appear to exemplify the veritable giants of the first class. The horned rays or *Cephalopteræ* of the Mediterranean Sea may thus attain an immense size, may measure twenty feet long, twenty-eight feet in width, and may weigh over a ton. Such were the dimensions of a specimen actually captured. At Marseilles large specimens of these fishes are often landed, and it may well be understood how cautious the Mediterranean fishermen are in attempting the capture of such veritable monsters of the deep. Equally interesting is it to find that the eggs of the skates and rays are enclosed in tough cases, which, under the name of "mermaid's purses," are often to be picked up in an empty condition on the sea beach. Should the holiday-maker by the sea be fortunate enough to find a "sea purse" with the embryo enclosed, he will be interested by the spectacle of the little skate or ray coiled up, head and tail together—the features of the adult, although represented in miniature, being still recognisable in the little embryo which lies imprisoned within the seaweed-like egg-capsule referred to.

A final feature of no small interest in skate-history, is that included in the remark that this family contains at least one member which finds a place in the lists of "electrical fishes." It is a well-known fact that certain fishes possess organs whereby they are enabled to give electrical shocks of surprising force and power. Such are the electric eels of South American rivers, and the Malapterurus of the Nile, from a specimen of which the writer recently received a shock which numbed his arm for several hours afterwards. The electric ray, well named the torpedo, and popularly known as the "cramp fish," is another example of these curious fishes. The torpedo and its kind are found on our southern coasts and in warmer seas. On each side of the head exists an "electrical organ," somewhat resembling a honeycomb in appearance, and consisting of structures richly supplied with nerves. It is notable that the more commonplace rays possess an inactive and useless rudiment of the electrical organ on each side of the tail. The production of electricity by this organ may be readily understood as involving merely a modification of the ordinary nerve-force of the body. When the nerve-force of our bodies is sent to muscles, it is converted into motion, the muscle being the organ which converts and transforms the one force into the other. So with the electricity of the fish. Nerve-force supplied to the special organ in question is converted into electricity, and thus serves as a means of offence and of defence as well. That the nerve-force of the body is the source of the electrical force cannot be doubted, since the shocks become less and less powerful as the nerve-force becomes exhausted through over-stimulation of the fish. The whole apparatus in the torpedo reminds one of the arrangement known as a "voltaic battery;" and the fact that in the skates and rays such a form of apparatus must have existed for untold ages prior to man's epoch, affords another illustration of the wise man's adage that "there is nothing new under the sun."

THE AUTOBIOGRAPHY OF A BARNACLE.

IN your seaside strolls, I dare say you have frequently met with specimens of the race to which I belong, whilst in the graving-dock of your nearest seaport town you may meet with us in hundreds attached to the sides of ships, like a race of parasitic dependents brought from some warmer clime. I do not know whether you have ever thought twice over our identity and nature. The question, "What is a barnacle?" is not perhaps an attractive one in the ears of most folks; and I dare say there are half a dozen ways in which humanity might reply to the query. There is, of course, a goose of the name, but the bird is no relation of mine. I should have called it a "goose" were that not its appellation already, on account of its somewhat far-fetched connection, even in name, with a family like ours. Max Müller will tell you, if you care to dip into his lectures, that the name "Barnacle," as applied to the goose, is in reality a corruption of the word "Hibernia;" and although certain wiseacres—notably one old Gerarde who wrote "The Herball"—used to assert that he and others had seen young geese growing within our shells, and that we in turn grew on a tree, I may simply assert such statements to be figments of Gerarde's imagination. We have no connection whatever with the geese. They are at one end of the animal world, and we reside nearly at the other extremity. So let us dismiss, once for all, the barnacle-goose as no relation of mine. But, in the second place, I have heard the name "barnacles" applied to a species of spectacles of large size and ancient make. If I have little connection with the goose, I have still less with the spectacles, and I need not delay by saying more of the unlawful associations which our name has now and then had attached to it.

But the question still remains, "What is a barnacle?" And, as I am about to tell you the story of myself, I may say, without being deemed over bold, that I am the proper person to answer the query. To begin at the beginning, let me ask you in turn whether you have ever noticed the little conical shells which grow by the thousands on the rocks at low water mark, and are crushed by the dozen as you scramble over the rocks in your seaside ramble? If you procure a piece of stone or an oyster-shell on which these little shells grow, and place the said stone or oyster-shell in water, you will see a sight worth looking at. From the upper part of the little conical dwelling-place will come forth a curious little set of plumes, which will wave backwards and forwards in the water with a regular and incessant motion. If you touch the shell you will find its tenant to take alarm. The little plumes will be at once withdrawn; snap! will go the little lid at the top of the shell; and the tenant in question will withdraw itself for a time into the retirement and obscurity of private life. Then, after a suitable interval, the door will be cautiously reopened, the plumes extended, and in a short time the activity of our small friend in the shell will be perfectly and completely resumed.

Now, this being in the shell is a poor relation of mine. He belongs to a subordinate branch of the barnacle family, although I admit he has most of the characters and belongings of our race.

He is called in familiar language the "sea acorn;" but scientific persons name him *Balanus*, and perhaps, out of compliment to the people who study us most and who know most about us, I had better use the latter appellation. Thus around the coasts of Britain our family is well represented, and, indeed, in well-nigh every sea you will find examples of the tribe. My special habitat is a piece of floating drift-wood, or the sides of ships; the graving-dock becoming, of course, a scene of the massacre of our race. We have been credited with delaying the passage of ships through the water by reason of our numbers, but this latter statement I regard as an exaggeration and a libel on our kind. It is not our fault if Nature has given us a special facility for attaching ourselves to fixed objects. Our feet are of no use—in our adult state—at least for swimming, and hence, unless you interfere with the mere fact of our existence, you must admit our right to dispose ourselves to the best advantage in our ways of life. Some members of the barnacle family, I may lastly remark, are somewhat peculiar in their choice of a habitation. One or two near neighbours of mine actually fix themselves to the backs of whales and the sides of sharks. Such an existence would not suit me; but, of course, there is no accounting for taste in barnacles any more satisfactorily than in human beings.

Having thus finished a brief survey of my friends and relations, I may now say something about myself. If you wish to understand me thoroughly and completely you should read Mr. Darwin's history of our tribe. That will show you that one of your greatest philosophers did not deem us beneath his notice, and he will tell you therein that there are a good many points in our history which present very deep puzzles and problems to the most learned of mankind. But to make my acquaintance in a superficial fashion is not a difficult matter.

I possess a triangular shell, enclosing my body, and attached to the fixed object—drift-wood or ship as the case may be—by a fleshy muscular stalk called a "peduncle." This "shell" of mine is a very different structure from the oyster's possession. I am not egotistical, but I make bold to say mine is the more complicated and handsomer shell of the two. It consists of some five pieces, two at the sides above, two at the sides below, and a lower piece called the "keel," because it occupies much the same position in my shell that the keel does in a boat. I told you that my relation the Balanus, or "Sea Acorn," possessed a series of beautiful plumes which waved continually in the water, and which could be protruded from the shell, and also withdrawn at will. I am similarly provided with no less than twenty-four of these appendages, which are called "cirri" by our friends the naturalists, and which popularly and collectively compose my "glass-hand." In this "hand" of mine there are twenty-four fingers, which I use as plumes to sweep the water around, by way of drawing food-particles into my mouth. I am, in fact, like a persistent beggar, for my hand is always open, and my commissariat is continually being replenished by the sweeping fingers in question. I may be misleading you, however, in speaking of these filaments as "fingers" and of my plumes as a "hand." Properly regarded, they represent my "feet." How this curious transformation comes about you will learn later on, but you may meanwhile rest content to know, on the authority of a great naturalist, that one of the chief characters of the barnacle race is found in the fact that we kick our food into our mouths with our legs. It is, I admit, not a seemly procedure to speak of, and savours too much of the acrobat to be thoroughly respectable; but you must not judge barnacles by a strictly human standard, and after all I do not see why a handy foot may not, for purposes of the kind just mentioned, be as convenient an organ as a hand.

As regards my internal economy, you would find that I am by no means of lowly structure, but possess the usual apparatus for maintaining existence such as you expect an animal of average rank in the kingdom to exhibit. It is true I have no distinct heart, but in the absence of that organ I contrive to live perfectly, and well. I am by no means an epicure, but I enjoy to the full the titbits which my "glass-hand" sweeps in from the outer world, and I possess a full and complete digestive system, whereby the wants of the body may be supplied. Neither am I of an unfeeling race, for we possess a very well-defined set of nerves in the shape of a double chain of nervous cords lying along the floor of my body. Organs of sense I do not set much store by, because, probably, I do not require them, being a stay-at-home being, and not resembling in disposition those near neighbours of mine, the crabs and lobsters, which are always on the move—especially the crabs. But I do possess a pair of eyes, not of very definite type, it is true. You would probably call them mere specks of colour, and so, indeed, they are; still, they serve my purpose, and the latter remark excludes all criticism of an unfriendly kind.

So much for my internal anatomy. What more need be said regarding myself, in reality, resolves itself into the history of my development, or, in other words, the story of how I came to be what I am. If you were to ask Mr. Darwin to which portion of my history he would attach the greatest value, he would reply, my development. This marked appreciation of my early history is easily explained. Mr. Darwin will tell you that in the history of the individual's production you may see, as in a moving panorama, the history of its race. Of course you may not agree with the eminent philosopher just named; but I know that in barnacle-circles his views are regarded as most satisfactory, because you observe they tend to bring us nearer to the aristocracy of the animal world, and to place us in virtue of our descent on a par with apparently much higher forms of life. My first appearance on the stage of time was in the form of an egg—a very minute, trifling thing, no doubt, but still an egg, with all the probabilities and possibilities, all the trials and sorrows, hopes and fears, of barnacle-life locked up within its narrow limits. After a few preliminary changes—not worth noting at present, save to remark that they tell me all living beings have to undergo similar transformations at first—I was fairly launched, in a literal sense, on the sea of life. The earliest impressions of which I have any recollection are those of escaping into the sea from the shell of my parent. Around me were swimming a large number of very curious-looking little beings, each possessing a body somewhat of triangular shape, ending behind in a very well-marked tail, and in front having two side-projections, resembling horns. "Well! you are a curious set of beings," was my first remark to these little comrades of mine. "Hear, hear!" said one of them; "why, don't you know you are one of us?" and of course the remark at once corrected any vain notions I might have entertained regarding myself. The queer creatures with the tails were, of course, my youthful brothers and sisters, who, like myself, had just been liberated from the care of our fixed and rooted parent—so soon, alas! are family ties snapped in barnacle existence. Here we were left to ourselves in our infantile stage, and without a guardian in all the days of our youth.

In front of my body I possessed a mouth, opening on a kind of raised margin, and around the mouth were set three pairs of legs, of which the two hinder pairs were cleft at their tips. Like the cyclops—the "water-flea," I mean, a far-off cousin of mine—I possessed a single eye. And thus provided, as the baby-barnacle, I was launched on my travels, being named by those kindly persons, the scientific zoologists (who are well-nigh the only persons who take an interest in us), a *Nauplius*. This term, please to recollect, is just the scientific name of a baby-barnacle. Swimming about day by day, and picking up whatever food-particles came in my way, I grew rapidly. My first coat or skin becoming too small, I had to cast it off, but found Mother Nature had already in her mindfulness provided another garment below the first. After moulting two or three times I approached the period of my youth. I became more sedate and less inclined to swim through the sea: and my next epoch began with my attaining a new livery as the mark and badge of my growing condition. I found myself, after a certain moult, in the possession of a body, which was unlike that of the Nauplius, and which, indeed, I could not at first recognise as my own. My body was now of oval shape, and I had attained to the dignity of a "shell." Not a very perfect shell—a small, folded down, thin kind of thing it was, just like that of a water-flea—nothing like the one I now possess, but still a shell; and I dare say I regarded myself as having advanced a stage in the world, very much as a young miss, who, having discarded short dresses, thinks she is somebody in her long skirt and train. But my changes were not limited to the development of a shell. My first pair of limbs had become wonderfully transformed, so much so indeed that I hardly knew them. No longer like limbs, they had become "organs of prehension," as my scientific friends say, or, in plainer language, things for holding on by. I had parted with the other two pairs which you will remember I possessed as the infant-Nauplius, and not even the stumps of them remained. But my fears as to my limbless condition were soon calmed by the growth of six pairs of curious feet, not by any means so elegant as the pair I had lost, but provided with stiff bristles, and thus very well adapted for swimming.

I imagined I was getting on in the world at a great rate, when, in place of my single eye, I found, on waking up one fine morning, I had two of quite a superior kind; but whatever feelings of congratulation I may have had on this latter point were somewhat dashed by the discovery that, in this second stage of my development, I had no mouth. How I nourished myself I cannot tell. Probably there was no need for much nourishment in this second stage of mine; but in any case there I was, mouthless, but provided with two big eyes, with a pair of long hold-fasts in front, and six pairs of feet. I was now the "Pupa barnacle," a term which I hear is meant to denote a similarity to the chrysalis stage in the insects. Internally, at this stage, my organisation must have proceeded apace. Two curious glands called "cement-glands" were beginning to be formed on each side of my digestive system, and these glands in due time came to open in my hold-fasts, or front pair of feelers. Next came an all-important epoch in my life. I am credibly informed that in higher life there is a process described as that of "sowing one's wild oats," and that this procedure, bearing no reference to an agricultural operation, is meant to indicate the free and ingenuous life of youth, prior to the invasion of the sobriety and decorous demeanour of mature life. At the time I speak of, my period of "settling down" had, all unknown to me, arrived. One day I found myself in company with about a dozen of barnacles in a similar stage of development to myself, clinging by means of our hold-fasts to a piece of floating wood. What we were doing there I do not suppose any of us could tell, but there we were, holding on to the wood, and more curious still, we gradually found that we were being fastened firmly thereto by the action of the cement from the glands I have spoken of. You have, I believe, a very useful fluid called "marine glue," warranted to withstand the action of water.

Well, our cement was such a glue; but when I remind you that we were being fastened head downwards by this cement to the wood, I think you will admit our position must have appeared floating somewhat ridiculous in the eyes of a disinterested observer.

Worse still, my eyes disappeared, and left me in total darkness. Of the changes which took place during this interval of blindness I can give no account. Suffice it to say that when I awoke to consciousness I discovered myself in possession of my perfect shell; and I found that my six pair of legs had each become divided to form the twenty-four fingers of my "glass-hand." I also saw that I was firmly attached to the floating wood by my fleshy stalk which had grown out of my hold-fasts and cement-glands—in a word, I awoke to find myself the barnacle you see before you. There are various persons belonging to the world of science who tell me that I am a good example of physiological backsliding. Well, so be it. I suppose by their "retrograde development," as they term it, they mean to declare that I am a less highly developed animal in my adult stage than I was in the days of my youth. As to that I say nothing; but I do say that a barnacle is a barnacle only when it is like me, and I maintain I am now in reality quite as typical and perfect a being in my way as when I roamed far and wide in the sea, and did not always think so seriously of life as I do now. At any rate I have one comfort—I am not nearly such a low animal as the Sacculinas, that attach themselves to crabs, and which, although beginning life like me as Nauplii, yet grow down into the condition of insignificant little sausages or bags, rooted to their hosts, the crabs, and showing little or no sign of life whatever. And although I cannot boast of being so high in the world as the crabs and shrimps, still I feel some comfort in knowing that the infant crab is very like the infant barnacle, whilst the young water-fleas and other beings quite of the upper classes begin life just as I do.

This reminds me of what I said long ago, that my friend Mr. Darwin thinks that when animals are alike in their development, they are to be regarded as true blood relations, and as chips of the same old block. Now of what particular block did the barnacles come, do you think, and which chips most resemble the barnacle family in their nature? The answer to this important question concerning our pedigree may be found by referring to the baby-barnacle, or *Nauplius*, with the triangular body and the three pairs of feet. You will think it a peculiar fact, no doubt, that such widely different animals as crabs, shrimps, water-fleas, and barnacles, are developed in exactly the same way. Yet it is nevertheless a plain truth. It would puzzle you exceedingly to say sometimes whether a Nauplius was a baby-barnacle, or a youthful crab, or a young water-flea—so closely do we resemble each other in early life. Your crab that crawls on the sea-beach has a splendid tail in early life, this appendage dwindling away, and becoming "small by degrees and beautifully less," until it appears as the merest vestige in the form of the "purse," tucked under the crab's body (which is all head and chest), and which children are fond of pulling down to see how much money Mr. Cancer Pagurus may possess. Thus a crab, who is very different from the barnacle in adult life, resembles me closely enough in youth. We begin life on equal terms, but he advances whilst I lag behind. Such, I am told, is often the way of the world in higher societies than mine. But, at any rate, you see quite plainly what I contend for. If we crustaceans, as we call ourselves—crabs, water-fleas, lobsters, barnacles, etc.—all begin life much in the same guise, as the Nauplius, or something very like it, it stands to reason that our original progenitor, and the founder of the whole, must have been something like the baby-barnacle itself. After such a revelation, you will not despise the barnacles, but think of us, perhaps, as a curious race of beings with a curious history of our own. And perchance you may likewise learn from my story that even in the humblest history there may be a great many more things than are dreamt of in your philosophy. Good-bye.

LEAVES.

No organs of plants are so common as leaves, and yet, strangely enough, there are few parts of a plant with the functions and uses of which ordinary people are less acquainted. It may therefore form a pleasant if not profitable study, if we venture to give some plain ideas concerning the structures which add so largely to the grace and beauty of our fair world. Our first remark regarding leaves may take shape in the form of the query, "What is a leaf?" To this it may be replied that a leaf is a side-expansion of the skin or integument of the plant. In this respect there is some analogy to be drawn between a leaf and the wing of an insect, which is also an extension of the animal's outer layer, and which, like the leaf, is supported by veins or ribs. How, in the next instance, is a leaf developed, and what is its origin and mode of growth? Like the stem of the plant itself, like the branch on which it is borne, like the flowers which crown the life of the plant, the leaf is developed in and from a "bud." One of the most curious studies of the botanist is that of tracing how leaves are folded in the bud. Each plant has its leaves folded within the leaf-buds in a particular fashion. Thus, for instance, in the oak the young leaf is folded from the midrib, in halves, so that the upper surfaces of the leaf are pressed together. In the vine and maple, beech and birch, the leaves are folded like fans when in the bud; and as every one knows who has watched a fern growing, the leaves of those plants are rolled up in a fashion which reminds one of the bishop's crosier.

Every leaf springs from a point of the stem which the botanist designates as a "node;" and it is interesting to note that the leaf-blade is as a rule spread horizontally, and with one surface to the earth and the other to the sky. It is a highly curious observation that in some plants the leaf appears to be actually twisted by nature; whilst in some Australian plants the edges of the leaf occupy the place of the flat surfaces, and are turned to the earth and sky respectively. To regard the mass of foliage seen on a tree as an orderly arranged series of organs, might seem to be a far-fetched thought. But the botanist assures us that leaves are arranged in each plant according to one of several modes. Thus in some plants we see the leaves placed opposite each other on the stem or branch; in others again, each succeeding leaf is placed above and opposite to its predecessor; whilst we may sometimes see a whole circle of leaves given off at one point—as in the glutinous goose-grass of our hedgerows. It is somewhat of a technical study to explain the manner in which the botanist constructs a formula to express the particular leaf-arrangement of any plant; but the importance of his work in this direction can be readily understood when we reflect that the true nature of certain parts of plants becomes known to us through the accurate determination of leaves and their arrangement. Thus a fir-cone is simply a collection of modified leaves arranged in a highly characteristic spiral manner. An onion and a lily bulb, and all other "bulbs," commonly mistaken for roots, are in reality "stems;" a fact proved by the modified fleshy or scaly leaves with which they are covered. So that we may in fact distinguish a root from a stem by the fact that the latter is capable of producing leaves, whilst the former has no such power.

Each leaf consists, as a general rule, of the stalk and blade—the "petiole" and "lamina" of the botanist; but a very slight exercise of our observation may serve to show us that sometimes leaves want stalks, and are attached directly to the stem of their blades. To properly understand the modifications in form which leaves may undergo, we require to bear in mind that in some plants the leaf-stalk may be well-nigh as broad as the blade of the leaf itself; and in some Australian acacias the leaf-stalks actually become modified to form leaves when the true leaves have withered and died away. These acacias represent the plants already alluded to as possessing leaves which are set with their edges vertically instead of with their flat surfaces to earth and sky. The manner in which leaves are united to the stem or branch occasionally produces peculiarities in plants. It is thus no mere poetic fancy to speak of the "light quivering aspen;" since we find that the leaf-stalk of that tree is flattened from side to side—that is, at right angles to the blade—and thus catches the lightest breath of wind, with the result of causing the leaves to tremble when the leaves of other plants are at rest.

The modifications which the leaves of certain foreign plants undergo may be of very extraordinary kind. Every reader must know something of the curious *Dionæa*, or Venus' Flytrap, a native of North American marshes, which possesses its leaf-blades divided into two halves, so that they may close together, when the sensitive hairs which stand erect on the leaf-blade are touched by an unwary insect. Not only does this curious leaf serve as an insect-trap, however. It acts as a veritable stomach, digesting and assimilating in perfect fashion the flies it captures. The Venus' Flytrap, moreover, is not alone in the peculiar use to which its leaves are put. The sundews, common in our marshes, capture insects, and digest them by means of the sensitive hair-like tentacles, which are provided with a viscid or glutinous fluid. So also in the Pitcher Plants and Side-saddle plants, the "pitcher" is a structure supposed to be formed by the large development of the leaf-stalk, whilst the blade of the leaf forms the lid. These latter plants also capture insects by aid of their curiously modified leaves. The leaves of certain plants may, however, be simply irritable and sensitive without being devoted to the capture of prey. Thus we know of the Sensitive Plant, of Shelley's charming poem, the "fan-like leaves" of which droop on the slightest touch, their leaflets becoming huddled together on the stalk. And it is noteworthy that the leaves of the Sensitive Plant may be chloroformed as if they were animals, and so as to utterly destroy their sensitiveness; the leaves recovering from the anæsthetic after the lapse of a suitable interval. The leaves of the Wood-sorrel are found to be sensitive in daylight when the leaf-stalk is smartly tapped; and in the Moving Plant of India the leaflets appear to be in a state of constant movement during the day, and even during darkness, the advent of which produces certain remarkable actions and variations, to be presently noted, in plant-life at large.

The statement of Goethe that every appendage of the stem of a plant is in reality a "leaf" of some kind or another, is not difficult of proof. One very plain demonstration of this fact is to be found in cases of "double flowers." The outer green part of every flower is called the *calyx*, and this portion is evidently composed of leaves. The coloured part of the flower, or *corolla*, composed of petals, also evidently consists of leaves. But the *stamens*, or little stalked organs seen in the inside of the flower, and which manufacture the yellow dust or *pollen* necessary for fertilising the "ovules" (or "seeds"), do not resemble leaves at all; and it might be thought that Goethe's maxim would fail when applied to the stamens. Where the course of ordinary development fails to afford a solution to the puzzles of nature, we frequently find the clue in cases of abnormal or unwonted development. Suppose, for example, that we trace the growth of the stamens in a double rose, such as the *Rosa centifolia* of the botanist. There we may see represented, in one flower, all the stages through which the petals become converted into stamens, and by means of which a leaf becomes folded and modified to form the little pollen-producing organ, or *vice versâ*. In the water-lilies the transformation of stamens into petals is well seen.

More common modifications of leaves are, however, to be noted in the shape of *tendrils*. The idea of a tendril as a climbing support is so well known, that the term has passed into the domain of poetic metaphor and imagery. The tendril becomes highly interesting to the botanist not merely because of its relation to the leaf, but from the fact that tendrils may be formed from organs and parts of plants other than leaves. A simple tendril is seen in the common pea, which climbs up the stakes placed for its support by aid of these organs. If we look at the leaf of the pea we may see that it is a compound organ, and consists of leaflets attached to a central leaf-stalk. At the extremity of the leaf, the leaflets disappear, and in their place we see the delicate thread-like tendrils. These latter organs are given off from the sides of the leaf-stalk, and we also note that the tip of the leaf is drawn out to form a tendril. Thus we readily come to the conclusion that the tendrils of the pea are formed by modified leaflets. Suppose now that we examine the vine. We find that in the latter plant the tendrils appear to be formed by veritable branches, and not merely by modified leaves; whilst certain other parts may in other plants be modified to assist a weak stem in maintaining its hold of a support.

The "veins" of leaves form well-known parts of these

organs, and the botanist has drawn certain important distinctions between the *venation* or arrangement of the veins in the leaves of different plants. If we look at the leaf of a nettle—having due regard to the powers of its stinging-hairs—of a lime-tree, of a primrose, or any other common tree or plant, we see that the veins form a network, the beauty of which is fully appreciated by those who make skeleton-leaves. In the leaf of a lily, of a grass, of a tulip, or of a palm-tree, we see that the veins do not unite but run parallel with one another, whilst in the hart's tongue fern, or any other fern with a broad frond, we may observe that each vein becomes forked as it is given off from the midrib of the leaf. Now, curiously enough, each of these three kinds of venation is characteristic of a great division of the vegetable world. All the highest plants (or exogens) have leaves the veins of which form a network. Parallel-veined leaves belong to the palms, grasses, lilies, etc.—the endogens of the botanist; and "forked" veins are only found in ferns. The character of a plant may therefore be determined in a general fashion, by merely looking at the veins of its leaf.

The microscope has made us acquainted with many interesting facts regarding the structure and functions of leaves. A thin skin exists on each surface of the blade, and incloses numberless little *cells* laden with green colouring-matter (or chlorophyll), and forming the delicate leaf-tissue, which, in its turn, is supported by the tough fibres of the veins. The minute cells of the upper surface of the leaf are much more closely packed together than those of the under surface. In the latter part of the leaf, spaces exist between the cells. Many of these spaces open on the under surface of the leaf by minute openings called "stomata;" each of these openings being guarded by two half-moon-shaped cells. These openings are the literal "mouths" of the plant. Through them gases are inhaled and exhaled, and thus serve for the nourishment and other vital actions of the plant. By means of the stomata also, the important act of "transpiration" is performed. In dry weather the stomata are closed, so that the plant may retain its moisture; but when the atmosphere is moist, and when the plant may obtain a due supply of water by the root, the stomata open and permit the excess of water to escape from the leaves in the form of invisible vapour.

The gas upon which plants depend for subsistence is, as our readers already know, the *carbonic acid* exhaled by animals, and of deadly character when rebreathed in any great quantity into the animal frame. This gas is a compound of carbon and oxygen; the latter, in its pure state, being the gas required for the respiration of animals. Bearing these facts in mind, we may ascertain the indebtedness of the animal world at large to plants, when we discover that by means of their leaves, plants absorb the noxious carbonic acid as part of their food; decompose it, that is split it up into its component carbon and oxygen; retain the carbon for food; and liberate or restore the oxygen to the atmosphere for the use of the animals. Plants are thus types of the unselfish in nature. But to perform this kindly office of removing carbonic acid from the air, and of restoring oxygen to us, two conditions are required. These are, firstly, that the plant must possess chlorophyll or green colouring-matter; and secondly, that it be exposed to light. Plants (such as fungi) destitute of green colour, inhale oxygen and give out carbonic acid like animals; and green plants exhibit a similar action in the dark. Thus it may be estimated how great a difference the advent of night brings with it to the plant-world; and we may also note the curious fact that the plant which acts in opposition to the animal during the day, becomes a veritable animal in its breathing when the sunshine disappears and the night falls.

THE AUTOBIOGRAPHY OF A FLY.

It is but seldom that a member of the insect race is permitted to address beings of a station in life superior to himself. But as the opportunity has been presented to me, I should be rude and somewhat neglectful of the interests of my race were I to allow it to pass without saying a good word for flies in general, and for the particular branch of the family to which I belong. We are usually regarded as a happy-go-lucky, idle race of beings. Even the Wise Man himself found in our apparent frivolity a subject of remark. Poets have selected me as the type of extreme foolishness, and the nursery rhymes of children do not fail to present me in the same light to the youthful mind. Hence I am reminded of a proverb which says, "Give a dog a bad name, and hang him." In the language of the fly-family, I should say, "Credit a fly with being a useless insect, and crush him." You lay traps for us, gilded outside and furnished with a sugary solution, for which, I must confess, we have a decided weakness. Only, I would also beg to remark, that the liking for sweets is at the same time a natural instinct of our race, and one, moreover, from which mankind, judging from the numerous emporiums of sweetstuffs I have observed, is by no means free. Sometimes, too, you poison us with a subtle paper, the aroma of which steals into our brains and nerves and paralyzes us; and in any and every way, from the employment of the chemist's art to the use of the clumsy duster, we are assaulted and pursued. This is very hard; but even Dame Nature herself, of whom we are all entitled to think kindly indeed, has ordained that we should fall victims to the traps laid for us by many plants, and to the deceit and cunning of certain near relations of ours, the spiders. Of the latter family, the less said the better. If we cannot boast of their superior brain and cunning, if we do not toil and spin as they do, we at least have clear consciences,—for I do not regard our occasional raids on the cream jug and sugar basin as anything more serious than the petty larceny and as the little perquisites which Dame Nature perfectly justifies in a world, wherein one of your great philosophers has told us there is a perpetual "struggle for existence." On the whole I am thankful I am not a spider; and despite the idea that these creatures are "superior persons" to the flies, I think, if you investigate their history, you will find not a few traits of character with which you will be extremely horrified, not to say perplexed. We live on perfectly amicable terms with each other, and actions for assault and battery are unknown amongst us. But they do say—and although this is gossip, still I have it on the best authority—that the lady-spiders maul and beat their husbands unmercifully. The poor gentlemen have not the life of the most miserable fly; and a near relation of mine told me that, on one occasion, when perched in a secure position, he saw an unfortunate male spider devoured by his mate. Now, we may be frivolous, but you will admit we are preferable to these cannibal neighbours of ours in more ways than one.

I have been told that when, in higher life, you desire to announce the absence of kinship between yourself and some other person, you say, "No connection with the party over the way." Permit me to say, likewise, that we flies have no relationship whatever with the spider fraternity. Many excellent persons who have not made our intimate acquaintance, are apt to class spiders and flies together. But I would remind you that we are "insects," whilst the spiders form a group which learned persons have named "Arachnidans"—a term derived, so I have heard, from the name of a foolish young person named Arachne, who challenged Minerva, the goddess of wisdom, to a trial of skill in spinning, and who was changed into a spider for her temerity. Be it observed then, that we are not spiders. They have eight legs, we have only six—a number, I make bold to say, more convenient than the former. They have no wings, we have two; and although most other insects possess four wings, still we find that with our two appendages we manage to get along very comfortably; and besides, you know, there are some higher creatures than ourselves who possess but two wings. Then the spider race have no feelers; we have a pair of very delicate organs of touch, and our susceptibilities are in consequence of a much more refined caste than those of the cannibal race just mentioned. They have a few paltry eyes scattered over the top of their heads. Did you ever see our eyes? No. Then just you look at the sides of my head, and you will see two great masses of eyes, the structure of which, seen through a microscope, will cause you to open your own organs of sight more widely than before. You would not imagine, I suppose, that I had about four thousand eyes. I assure you that is the case. The fly race is not given to mendacity, but if you doubt me ask your friend the zoologist. He will tell you my statement is perfectly correct. So that when you attempt to exterminate us in our little attentions to the sugar bowl, you can well understand why you should so seldom catch a fly. We see you long before you think we notice your movements; and as for eyes in the back of our head—well, we possess them all round our heads, and hence we are just as wary as Nature intended we should be.

The other points of difference betwixt the spider race and ourselves may be briefly summed up by stating that the former do not come into the world in such a curious fashion as we do. But of this more anon. And they breathe differently from us; whilst, their heads and chests being stuck firmly together, you will admit they cannot possess that ease and grace which we display in the regions just mentioned. I shall therefore say no more of the spiders, now that I have satisfied you we are a distinct race of persons. And I shall now ask your attention to what I believe to be a much more important topic—I mean myself.

Of course there are flies and flies, just as there are Smiths and Smiths amongst yourselves. My family is one of the most typical. Our especial cognomen is *Musca,* and my own twig of the family-tree is the *domestica* branch. Hence, when I am at home, I am known as *Musca domestica,* which is the scientific name for the Common House-fly. Some of my nearest relatives —cousins you would call them, I dare say—are also well known to you. There is the " blue-bottle," a term I hear often applied in derision to preservers of the peace in higher life— I do not know why; and there is the flesh-fly, with whose tastes I do not agree, although the species in question has its own uses in nature's economy. Even so notorious a fly as the "Tsetse" is a far-off cousin of mine, and I am reminded by its existence, and by the fact of its poisonous bite, that I should be charitable in speaking even of those reprobates the spiders. The name " fly " is much abused in nature. This honourable distinction is applied without any real cause to such parties and insects as the dragon-flies, may-flies, and day-flies, and to other members of the insect class as far removed from me and mine as you are from the Chinaman or the Tartar. The day-fly is a poor thing which passes its early days in water, comes out of its shell in the morning, and dies at night. I have attended a large number of their funerals even in the afternoon. So that these far-off friends of mine never seem to get beyond the infant stage of existence, whilst we attain a respectable age. We live at least for a summer, unless the *papier-mouché* deludes us to a premature end, or the fly-trap checks our budding hopes and aspirations. Many of us even sleep through the winter, when we can discover a secure bedroom and some kindly shelter; and we may thus appear in the next spring, like giants refreshed by a long winter's nap. Flies thus are a very distinct race, with their two wings—dragon-flies and day-flies have four, but they do not fly one whit better than we do—with our distinct globular heads, our big eyes, and our curious mouths, of which more anon.

You ask me what has become of our hinder pair of wings. Do you know where last summer's leaves are, or where the rainbow goes when it disappears from your gaze? Do not think my query impertinent, for really, where our hinder wings have gone, or why they have disappeared, nobody knows. There is a legend in the fly-family that once we did possess four wings. And I must say that some colour is given to this supposition by the fact that we possess two curious little appendages where the missing wings should be. Some people call these appendages "poisers" and "balancers," though why they should have received this name is more than any sensible fly to whom I have mentioned the matter could tell. Somebody has evidently thought that we "balanced" ourselves by aid of these filaments—as if, indeed, we were as weak in the head as a human rope-dancer or acrobat. But there these poisers are, and how they came there, or what they are, no one can definitely say. I myself believe that they are the rudiments of our hind-wings, "which grew small by degrees and beautifully less," by order of Nature, until we were left with two wings; and, as I maintained before, I regard ourselves as superior to the insects with four.

It has been reported to me that human physiognomists are largely given to judge human character by the shape and form of the mouth. Now in fly existence, and indeed in insect life at large, there is a deal of character to be found in the latter region. Take those sombre gentlemen the beetles. They have a mouth wherein is plenty of jaw. Then there are our delicate lady-friends and fops, the butterflies; they have the longest tongues you ever saw. The bees and wasps are half-way between the beetles and the butterflies, and they are really a very clever family, being able to do a great deal of very difficult work with their mouths. Though a somewhat sharp, ill-tempered, and easily-provoked race, I still respect the bees and wasps, but they certainly owe a good deal to their mouths. Now, where do the flies stand in the matter of their mouths? I reply, as a kind of offshoot of the wasp and bee type. Let me sum up our belongings for you. Watch me alight in your sugar bowl, and keep your eye steadily fixed on my head. As soon as I drop down on the crystalline particles in the basin, you see an organ, that looks almost like one of my legs, folded down from under my head, and you may see me scrape up the sugar with this long spoon. Now that is my tongue, and a very fine tongue too. It is formed by what in the beetle exists as a mere under-lip to the mouth, and you see that the end of my tongue is very curious. It is broad and leaf-like, and opens out in two joints, which are unbent in a very complicated manner, which I can no more describe to you than you could tell me the structure and mechanism of your tongue. But by aid of this broad leaf, I can rasp down your sugar particles, and I manage in a very short time to make a very hearty meal of whatever substance I may be permitted to partake. You will now be able to understand—although in saying so I am, perhaps, injudiciously showing you a grave fault of ours—why, after a hot summer, when our population has been very much increased, the nicely bound books on your drawing-room table (where, of course, they exist only for ornament), or your beautifully polished furniture should be scratched. It is a bad habit, I know, but we cannot help it; when we alight on any surface we must touch and rub it with our tongues. The rough surface of the tongue acts like a fine file, and causes you many sighs that flies are permitted to exist. Blame Nature, my dear friend, for so providing us—do not blame us. We are just like yourselves, the creatures of habit; so please be charitable, and reflect rather upon the wonder of our tongue than the damage we do by its aid.

I am afraid I shall not have time to tell you very much more about myself. You may think me an egotistical insect, and I do not deny I have a good opinion of our race. Whilst I am not singular in my behaviour that when I get a good topic I like to do it justice. Still, as you desire it, I shall give you a few more particulars regarding fly-economy and ways; and I have yet to tell you of the most curious part of our history, namely, how Nature manufactures her flies.

Have I a heart? Yes, and a pretty big one too. It lies along my back, and goes on pumping from morning till night, just as your own does, distributing the blood through my body. I have no lungs, but everywhere through my frame runs a curious set of delicate tubes, and into these tubes air passes by several apertures; so that I breathe all over my body, and, although somewhat puffed up and airy through this arrangement, I feel the advantages of its presence in rendering me light for flying. The work of my muscles is also rendered less tiring. You would hardly believe how many times I move my wings in a second. A wonderful man, M. Marey of Paris, held us captive, and then calculated that our wings in this position moved 330 times per second, and that they describe a beautiful figure of 8 in their motions. When I increase the vibrations of my wings to 352 times per second, I produce a musical sound which I am informed corresponds to F. And you know from experience how I can ring the changes on notes when I buzz. You can distinguish the angry "buzz" from the good-natured "hum," and the excited sound from the placid easy-going note. Is there very much difference after all between "the expression of the emotions" in the man and in the fly? Of my legs, I need not say much, except to remind you that my feet consist of hairy pads, not very elegant, I admit, but enabling me, by aid of their tube-like hairs and the adhesive cement I can produce, to walk body downwards from the ceiling or to run with ease up and down your walls. But this last is a sore subject with housewives, and I will not pursue it further.

Last of all, what about my development? Well, I suppose you know something about my early history. I am not ashamed to own that I began life as a maggot of some kind or another. I fancy you would not have recognized me, had you seen me in the days of my youth, not to speak of those of my infancy. But, nevertheless, I was worth studying. I had no legs, and I am ashamed to say I was a voracious youngster, eating almost everything that came in my way. Amongst the furnishings of my body in this stage were certain organs called *imaginal discs*, arranged along the sides of my frame. I took no account of these until I became the chrysalis, or pupa, which means, as you know, that I left off my voracious habits. Although I had got rid of many a coat and skin previously to the commencement of this stage, yet I retained my last covering, and lay quiet and still within it, just as the moth or butterfly lies motionless in its cocoon. Now I saw the use of these imaginal discs. Can you believe it, I seemed to undergo a kind of dissolution, and to be rebuilt up like a Phœnix from the ruins of my frame? These discs became, some of them, the legs I now possess; others of them gave rise to my head; and others again to my wings. The only part of my infant body which was retained and used in the production of my present frame was the tail, which, with a little touching up at the hands of Nature, became the comely appendage I now possess. Then a day came when the rebuilt body was complete, and as the old skin of my childhood was burst and cast aside, I emerged into the world as *Musca domestica*—the perfect fly. Such a strange history in my humble opinion is only paralleled by that which ends our eventful lives and yours, when our elements are once more dissipated hither and thither to enter, it may be, I am told, into new combinations in the world of life.

My tale is ended. I hear a familiar "hum" close by, which warns me that a near friend and neighbour has discovered a store of sweets of which he kindly invites me to partake. We must make the most of our time you know. Thank you for the patient attention you have given to my story. May you cherish in future none but kindly feelings to the race of flies, and if you care to know more of our history you will not find your labour in vain. Though I say it myself, we are a curious set of beings; and you see there may be something to wonder at even in our common acquaintances. This last I consider is a wise remark, applicable to other lives than those of flies. Fare you well.

ABOUT KANGAROOS.

THE visitor to our zoological collections naturally pauses a while before the kangaroo sheds, to remark the curious aspect of these animals, or even to gaze at beings to whose history attaches much that is strange and interesting. The mere look of a kangaroo is, to say the least of it, ungainly and awkward in the extreme. The animal somewhat resembles the frog in the extreme development of the hind limbs as compared with the front members, and when at rest sits in much the same position as the amphibian, only differing from the frog or cat in that its fore limbs are completely free from the ground. Resting in its cage the kangaroo sits on a kind of tripod, the two hind limbs and the strong tail forming the three legs of its support. Moving about in its den the animal progresses in awkward fashion, hopping on its two hind limbs, and occasionally assisting its movements by tilting itself over for support upon its short fore limbs, but invariably coming to rest upon the tripod once again. The non-zoological visitor to the kangaroos is, as a rule, perfectly conversant with the fact that they come from Australia—that curious continent which gives us the *Ornithorhynchus*, or duck-billed water-mole, and other curious creatures. The animal just mentioned, indeed, is a near neighbour of the kangaroos, and presents a strange appearance in that it possesses a duck-like bill and webbed toes. So curious was its outward aspect that when first brought to England, about the close of last century, it was regarded as a manufactured monstrosity, but more exact examination of the animal served to dissipate the erroneous impressions, and to establish its position as one of the lowest quadrupeds. With the opossums—which, by the way, are limited in their range to the New World—the kangaroos also possess near relationship; and the wombats, koalas, Tasmanian devil, and like beings, hail them as kith and kin. We may learn much, not merely respecting the quadrupeds at large, but regarding the manner in which the existing population of this world has been distributed and arranged, from a simple study in zoology, such as that we now purpose to undertake. Let us therefore try, firstly, to gain some ideas regarding the broad structure of these animals, and concerning the relations of the kangaroos to their own kith and kin and to the world which they may especially call their own.

That the kangaroo is a quadruped or mammal, and that it therefore belongs to the same great class which includes man as its head, are facts known to every one. But such information, whilst leading us to expect that between the highest animals and the kangaroos there should exist certain broad likenesses of structure and function, also prepares us conversely to expect to find marked differences between the kangaroos and most other quadrupeds. It may be said that man and the kangaroo agree in the broad structure of their bodies. Their bodies, along with those of all other quadrupeds, conform to a general type or plan which may be said to run through the whole class of mammals. But apart from this broad likeness, there are many and important differences to be discerned upon a very short acquaintanceship with the lower forms; and to some of these differences and your characteristic belongings of the kangaroo tribe we may now direct attention.

All kangaroos—and of the race there are various genera and many species—agree very closely indeed in their general structure and appearance. It would require no scientific training to enable an observer to parcel out the kangaroos from all other quadrupeds. True, there are the "kangaroo rats," belonging to the kangaroo family, which are, perhaps, strictly speaking not true kangaroos; and there are the tree kangaroos of New Guinea, in which fore and hind limbs are nearly of the same size, and which possess scaly tails, not used as supports after the fashion of the common species. But even these animals might justifiably enough be called "kangaroos," and the naturalist places them in the kangaroo family, to which he gives the name *Macropodidæ*. The representative family (or generic) name of the kangaroos is *Macropus*, a term meaning "large-footed," and the derivative of which we shall presently note. The members of the family derive their special names from some peculiarity of colour, size, or structure. Thus we speak of one kangaroo as *Macropus major*, of another as *Macropus rufus*, and of a third as *Macropus Brunii*. This is saying much the same thing as if we were dealing with a race of Smiths, calling one group the London-Smiths, another the Edinburgh-Smiths, and a third the Dublin-Smiths. When we come to the tree kangaroos we speak of them as the *Dendrologus*, and such a variation of name implies the difference which we might regard as existing between our friends the Smiths and the Smythes. They really spring from the same family tree, but the variations in personal features and structural history have necessitated the separation of the tree kangaroos into a distinct genus or group of the kangaroo family. And similarly with the kangaroo rats, and with the rock kangaroos, and other branches of the family—we recognise their relationship to the kangaroos with which we are so familiar, but we also note their differences, and make allowance accordingly for their removal to a little distance from the heads of the house. The only animals which so closely resemble the kangaroos that they might be mistaken at first sight for our "long-footed" friends, are the little creatures named "jerboas," which occur chiefly in Northern Africa, and which are also represented in North America. These are little animals allied to the rats and mice, and included in the group of the *Rodents,* or "gnawers." When the kangaroos were first seen, indeed, their likeness to the little jerboas—which likewise sit upon their long hind legs, and leap like the kangaroos —was duly remarked. But the naturalist would point to many and important differences between jerboas and kangaroos; these differences including variations in bones, teeth, brain, and many other points. Hence the resemblance in question is at the best but superficial, as also is that between the kangaroos and those curious little creatures the elephant-shrews of Africa, which are really little shrew-mice, but which also possess a miniature proboscis, or elongated nose, and long hind legs like our Australian animals.

So much for the family resemblances of the kangaroos. A word or two concerning their discovery may not prove uninteresting, if only by way of accounting for the origin of the name. In 1770 Captain Cook visited Botany Bay in the *Endeavour,* which had been despatched in 1768 on a scientific mission. In the course of the voyage, and when anchored in Endeavour River, an exploring and foraging party returned to the ship with the news that they had seen a new and curious animal, of a mouse colour, and about as large as a greyhound, which moved with surprising dexterity and swiftness. This animal was seen next day, on which occasion also one of the seamen brought the surprising intelligence that he had seen the devil!—this information relating to an animal which he said had horns and wings. The animal proved to be minus the horns (which were, no doubt, its ears) but to possess wings, and appeared in the shape of a large fruit-eating bat. The new animal of the mouse-colour and of the size of a greyhound was duly seen by Captain Cook himself, who remarked its long tail, and also that it leapt like a hare or deer. On Saturday, July 14th, a Mr. Gore shot one of the new animals, which was ascertained to be called "Kangaroo" by the natives, and which was likewise proved to be remarkably good eating at the voyagers' dinner of Sunday, July 15th, 1770. Such was the description given by Captain Cook of the now well-known "kangaroo." Antiquarian researches in zoology, however, inform us that De Bruins, a Dutch traveller, saw a kangaroo as early as 1711. This animal was kept domesticated at Batavia, was named "Filander," and appears to be the species now called *Macropus Brunii*, after its discoverer.

The kangaroo's personal characters are both easy and interesting of study. The great length of the hind limbs as compared with the fore limbs has already been remarked, and the resemblance between the human arm and the kangaroo's fore limb is very close, inasmuch as both possess five fingers. The hind limb, however, is provided with a different number and a widely varied arrangement of its toes. The name "long-footed" applied to the animal is fully deserved, since the bones of the instep are exceedingly long, and upon this lengthened part of the foot the animal chiefly rests. But more noticeable are the toes. These number four in all, but two of the four toes appear to compose the really useful part of the foot. Of these two big toes the inner one is by far the larger, and is provided with a large claw or nail. On the inner side of this large toe in turn we find two other and extremely small toes, which are bound together in one fold of skin, and which clearly represent the second and third toes in man's foot. So that a kangaroo possesses all the toes we see in man, with the exception of the first or great toe, which is completely absent. This foot the animal uses as a means of defence, frequently killing dogs with a single blow. One of the most remarkable features regarding the kangaroos and their neighbours consists in this disposition of their toes. It is somewhat surprising when we think of it, that in the foot of a kangaroo used for leaping, in that of its neighbour, the koala, used for climbing, and in that of the ground-living bandicoot, we should find essentially the same composition of foot. This resemblance and conformity to one type, beneath varied uses and ways of life, can only be reasonably explained by the theory that these varied beings are descended from a common ancestor, and this theory, as we shall see, is supported by other facts of kangaroo existence.

Not the least interesting part of kangaroo history is included in the details which relate to the early life of these animals. Born in a weakly state, the young, as every one knows, are carried and protected within the pouch, or *marsupium*, of the mother for a considerable period after birth. We know that the young of a kangaroo, which stands over six feet high when full grown, are about an inch long at birth, and hence we perceive the necessity for their protection until they are of an age to shift for themselves. The young are transferred to the pouch, and are there duly protected and fed by means of the milk secretion of the parent. Even the throat of the young is so constructed that in its early and feeble condition it can obtain its nourishment without incurring any danger of suffocation; and we may perceive in this latter fact an evidence of that complete adaptation to a singular manner of life which is so frequently demonstrated by the studies of the naturalist. The "pouch" in which the young are protected is supported upon a couple of bones, which may be said to be peculiar to the kangaroos and their neighbours. These bones arise from the brim of the haunch-bones, and in their nature they may be regarded as essentially differing from the true skeleton. They represent parts which in other animals exist as the tendons or sinews of certain of the muscles in front of the body. The observation that the bones of the "pouch" are merely altered sinews, again presents to our notice the consideration that nature has adapted these animals for their peculiar life, not by the development of new structures and parts, but by the modification of parts which are common to all animals. It is noteworthy that an adaptation somewhat similar to that seen in the pouch of the kangaroos and their neighbours is seen in those curious little fishes common in our aquaria, and known as *Hippocampi*, or "Sea-horses." The males of these fishes possess a pouch, in which the eggs are not merely contained, but in which the young are also thereafter protected. The most curious feature of this latter relationship betwixt parent and young, however, consists in the fact that it is the male fishes which tend and nurse the progeny—thus reversing the common rule of animal existence.

The internal anatomy of the kangaroo presents many points of extreme interest to the zoologist and anatomist, but which may be but lightly touched upon, if mentioned at all within the limits of a popular article. Thus the lower jaw of the kangaroo and its neighbours is bent inwards, or "inflected," as the technical term runs, at its lower and hinder portion, such a peculiarity being of high importance as a character of the group. The kangaroo is well provided in the matter of teeth, and these organs are adapted in turn for their work of cropping and bruising the grasses and other vegetable matters upon which the animals feed. There are six front or cutting teeth above, and two cutting teeth below; the latter pointing straight forwards. No "eye-teeth" exist in the kangaroos, but five grinders are seen in each half of the upper jaw, and the same number exists in the lower jaw behind. Thus, these animals are provided with twenty-eight teeth, being only four less than man. The true, or American opossums—not to be confounded with the "opossums" of the Australian colonist, which latter are merely species of phalangers—possess on the other hand almost double the number of teeth found in our kangaroos. In some of the opossums fifty teeth are found, and they are perhaps most notable as possessing a larger number of cutting or front teeth than any other animals. In some of the opossums, it may be likewise mentioned, the "pouch" is represented by a mere fold of skin, useless for protecting the young, whilst the bones of the pouch, however, are well developed. In such a case, the opossum's habits fully compensate for the want of her probable nursery, in that the young are carried on the mother's back, and obtain a secure lodgment thereon by twisting their tails around hers.

Concluding thus the personal history of the kangaroo, we may briefly glance at the characters of the "order" of animals to which it belongs, by way of introduction to the past history of the kangaroo race. These animals agree with the opossums of America, and with the bandicoots, koalas, and other Australian animals, in possessing the pouch with its characteristic bones, and in the possession of the "inflected" jaw just alluded to, as their principal characters. Accordingly the naturalist classifies all of these animals to form a single "order," called the "Marsupialia," or that of the "pouched" quadrupeds, which has Australia as its head-quarters, and which possesses but one single family outside the boundaries of that island-continent—namely, the opossums of America. Now, it may be fairly enough asked, have we any record in history to show how Australia came to be the home of marsupial quadrupeds; how the opossums came to settle down in America, and far apart from their only kith and kin in Australia; and how marsupials are absent from all other parts of this world's surface? Without presuming to overrate the importance of our present study, we may safely say that the answers to such questions deal with some of the most important phenomena in the past history of our globe, and bring us, through a simple study such as ours, within the grasp of a deep philosophy. Let us once again briefly consider the problem before us. We are dealing with the case of a peculiar order of quadrupeds, named "marsupials," from their possessing a "pouch;" we find these to be confined to Australia, with the exception of a single family, the opossums which occur in America. On what theory may we explain satisfactorily, two facts—firstly, the limitation of the kangaroos and their neighbours to Australia, and secondly, the exceptional nature of the home of their opossum-friends in the New World?

To answer these important queries, we must pass firstly to the province of geology and to the history of fossils. The naturalist takes leave of us for the present by reminding us that the marsupials are lower quadrupeds than our cows, horses, dogs, cats, and ordinary animals; and he also begs to remind us that when Australia was first colonized, no other or higher quadrupeds —save perhaps a bat or two—were found there. The sheep, cattle, horses, dogs, and other familiar animals now found abundantly in Australia, are all importations, and not native products. So that we begin by esteeming our kangaroos and their neighbours as mammals of a low type in truth, but nevertheless as representing in their way the original quadruped population of Australia. Geology now takes up the thread of the story. Australia, it tells us, is as practically distinct in its animals to-day as it was of old. A little channel, called the Straits of Lombok—fifteen miles wide, but a channel of deep water—divides the Indian Region, as we term it, (consisting of so much of the Malay Archipelago, with its monkeys, its rhinoceroses, its tigers, etc.), from the Australian Region, in which, as we have seen, monkeys are unknown and higher quadrupeds totally wanting as native animals. The geologist continues his tale, and shows us that the lowest quadrupeds are older than the higher ones, and that the marsupial animals occur as fossils long before our familiar quadrupeds were in existence. The marsupials and their neighbours were, in fact, the first quadrupeds to appear on the earth's surface; the higher animals being children of a later growth.

Next in order, the geologist tells us that the first traces of marsupial life appear as fossils in those rocks which are called the Trias, and which are much older than the far-back Chalk Rocks themselves. Indeed, in the Stonesfield Slates lying above the Trias, we find the remains of a marsupial which must have been remarkably like the little banded ant-eater alive in Australia to-day. But far more important than all else is the information which next comes to hand, namely, that *we find the fossils of marsupials in Europe and America, thus proving that in the Triassic and succeeding period they had, if not a worldwide distribution, at least a very extensive range over the earth's surface as it then existed.* In these words we have emphasized lies the key to the mysteries and curiosities of marsupial distribution to-day. In Australia we do not find the fossil remains of any other quadrupeds save marsupials, thus proving that no other mammals save those allied to its existing population have ever been tenants therein. We do find in Australia, however, the fossil remains of kangaroos, and like animals, differing from their living neighbours in their immense size. Think of a kangaroo whose head alone was about three feet long, and you may conceive of the race of marsupial giants which inhabited Australia in *geologically* "recent" times, and of which our kangaroos and their neighbours are the pigmy descendants.

In the Triassic period, then, and in the Oolite, a succeeding epoch, it is certain that marsupials and their allies were the only quadrupeds developed on the face of the earth, and that they overran the world's surface; representing in their way the varied quadrupeds of to-day, and leaving here and there the fossil relics from which the "coming race" of mankind would construct their history. We see Australia—then joined to what we now name the Asiatic Continent—obtaining its marsupial population like the rest of the world. Next we perceive Australia to become detached from Asia, its marsupials being thus cut off from all subsequent communication with their neighbours elsewhere. Soon the higher quadrupeds begin to appear however, and the marsupials, which had hitherto held undisputed sway of the world's surface, come off defeated in the "struggle for existence." The higher and stronger quadrupeds come to possess the earth, and the wasted marsupials, well-nigh killed off in all parts of the world save Australia, at length die out entirely, with the exception of the nimble opossums, which, finding originally a safe home and haven in the New World, have lived and flourished there, since after the close of the Eocene period, when their reign in Europe came to an end. To the question, then, why kangaroos are only found alive in Australia? we reply, because, on account of the early severance of Australia from other lands, they have there been free from the inroads of higher and stronger animals. To the query, why are the opossums, of all marsupials, found in America alone? we answer, because they represent the surviving remnant of the marsupial population which once overspread the whole earth, but which died out in Europe at the beginning of the Tertiary period, and which now flourishes (as the opossum family) in America, since the "struggle for existence" has not been too hard for the welfare of their race. The opossums apparently did not migrate to Australia in the Triassic period to form part of the original stock from which our kangaroos and their allies are derived, and probably they represent a later development and a highly modified race of the marsupial group.

Thus, when we next look at our marsupials, we may in our mind's eye once again see the world peopled by that curious race of beings; once again we may see the conifers, tree-ferns, and cycads growing around us, as in the days of the Triassic and Oolitic worlds; once again we behold the spine-bearing fishes and the Port Jackson sharks in our seas; and thus in field and forest, lake and sea, the scientific imagination pictures for us series after series of strange forms succeeding each other in the "files of time,"—filling our earth with the curious array of quadruped life, at the head of which stands the last creation Man, and at the base of which dwells our friend the Kangaroo.

ON GIANTS.

FROM the earliest times, man has taken a deep interest in the marvellous, and especially in that aspect which relates to the production of abnormal beings of his own kind. References in ancient literature to the existence of giants and dwarfs are by no means rare, and even in the records of the sacred historians we find mention made of beings of abnormal stature, since we are informed that "there were giants in the earth" in patriarchal times. Henrion, a Member of the French Academy of Sciences, published in 1718 a work in which he argued for the great decrease in stature and physical conformation generally which had taken place in the human race between the Creation and the advent of the Christian era. In this curious treatise, the learned, but somewhat credulous, author informs us that Adam was 123 feet 9 inches in height, whilst Eve's stature is asserted to have been 118 feet 9 inches and 9 lines. The exactitude of the Academician's calculations forms a noticeable point in the recital; whilst no less remarkable is his assertion of the inexplicable degeneracy which the race seems to have undergone within a comparatively short period. Noah, we are told, attained a height of only twenty-seven feet; Abraham was barely twenty feet in stature; whilst Moses is alleged to have measured only thirteen feet in height. Henrion takes care to add that in his opinion the advent of the Christian era prevented the continuous decrease which had hitherto prevailed, and records his thankfulness that humanity was not permitted to become represented by infinitesimal or microscopic specks. The ancient and mediæval accounts of human giants are intermingled with much that is problematic, and in some cases absolutely fabulous. We are assured, however, that the height of Funnam, a Scotch giant who lived in the time of Pope Eugene II.—this pontiff's death having occurred in the year 827—was eleven feet; whilst in 1509 there were discovered at Rouen the remains of the Chevalier Rinçon, whose skull was alleged to have been capable of holding a bushel of wheat, whilst the length of his shin-bone is stated at four feet. In 1705, the skeleton of a hero named Bucart was disinterred at Valence, the remains measuring some twenty-two feet in length. These cases of huge development may very appropriately be capped by the Sicilian story of a human skeleton which was gravely maintained to measure three hundred feet in length; whilst, with the apparent object of giving additional veracity to the recital, this giant's walking-stick was alleged to have also been found, the length of this appendage being given at thirty feet.

We must naturally allow much for the credulity of the age in which these and similar instances of human giants were not only related, but also believed in. But again we find that ignorance of natural objects, and the then infantile stage of natural science, may together be credited with inducing an implicit faith in such legends. Sir Hans Sloane, of British Museum celebrity, was one of the first to express his opinion that the remains described as those of human beings of immense stature, were not those of men, but of some huge extinct animals; Sir Hans' ideas being met, in the spirit of the age, with a fierce opposition of a pseudo-religious kind. He was charged, through the expression of his opinions, with impugning the authenticity of the Scriptures, and with heresies of like kind. But those who thus had their beliefs "nail'd wi' Scriptur'" were rather disconcerted a little later by the announcement that Cuvier, through the exercise of his talents in the investigation of fossil remains, had declared the remains of the supposed human giants to be those of extinct animals, which were no doubt also giants in their way, especially when compared with their existing representatives. Thus fossil sloths and elephants of large size had been doing duty for giants of the human race; and the teeth of human giants, which used to be so conspicuously displayed in museums, were relegated to their proper sphere under the description of the armature of elephant's jaws.

The consideration of some of the best-authenticated cases of mankind having attained in modern times a very large stature, may be fitly prefaced by a brief account of several groups of lower animals in which individuals are known to occasionally exhibit gigantic proportions, since such a study of comparative development will assist us in obtaining some clear ideas regarding the prevalence of giants in lower life. In some of the lowest groups of the animal series, giant species, or members of species which are ordinarily of small size, may sometimes be developed. Most readers know something of the zoophytes—those curious plant-like animals, which are so frequently cast up on our shores, and which may be obtained in great quantities by dredging all round our coasts. These organisms ordinarily measure a few inches in length, but certainly the largest of them must shrink into insignificance when compared with the giant zoophyte obtained by the dredge of the *Challenger* off the coast of Japan, and again off Honolulu. This organism measures seven feet four inches in height, its stem has a diameter of half an inch, and the mouths and tentacles of some of its included animals measure nine inches across. This truly is an example of a veritable giant-race; and it forms not the least curious feature of such a being to consider that we are thus presented with an example of a literal zoological tree, consisting of numerous animal forms, which, however, unlike the vast majority of their neighbours, grow up in the strange similitude of a plant.

Passing by, with a mere mention, the instances of some giant sea-worms, some of which—such as the *Nemertes* of the zoologist—may attain a length of forty feet or more, we may note certain extraordinary and instructive cases of large developments amongst molluscous animals. Shells may vary greatly in size, as the visitor to any large museum may observe, but probably the largest known shells are those of the Giant Clams (*Tridacna gigantea*) of the Indian Ocean, the shells of which may measure a yard and a half in length, and weigh 500 lbs. The contained animal may attain a weight of 20 lbs., and forms a description of oyster of tough but palatable kind. In the church of St. Sulpice at Paris, large specimens of these shells are to be seen, the valves being used for fonts. Unquestionably, however, the cuttlefishes constitute a group, around which our interest must centre in regard to the huge development of many of these forms, and to the curious historical and legendary aspects with which the question has become invested. The student of classical lore will be at no loss for instances of giant developments of cuttlefishes, since Pliny and other writers give full accounts of some monsters which were alleged to exist in these early days, and to cause fear and terror to reign supreme in more than one maritime state. Pliny, in his Natural History, relates the history of one " polypus," or cuttlefish, which exhibited a singular liking for salted tunnies, since it was said to emerge at night from the sea, and carry off its booty from the curers' stores. Another cuttlefish is described as having haunted the coasts of Spain, and devastated the fisheries. This creature was finally captured, and, as the incident is told by Pliny, the body weighed 700 lbs., the arms surrounding the head measuring ten yards in length. Ælian, whose period dates from A.D. 220 to 250, relates the history of a cuttle, which resembled Pliny's monster in its affinity for cured fish, since it also made raids on the fish-curers' stores, and obtained its booty by crushing the barrels in which the preserved meats were contained.

The naturalists of the Renaissance were certainly not behind their classic predecessors in their recitals of giant cuttlefishes, and it becomes exceedingly difficult, or even impossible, to separate out the real from the fabulous in dealing with the records of some of the mediæval writers. The legends of Northern Europe, for example, have long credited the Northern Seas with affording refuge to a large monster of cuttlefish-nature, to which the name of the "Kraken" has been applied. A worthy but credulous ecclesiastic, Eric Pontoppidan by name, and Bishop of Bergen by office, propagated—no doubt with the best intentions, and with a firm belief in his recitals—many astonishing ideas and theories regarding the existence of the Kraken. In his "Natural History of Norway," published about 1754, he tells us that this Kraken was "liker an island than a beast," and suggests that the appearance of the animal, as it lay almost submerged in the water, lured unwary mariners to a dreadful fate; these persons landing to be submerged on a moving mass instead of standing on a firm island.

Another writer and churchman, Oläus Magnus, in his "Historia de Gentibus Septentrionalibus," dating from 1555, also relates many curious tales of the Kraken and other gigantic forms; and in the case of the latter writer, it is even more difficult than in the study of Pontoppidan's works to separate facts from fiction.

But of all the mediæval writers who drew largely upon imagination, Denys de Montfort was probably the most notable. This writer had infinitely less excuse than his contemporaries for perpetuating errors, since he was one of the assistants in the Natural History Museum of Paris, and thus claimed title to possess scientific knowledge and accuracy. Notwithstanding his scientific pretensions, however, De Montfort, in his "Histoire Naturelle Générale et Particulière des Mollusques," propagated many ideas of erroneous, not to say ludicrous, kind, regarding the occurrence and power of giant cuttlefishes. Thus, he boldly asserts the existence of a giant "poulpe" or octopus, which, as demonstrated by a most sensational engraving, he alleged to be capable of destroying ships wholesale, by dragging them beneath the waves with its arms. A three-masted barque of considerable dimensions is thus represented as being devastated by a "poulpe" of giant size, although it is related that the crew managed to escape destruction by severing the monster's arms with hatchets. Nor was De Montfort contented with this endeavour to deceive his readers. Report says that this worthy declared his intention to make the poulpe destroy a whole fleet, if the story of his one entangled ship was accepted; and report appears to have spoken truly in this instance, since, in the second volume of the work referred to, he informs his readers that six French men-of-war, captured by Admiral Rodney on the 12th of April, 1782, were engulfed by giant cuttlefishes, along with four British ships which acted as convoy to the prizes. The actual facts of the latter incident, as officially recorded, show De Montfort's assertions to be utterly false.

The six prizes arrived safely at Jamaica, but on their subsequent voyage to England were greatly damaged by a violent storm, in which it is needless to remark the "colossal poulpes" of De Montfort played no part.

As a last example of a tale of giant cuttlefishes, in which elements of discrepancy and exaggeration are plainly discernible, we may select the recital alleged by De Montfort to have been obtained from the lips of Captain Jean Magnus Dens, a worthy navigator who hailed from Dunkirk, and who made voyages to the Chinese Seas. Being becalmed on one occasion in mid-ocean, Captain Dens, like an energetic master mariner, set his crew to work to scrape and paint the sides of his ship. During the performance of this operation, a giant cuttlefish was alleged to have risen from the depths close to the side of the vessel, and to have carried off two of the sailors, whilst it seized a third with one of its arms; the startled crew, however, by aid of hatchets and prayers to St. Thomas, their tutelary saint, succeeded in releasing their comrade by cutting off the intruding member. The length of the arm thus severed, is stated by De Montfort at twenty-five feet, whilst its thickness is said to have equalled that of Dens' mizen yard, its suckers being as big as saucepan lids. Probably Dens did actually encounter a cuttlefish, and it is possible he may have engaged in battle with it.

It is fortunate that in scientific records, written or compiled by men whose character as observers and as faithful recorders of what they saw is above suspicion, we possess evidence to show that giants of the cuttlefish race do unquestionably occur in various seas; whilst, as will presently be related, the examination, within the few past years, of the remains of several huge cuttlefish-forms has placed their occurrence within the domain of sober zoological fact. For example, Peron, a celebrated

French naturalist and explorer, relates, in his "Voyage of Discovery," that he saw in the year 1801, off Van Diemen's Land, a cuttlefish which possessed a body of the size of a barrel; the length of the arms being estimated at six or seven feet, and their largest diameter at six or seven inches. Quoy and Gaimard, whose reputation as observers and travellers of a past generation is world-wide, assert that in the Atlantic they fell in with the mutilated remains of a gigantic squid or calamary—a kind of cuttlefish represented in our own seas by specimens attaining a maximum length of $1\frac{1}{2}$ feet or so—the original weight of this specimen being roughly estimated at 200 lbs. The learned Professor Steenstrup, of Copenhagen, relates that many years ago a large calamary was cast upon the Danish coast, the length of this specimen being set down at twenty-one feet, the tentacles adding an additional eighteen feet to the latter measurement. In 1854 Steenstrup met with a second case of like kind in the shape of a large cuttle which was thrown ashore on the coast of Jutland; the length of this specimen being at least fully equal to that of the previous instance.

A singular and interesting incident in the voyage of the French war-steamer *Alecton* was afforded by the discovery, on the 30th of November, 1861, of a giant calamary, between Madeira and Teneriffe. The body of this specimen was said to attain a length of sixteen or seventeen feet, minus the arms. The animal was met with floating listlessly on the surface of the sea, and, as became a gallant sailor, Commander Bouyer, of the *Alecton*, gave the cephalopod battle. The harpoons, however, tore through the soft flesh of the animal, whilst the bullets fired at it simply imbedded themselves in the mass without doing much apparent damage to the creature. The crew of the *Alecton* succeeded in passing a noose around the tail-fin of the monster—this fin being shaped somewhat like an arrow-head—

so that the rope was firmly retained by the fin, and considerable pressure could be thus made on the animal's body by pulling at the rope. Unfortunately, the softness of the body, together with its dead weight, defeated the intentions of the crew; for they succeeded in pulling on board the tail-fin and tip of the body, leaving the maimed giant, minus his tail, to disappear in the deep. The portion thus captured weighed about 40 lbs., and the French consul at Teneriffe, in his report of the matter sent to the French Academy of Sciences, relates that he inspected the captured portion two days after the occurrence.

Some of the most interesting cases in which huge cephalopods have been met with, however, are recorded in the narratives of British science. On the 25th of April, 1875, a large cuttle-fish was met with basking on the surface of the sea of Boffin Island, Connemara, by the crew of a "corragh"—this latter being a boat constructed of hoops and tarred canvas, and somewhat resembling the "coracle" of early days. The fishermen, knowing the value of cuttle-fish bait, attacked the animal, and, after a hard chase, lopped off several arms, together with the head, the body being allowed to sink. It is due to the intelligence and care of Sergeant O'Connor, of the Royal Irish Constabulary, that portions of the tentacles and the beak were transmitted to Dublin for preservation in the museum of the Royal Dublin Society, and from the description of these valuable relics by Mr. More, assistant naturalist in the above museum, we extract the following particulars. This specimen, like all other species of squids, had ten arms, two of these, named tentacles, being very much longer than the others, and possessing suckers at their extremities only. "A good part of both tentacles, one short arm, and the great beak entire," says Mr. More, "have reached Dublin, and there remains very little doubt that we have now to deal with a second example of the famous *Architeuthis dux* of Steenstrup;" this latter being the appellation that the Danish naturalist gave to the specimen which, as already remarked, was cast ashore on Jutland in 1854. The following particulars are given of the dimensions of the Irish specimen:—"Tentacles thirty feet long when fresh (fourteen and seventeen feet can still be made up from the pickled pieces). A few distant, small, and nearly sessile (unstalked) suckers occur at long intervals along the inner surface of the peduncle," or stalk of the tentacle. The expanded termination of the suckers, "measuring 2 feet 9 inches in its present shrunken state, is occupied in the centre of the palm by two rows of large stalked suckers nearly one inch in diameter, fourteen in each row; an alternating row of fourteen smaller suckers (half an inch in diameter) occupies the margin on each side of the palm. . . . These outer suckers are each armed with a denticulated (or toothed) bony ring of some twenty-eight teeth, pointing inwards. . . . The short arm is quite spoiled for examination; all the horny rings are gone, and the suckers themselves are scarcely represented. This arm measured eight feet in length, and fifteen inches round the base when fresh. The beak has a strong, wide tooth about the middle of the edge of the inner mandible (or jaw), and a much narrower notch on the outer mandible on each side. The head and eyes were unfortunately lost." We have thus sufficient details afforded even by the imperfect and cursory examination of these remains, to assure us that a cuttlefish, which might well be termed a veritable giant of its kind, when compared with its ordinary neighbours, was actually captured and despoiled. At Dingle, in Kerry, some 200 years ago, a gigantic cuttlefish was stranded. This latter is described as having been nineteen feet in total length, whilst the size of the animal is stated to have equalled that of a large horse.

In October, 1873, two fishermen met with a large cuttlefish which was floating quietly near the eastern extremity of Belle Isle, Conception Bay, about nine miles from St. John's, Newfoundland. Thinking the floating mass was the remains of a wreck, the men grappled it with a boothook, the formerly inert mass at once waking up into life, and appearing as a huge cuttlefish, which threw its two long arms across the boat, these arms, however, being at once severed with an axe. The animal then moved off into deep water, ejecting in its retreat a quantity of the inky fluid which these creatures elaborate by way of a protective secretion, capable of being quickly diffused in the surrounding water, and of thus serving as a cloak of darkness under which escape may be effected. A portion of one of the amputated arms is preserved in the museum at St. John's; and Professor Verrill, of Yale College, U.S., estimates, as approximate and comparative measurements, the length of the body at ten feet, its diameter at 2 feet 5 inches, whilst the length of the long tentacles is set down at thirty-two feet, and that of the head at two feet. Another specimen was captured in Logic Bay, Newfoundland, in November, 1874, a photograph of the head and arms having been taken of this cuttlefish. From the representation of this cuttlefish we may gain an idea of its gigantic size; and the actual measurements fully confirm the opinion formed regarding its great dimensions. The body exceeded seven feet in length, the tail-fin was twenty-two inches broad, the two long tentacles were each twenty-four feet in length, the eight short arms were each six feet long and ten inches in circumference at the base; whilst the number of suckers was computed at 1100, and the great eyes measured four inches in diameter. Professor Verrill has also given details of the stranding of another giant of this class at Grand Bank, Fortune Bay, Newfoundland, in December, 1874, this locality being apparently specially favoured in respect of its cuttlefish visitors: the abundance of cod and other fishes adapted for cuttlefish dietary affording a ready explanation of the latter fact. The total length of this last visitor to the Newfoundland shores is given at forty feet; the long arms making about twenty-six feet of this measurement, whilst the largest suckers were about one inch in diameter.

It would thus appear to be not only a settled fact that cuttlefish giants are actually developed, but that these monsters belong to new and distinct species, and may therefore be regarded, in the opinion of many naturalists, as presenting us with literal races of giants.

From the cuttlefishes to the true fishes is a transition of an easy nature both in a popular and in a zoological sense. Amongst the fishes very large individuals are developed in a normal and natural fashion—such dimensions as twenty or even thirty feet in length being common in many sharks. But with other groups of fishes, gigantic individuals belonging to species the members of which are ordinarily of small dimensions are frequently developed, these latter instances being typical cases of giants arising from amongst their normal-sized brethren. For example, amongst the flat fishes specimens of very large size are by no means of unfrequent occurrence. The turbot, possessing an average weight of 6 or 7 lbs., has been known to weigh 70 lbs., whilst the halibut, which attains an ordinary length of four or five feet, has been found to measure seven feet in length. A specimen of this fish was captured on the coast of Caithness in February, 1877, which measured 7 feet in length, $3\frac{1}{2}$ feet in breadth, and 1 foot in thickness, its weight being 231 lbs. Even the familiar cod may attain very large proportions. At Lochiel Head, on the west coast of Scotland, says a correspondent of the *Oban Times* (dating about 1876), a large cod was recently captured, the length of the fish being 9 feet 2⅛ inches, and its circumference 3 feet 2½ inches. One can well understand the truth of the remark appended to the statement, that some of the oldest fishermen declared that they had never seen such a monster taken before. The conger eels may sometimes be developed to a size in which they approach the dimensions of very large snakes, whilst those elongated fishes, the "tape" or "ribbon fishes," attain a normal length of ten, eleven, or even thirteen feet: and the writer has recently put on record a case in which a specimen attained the enormous length of sixty feet.

Reptiles frequently attain large dimensions, but more commonly as a result of normal growth than of spontaneous and unusual development; and some extinct birds, such as the Dinornis of New Zealand, must have exceeded their neighbours in size to as great an extent as the reported human giants of old overtopped their nearest relations. This is particularly the case with one species of Dinornis, the leg bones of which, found in a fossil state, are described by Owen as being equal to those of the elephant in size, whilst the total height of the bird must have exceeded ten feet. Extinct species of sloths and armadillos bear a similar relation to their living neighbours. The Irish elk of recent deposits overtops the stateliest living deer; and the extinct mammoth, in respect of its size and bulk, might fairly rank first amongst the elephant kind.

Man, as the head of the animal series, presents us with not a few interesting examples of large or even extraordinary physical development, whilst the subject of human overgrowth assumes an additional interest in the light of an inquiry into the peculiarities of character which attach themselves to rarities in the shape of giants of the human race. Of such tall persons it is noticeable that by far the greater number belong to the male sex. Giantesses, in fact, are but rarely met with in proportion to the number of giants of whom due record has been preserved. In the reign of Edward III., Long More, or Mores, an Irish giant, attained the height of 6 feet 10¼ inches. Queen Elizabeth had a Flemish porter who attained the height of 7 feet 6 inches; this height being exceeded by John Middleton, or the "Child of Hale," as he was called, who was born in 1578, and who measured 9 feet 3 inches. C. Munster, a yeoman of the Hanoverian Guard, who died in 1676, attained a height of 8 feet 6 inches; Cajanus, the Swedish giant, who was exhibited in London in 1742, attained a height of nine feet. The most celebrated of living giants are the famous Captain Bates, a native of Kentucky, who attains a height of eight feet; his wife, *née* Miss Anna Swan, who was born in Nova Scotia, also measuring eight feet in height. Many of our readers will remember the exhibition of the two latter persons a few years ago in London. Chang-wu-gon, the Chinese giant, is also still alive; this tall Celestial measures 7 feet 9 inches in stature.

The details of giant-life exhibit many curious features. Contrary to expectation, and against the spirit of the old legends, our modern giants are, for the most part, persons of a singularly mild disposition, and exhibit, as a rule, the most amiable of tempers. Nature in this respect, indeed, appears to preserve a wonderful and admirable balance of power in imbuing persons of great physical development with an equable temperament; whilst the dwarfs and pigmies of our race are usually inclined to exhibit a disposition the reverse of benevolent or mild. Probably the only giants of past days concerning whom details of a thoroughly authentic character have been preserved are Patrick Cotter, *alias* Patrick Cotter O'Brien, and Charles Byrne, both individuals hailing from the sister island. Curiously enough, there is preserved in the museum of Trinity College, Dublin, the skeleton of a third Irishman, named

Magrath, whose case attained some notoriety in consequence of a Doctor Campbell's statement, in his work entitled "A Philosophical Survey of Ireland," that Magrath's growth was caused by Bishop Berkeley's experiment of feeding the lad. There exists little or no foundation for this statement, which probably arose from the fact that Magrath, having at the age of sixteen attained a stature of over six feet, and being poorly fed, presented a fit case for the exercise of the kindly bishop's charity. He accordingly caused Magrath to receive a liberal diet for about a month, this treatment restoring the overgrown lad to health. At his death Magrath measured 7 feet 8 inches.

In the *British Magazine* for 1783, the death of Charles Byrne, one of the giants just mentioned, is duly chronicled. From this source we learn that Byrne measured exactly eight feet in height in August, 1780; whilst "in 1782 his stature had gained two inches, and when dead his full length was 8 feet 4 inches." His death, sad to relate, is alleged to have been caused by excessive drinking, "to which," says the writer in the *British Magazine*, "he was always addicted, but more particularly since his late loss of all his property, which he had simply invested in a single bank-note of £700. In his last moments," continues the narrator, "he requested that his remains might be thrown into the sea, in order that his bones might be removed far out of the reach of the chirurgical fraternity; in consequence of which," we are further informed, "the body was put on board a vessel, conveyed to the Downs, and sunk in twenty fathoms water." Byrne died, it is necessary to add, in Cockspur Street, Charing Cross, at the age of twenty-two. The statement that the remains of the giant were buried at sea is quite erroneous, since, after all, the "chirurgical fraternity," represented by the famous John Hunter, contrived, after much trouble and the expenditure of a considerable sum of money—

stated at £500—to obtain possession of the body, and the visitor to the magnificent Museum in Lincoln's-inn-Fields may have the pleasure of beholding the skeleton of the once famous Byrne occupying a place of honour in the osteological department. It is interesting to note that Byrne appeared on the stage in 1782, at the Haymarket Theatre, in the summer pantomime of "Harlequin Teague, or the Giant's Causeway"—a title strongly suggestive of Byrne's prominence in the production.

The history of Patrick Cotter, who was born at Kinsale in 1761, shows that giants are by no means exempted from the cares and worries which beset ordinary existence. His parents were poor persons, of ordinary stature; and his father leased him for exhibition to a showman at eighteen years of age, for a period of three years, at the rate of £50 per annum. Arriving at Bristol, Cotter demanded some extra remuneration for himself; and the showman being disinclined to grant his request, Cotter refused to allow himself to be exhibited, with the result of being incarcerated as a debtor. His case, however, being made known to some benevolent person, Cotter was liberated, by the contract between his father and the showman being declared to be illegal; and, proceeding thereafter to exhibit on his own account, he realised the sum of £30 in three days.

Cotter adopted the name of O'Brien in order to strengthen the fiction, set forth in the bills, that he was "a lineal descendant of the old puissant King Brien Boreau," and that he possessed, "in person and appearance, all the similitude of that great and grand potentate." His height was stated at "near nine feet," although a memorial tablet in the Trenchard Street Roman Catholic Chapel, Bristol, informs us more truly that his stature only exceeded "8 feet 3 inches." Cotter died at Clifton on September 8, 1804, having realised a modest competence by exhibiting himself, and having secured, we are told, the respect of the entire community by his well-regulated conduct. Like his countryman Byrne, Cotter was exceedingly anxious that his remains should not fall into the hands of the anatomists, and gave directions that his grave should be built in with bricks and secured with iron bars.

At the end of March, 1877, there died, at the age of forty-nine years, at the Five Arrows, Waddesdon, near Aylesbury, the "Buckinghamshire Giant," a person named William Stevens, who merited his appellation of giant rather from his immense weight than from his unusual stature. He went to reside at this tavern some four years before, at which time he weighed eighteen stones. From that time his life was spent in eating and drinking, and in exhibiting his increasing weight to interested observers. At his death he weighed thirty-five stones, and measured 6 feet 8 inches in height. Most readers will express surprise that the fatal issue was so long delayed in this rather melancholy case, in which an abnormality in physical development had operated decidedly to the prejudice and injury of the unfortunate subject. And, despite the interest with which the physiologist must regard such cases, it cannot be denied that they present a reverse aspect which offers by no means pleasant food for reflection to the student of poor humanity at large.

THE POLITY OF A POND.

"Nothing to do," you say. Well, the mental condition implied by these words is nearly if not quite as deplorable as that involved in the related statement "nothing to wear." True, it may be, as you point out, one cannot spend existence looking out of a window surveying the meadow-lands and fields of the quiet, flat Thames county of Oxon. One tires also of running water, and your sketch-book has already acquired most of the choice " bits " of copse and field, and well-nigh all the views of those tall poplars that you care to paint. The trout in the Thames are lazily inclined to-day, and even with ancient Izaak himself for good company, the art piscatorial might tempt you in vain. A sad disorder truly, this *ennui,* which, I take it, is the fashionable name for the complaint affecting the nothing-to-do constitution and its subjects. What say you, then, to a stroll towards the copse by the pollard willows yonder? "For what purpose?" you ask. Come and see. I have an idea I shall pass a pleasant hour or two over the fruits of our journey. You agree. A moment then, for preparation. There is a stowing of phials into empty pockets, and the placing of a pocket lens in a secure position. Then comes a linen "hand net" mounted on a stick, such an apparatus as a fisherman would scoff at, and which, exhibited before the eyes of nephew Charley—a great authority in the capture of small fry by many cunning expedients—would subject me to ridicule of peculiarly sarcastic kind, as the inquiry "where I am going a-fishing" is made.

The pollard willows mark the terminus of the expedition, and these trees loom near enough at hand. Just beyond them is a pool—you know it well. For that pool we are to depart, on a scientific mission bent. You look alarmed at the mention of the word "scientific;" but there is no cause for fear. I have no intent to inflict a science lecture upon unwilling ears; and truth to tell in holiday times, the memories of lecture notes, and blackboards, and diagrams, of chalk, of a long pointer, and of other paraphernalia of the order scientific, are not over-welcome, because of their reminding one of a return to the "Grad-grind" philosophy of busy life, and because of their making holiday scenes like the present vanish into mere thin reflections of pleasant times. No, my friend, there shall be no "science discourse for one" on this occasion. But you asked me to invent an employment for an idle day. You besought me to relieve the tedium of an aimless hour in a country life. And I reply by conducting you to a favourite hunting-ground of mine, whence I gather the treasures that constitute the liberal "harvest of a quiet eye." Here we are at the spot in question. You look around, but see nothing very attractive. Possibly not. But sit down on the bank. The willows behind will screen you from the sun. Permit me to introduce you to a rich pasture for the cultivation of an idle mind—a pond, and its "tenants at will."

We find in our pond a very fair example of a locality which, dull enough to the unimaginative eye, may present the scientific mind with food for reflection for many days to come. Vast stores of microscopic wealth lie hidden before you; and a zoological treasure-house, as well as a choice botanical herbarium, is included in the apparently dull prospect and within the weed-bedecked limits of our pond. How thickly the osiers and flags grow in the furthest corner of the watery domain. Those flags that seem to have been irregularly cropped by some careless reaper betoken the nocturnal dietary of the water-voles, which steal out silently by night and nibble the reeds with a relish that can best be imagined by those who have seen these rodents feed. The duckweed grows thickly, too, beside us, and canopies over a moiety of the pond, affording a grateful shade and shelter to many a denizen of these waters, and likewise a broad leafy platform whereon a perfect crowd of insects gather to discuss the matters that most interest the aerial state and life. The water-plantain, doubtless an emigrant from the near river, appears to flourish within the quieter circle of the pool, and now and then you may see its stems disturbed by the energetic leaps and hops of one or two frogs that seem to be amusing themselves in athletic feats in the far corner of the pond.

The water in the warm days of summer has acquired a green hue of very decided kind, and here and there you see thick patches of the plant-life that will soon become

"The green mantle of the stagnant pool."

This lower plant-life—the swarm of *Confervoid* species—flourishes apace beneath the kindly influences of the summer sun. Composed of minute cells, each containing its quota of *chlorophyll*—the green colouring matter that enchants and soothes your eye wherever you turn in living nature—the mass of lower plant life extends its limits with a rapidity that almost defies calculation. Not Jonah's gourd grew with such rate of cell-multiplication and increase as your lower plants; and friends botanical will tell you, in language more learned perhaps than plain, of the mysteries of "zoospores" and "swarmspores" and "oospores," by which names they mean to indicate the curious little bodies discharged from the parent-cells, and which after a free-swimming existence perpetuate these lower plant species. Is it not curious to think that these lower plants begin life as active free-swimmers; so like animalcules that the non-technical eye regarding them through the microscope would receive with legitimate doubt the assertion of their plant nature? Could you glance with microscopic gaze beneath the green scum of the pond, you would find a teeming population of these moving seeds or "spores" of the lower plant life that grows therein; and doubtless hereafter we may see these spores at home, as well as some other notable forms of plant-life that find in pools, ponds, and ditches a local habitation, as well as— from the botanist—a polysyllabic name. These lower plants of our ponds are technically called *Algæ*. They are included in the family circle of the seaweeds and their kin, and thus we find included in the same family group forms which may be of very large dimensions, like the great tangles or the Gulf-weed occupying its acres upon acres of the Atlantic; and plants which on the other hand may descend to the extremes of minuteness, and which are known only to the microscopist who has sought out knowledge from the very confines of the world.

It is these Algæ which, under other forms, occasionally perplex the simple-minded amongst us by suddenly dyeing our pools a deep red hue, through the rapid multiplication of their red-coloured species. And then is penned an epistle to "Mister Editor," announcing the fact of the amazing phenomenon of blood-red water having appeared in the pools and ponds, and begging that the editorial "sweetness and light" may be cast upon the event in question, as an assurance that the portent is neither a bad omen, nor one of coming disasters or of wars and rumours thereof. So also when the fir-trees and conifers at large discharge their yellow "pollen," which is blown by the wind for miles, the appearance of this "yellow rain" perplexes the soul innocent of elementary botany, and drives superstitious folks to the borders of despair. From all of which circumstances we may draw the conclusion that it behoves us to seek a little of the wisdom that is in natural science, by way of understanding some of the common events which occasionally disturb the peace of mind of communities by no means invariably of primitive kind.

But now let us "go a-fishing." No thoughts of lazy pike or perch or of the humbler roach engage our mind. Our "fishes" are of humbler grade, and such as the angler wots not of, whilst the fare I may offer you as the result of our operations is not physical but mental. With the improvised "bag-net," let us obtain some of the green scum which lies just within reach, and then let us fill our phials with samples of the pond water, glancing here and there as we travel round its banks for traces of samples of such rarer kind as may be represented in the miniature world before us. A wide-mouthed jar receives a portion of the pond's "green mantle," and phial after phial is duly filled with specimens of water and of sundry living and moving things which disport themselves therein. Already our harvest seems promising. The "bag-net" has swept into our phials more than one water insect, and sundry green specks which we see rolling over and over upon themselves betoken a rich treat at home in the way of microscopical examination. A bit of pond-weed and one or two water-leaves have now been secured for the sake of the chance population to which they afford shelter. Of water-fleas we have a plenteous store, and I should be afraid to say anything about the number of animalcular treasures, the existence of which you will have to take on trust, for the present at least, until the object-glass at home shall reveal their whereabouts and nature.

We may now retrace our steps, laden with what to the popular mind seems too often so much "rubbish," but in which the gaze of a very elementary philosophy may reveal much that is curious, a great deal that is inexplicable, and everything that is interesting. The picture drawn so happily and with such deft touch in the "Ingoldsby Legends," of the "man of a very contemplative mood," who

> —would pore by the hour, o'er a weed or a flower,
> Or the slugs that come crawling out after a shower,"

is one which, in respect of the apparently absurd nature of the search after knowledge, meets with the sarcastic approval of the work-a-day world. And the misguided man who,

> "Instead of enjoying a sociable chat,
> Still poking his nose into this and to that,
> At a gnat, or a bat, or a cat, or a rat,
> Or great ugly things, all legs and wings,
> With nasty long tails armed with nasty long stings."

is regarded, as a rule, as a person who may be an enthusiastic observer of nature indeed, but with whose proclivities polite society need not be expected to exhibit much or any sympathy. Scientific philosophy happily carries its own reward, however, and is in any case thoroughly removed above the popular criticism whose world simply exists in the commonplaces of life after all. And so consoling ourselves with the knowledge of our advantages, we trudge homewards, halting for a moment at the brook—a tributary of the larger river that rolls past the mill —to look at the "caddis-worms" that struggle in its bed, and to add some of these beings to our store of curiosities.

Arranging our apparatus in suitable array close by the window, with a fine southern exposure lending us a brilliant illumination for our microscope mirror, we proceed to the business of learning something regarding the teeming population of the waters we have left. Dip the first with a phial of green water presents us with an object of interest. Rolling round and round upon itself in the field of vision, in company with several companions and with other forms of lower life, you perceive a living globe, fringed, as you can see after attentively watching it, with a series of delicate filaments we name *cilia*. What is this curious living sphere which exists by the hundred in the pond? Is it an animal, as by its movements you might at first sight suppose, or is it a plant, as its green colour might lead you to believe? Can the botanist claim it as his own, or the zoologist adopt it as a foster-child? Had you asked these questions some years ago, you would have been told that the zoologist was its proper guardian. In this light it was regarded as an animal form, and was named the *Globe Animalcule* (*Volvox globator*). But nowadays we have grown wiser, and knowing that Volvox is a true plant, despite its absolute freedom and motion, we hand it over to the botanist, who places it in that large family circle, known as the *Algæ*, to which group you have already been introduced. Placed thus in the vegetable kingdom, and amidst its lowest members, the question still remains, what is this *Volvox*? In diameter it averages the one-fiftieth part of an inch—dimensions which may be considered gigantic when compared with many of the animalcules disporting themselves beside it. Imagine a clear globe, dotted with little green specks placed at tolerably regular intervals. When the light is skilfully disposed, these green bodies are seen to be connected by delicate lines, the Volvox externally resembling a kind of network, with emeralds at the angles of the meshes.

But let us look more closely at these green bodies. Each when examined separately is pear-shaped, the stalk end of the pear abutting against the edge of the volvox globe, whilst attached to this end we find two delicate filaments, representing microscopic eyelashes—the *cilia*. The cilia, by aid of which the Volvox swims, are therefore the belongings of these green bodies, each of which is called a *zoospore*. How cilia move? why they vibrate with unceasing regularity? why they continue to move for a longer or shorter period after the death of the being to which they belong? how they thus act in utter independence of the nervous system? are amongst the deep puzzles of modern physiology.

But what of the green zoospores of which the Volvox appears to be composed? In the early days of the microscope, they were regarded as animals; a certain bright red spot occasionally seen in some of these green bodies was named an "eye;" and some hollow spaces were credited with performing the function of stomachs. But the bright red spot is known to occur in many other lower forms of both plant and animal nature, and whilst, it is true, its appearance seems compatible with the idea of its being a rudimentary "eye," its mere presence is no criterion of the animal nature of its possessor. The clear spaces —which are seen to "beat" as if they were little hearts—are likewise the common property of lower animals and plants, but their function is unknown. There is thus no ground for supporting the animal nature of Volvox; whilst on the other hand, when we survey the Algæ family at large, we find that the "zoospores" are very typical belongings of that group. The zoospores discharged from other freshwater plants of lower kind, exactly resemble those of Volvox, which may thus be regarded as a colony or collection of these green bodies. You must not neglect to notice, however, that within the Volvox you may discern some half-dozen other small green spheres, which often revolve on their own account, as their possessor rolls onwards on its course through the waters. When you gain a nearer glimpse of these little green spheres, you see that they resemble the Volvox in every respect, save in size. They are, in fact, the progeny of the plant, and have been facetiously named the "daughters" by the botanical world; and occasionally we may find that within the "daughter" Volvoces other progeny may in turn be discerned; three generations of these organisms being thus associated together in singular combination.

How has the process of multiplication been carried out? To answer the query we must study the emerald "zoospores" once more. At certain periods, a zoospore may be seen to divide itself into two or more parts, and a series of new cells is formed by the division of one. Ultimately the green cells thus produced become zoospores, develop cilia, and assume their place as essential parts of the new Volvox, which has thus been produced from a zoospore of its parent. When thus developed, the young Volvox is at first attached to the wall of the parent-globe. Soon it detaches itself, and rolls about in the parental interior, whilst it will be ultimately liberated and allowed to escape into the world of waters around, but not before it has itself given origin to "daughters" of its own.

So much for the "*Globe animalcule,*" which belies its popular name in that it is a veritable plant. We shall dip into another phial close at hand, and with our "dipping tube" we may secure one or two of the little specks you can see moving about so actively within the limits of the jar. This feat accomplished, and the objects in question safely transferred to our slide, you may enter upon a study of animal life, and that of by no means the lowest grade. You now see a curious little being, which authority in matters zoological has compared to a split pear in shape. It certainly possesses a head which is pear-shaped, and a tail which is pointed; and you see that the head, moreover, is covered by a large shield. In front you will be able to discern a single black speck placed in the middle of the head. This is the eye. And you may see that the creature possesses two pairs of feelers, one pair being much longer than the other. A neighbour swiftly paddling its way in the neighbourhood of our prisoner is seen to propel itself by the long pair of feelers, like a waterman pulling a pair of oars. The animal in external appearance is certainly a curious creature. You ask the nature of the animal we have been regarding, and I reply, the *Cyclops quadricornis*, or in plain English, "the four-horned water-flea with the one eye."

There are few persons who have not heard of the water-fleas, which, despite their name, are not insects, but poor relations of the crabs and shrimps. Indeed, looking at the Cyclops generally, there is to be perceived an indistinct resemblance to a shrimp. Interesting in many ways is the animal before us. It possesses neither heart nor breathing-organs, but contrives through adaptations of nature's own devising to bustle through life—and water-fleas certainly spend their existence in a state of perpetual hurry—without these organs. Well provided in the matter of jaws and limbs, is our Cyclopean friend. At least three pairs of jaws are represented, and the feet number five pairs. I do not know whether the argument for "woman's rights" has ever been supported by comparative anatomy, but an enthusiastic advocate of the removal of the disabilities of the weaker sex, might find the facts of natural history to support his argument very materially, even admitting that opponents might deem his comparison transcendental and his premises wrong. I refer to the fact that the superiority of the male sex is not universal in the world of animal life. Mrs. Cyclops is a magnificent creature as compared with the partner of her joys and sorrows. Mrs. Araneina, the representative of the spider family, is not merely much bigger than her mate, but is a fearful shrew, and sometimes goes the extreme length of eating and devouring her "puir man," as runs the Scottish familiarity for designating a henpecked husband. Lady Rotifer of the Wheel-animalcule family—a branch of the animalcules of high repute in the social scale—is a very superior person as compared with Lord Rotifer. The latter is not only smaller than his partner, but if the wonderful and curious fact must be told, he is a deformed and insignificant person; possessing no internal anatomy to speak of, and presenting a living realization of the old lady's comment on her minister's discourse, in respect of the said discourse lacking vigour and having "nae vitals." And last of all, to bring the facts nearer home and to the vertebrates themselves, one may point to the female eagles and falcons as being larger and more powerful than their lords and masters.

To return to Mrs. Cyclops, we find that the gentler sex is readily recognizable by the presence of two curious pouches attached one on each side of the tail. As we peer into these receptacles we see that they contain numerous little round bodies, the future progeny of the Cyclopean family in the shape of eggs. Thus the mother Cyclops may actually count her progeny before they are hatched, since during the process of development, they are carried about in the double cradle just mentioned. When hatched, Cyclops, junior, appears at first as a little three-jointed animal, possessing a pair of legs to each joint. Then the hinder portion of the body grows backwards, and becoming jointed forms the chest and tail. Moult after moult takes place; and finally the first three pairs of legs which the young Cyclops possessed become the four feelers and the two large jaws of the adult water-flea; the eye, originally double, having meanwhile grown single.

Another application to our phials is found to result, after a careful scrutiny of their contents, in the discovery of certain other Crustaceans which rejoice in the common title of Water-fleas, although, indeed, they belong, zoologically regarded, to very distinct and different families. Here, for example, is *Cypris*, which in point of its common occurrence rivals its one-eyed neighbour—although, indeed, Cypris itself has but a single eye, or at most an imperfectly divided one. But you see at once the marked difference between Cypris and Cyclops, since the former has its body enclosed in a double "shell," that at first sight reminds you of a miniature mussel. This "shell" of Cypris is really worth your study. You observe that it consists of two halves joined by a hinge along the back, and it can be opened and shut by the action of special muscles, the existence of which mechanism in such a small body, is, in itself, a source of legitimate wonder. Cypris has but two pairs of really useful swimming feet, but its jaws are complex, and like Cyclops it wants a heart. The eggs in the Cypris are carried within the shell, the outer egg-sacs of the Cyclops being unrepresented here. But Cypris-development waxes in complexity over that of Cyclops. No less than nine different stages have been described, so that the nine stages of Cypris may parallel somewhat the seven ages of man.

The Cypris-tribe present us with an antiquity and descent of highly respectable kind. These little shelled tenants of our ponds must have literally swarmed in certain fresh and salt waters of the past. As early as Silurian times, we find near neighbours of Cypris represented as fossils through the preservation of their "shells;" and Cypris itself makes its appearance tolerably far back in the geological record. One more example and we may leave the further knowledge of the Water-fleas as a matter for personal cultivation. This time the specimen is of larger size and more curious shape than before. You observe the branched feelers in front of the head. These organs enable you to pronounce the form before you to be the "Branched-horned water-flea" (*Daphnia pulex*). Differing from its neighbours Cyclops and Cypris in the character of its feelers, by means of which it swims, we find it to possess a shell composed of two halves. Like Cyclops it has a single eye, and the gills or breathing-organs are borne on the five pairs of legs attached to the chest. The Branched-horned is also peculiar in other respects. Messieurs the Branched-horned are few in number and small in size when compared with Mesdames, as in the neighbouring families of the Water-flea race. The young Daphniæ are produced from eggs, but the study of their development reveals certain peculiarities worth notice. The ordinary eggs—called "summer eggs"—vary from ten to fifty in number, and are retained within the shell until the young Branched-horns are developed. The "winter eggs," on the other hand, number two, and these ultimately pass into a chamber in the back of the shell, known from its shape as the "saddle." This saddle-shaped cavity is cast off at the succeeding moult of the animal, and sinks to the bottom of the water with its contained eggs. In the returning spring, the eggs are hatched and the Daphniæ are duly developed. Such a contrivance appears to exist for the purpose of continuing the Daphnia-race during the cold of winter. Related to our Water-fleas may be mentioned the curious Brine shrimps (*Artemia*) which live in the Salt Pans at Lymington, in a briny solution of sufficient strength to pickle beef, and which also occur in the Great Salt Lake at Utah, and in other salt lakes in both hemispheres. The Fairy shrimps which, with their clear and transparent bodies, seem to flit through the fresh waters they inhabit, are also related to our Water-fleas, whose brief history may thus be concluded.

If our microscopic researches have interested you so far, let us look at the fragments of pond-weed and confervoid scum we have secured. No better field for microscopic inquiry exists than the weeds of the pond, or in the "green mantle" of its surface. Each leaf then becomes a veritable world of lower life, and teems with a varied population of both plant and animal life. We snip off a small fragment of this water-weed, adjust it amidst a few drops of its native element on the microscope-slide, and then behold a scene so busy and so full of bustle, that we are tempted for a moment to think that the noise and din of the miniature world before us should find its echo in our own existence. There, attached to one side of the fragment, you see a colony of Bell-animalcules, or *Vorticellæ*. Each consists of a bell-shaped head supported on a stalk, the head being fringed with moving *cilia*, similar to those you saw in Volvox. Very busy are the Bell-animalcules to-day. Everywhere around them there is stirrage of the particles which float in the water; and now and then some free-swimming animalcule, coming within reach of the ciliary currents, is whirled round and round in a veritable vortex until it collides with the bell-shaped head, which immediately seems to disappear as if by magic. The stalk is highly contractile, and coils itself into a spiral form whenever the head is irritated, releasing and straightening itself when the alarm is overpast—the action, indeed, reminding you most of all of the behaviour of the spirally coiled wire that constitutes the chief mechanism of a Jack-in-the-box. A tap on the glass slide causes the whole colony of bell-heads to disappear, but a moment later they sweep out again, their stalks uncoil, their cilia vibrate, and the busy work of sweeping food-particles into the mouths is resumed. And you will please bear in mind that all this activity and sensation takes place and occurs without the vestiges of nerves. Sensation in lower life you see to be performed in entire disregard of the fact that nerves are utterly wanting—a general sensitiveness of the body-substance doing duty in a perfect fashion for the defined sensory apparatus of higher forms. The presence of such a colony of active beings must be a sad aggravation to more peaceably inclined animalcules, which, as you observe, are swept hither and thither, not by "winds of doctrine," like certain unstable particles in your world and mine, but by veritable and strong currents excited and maintained by the ever-active cilia that fringe the "bells."

A new form, however, looms across our view. Paddling its way once again by the ever-recurring cilia, like some large vessel amongst small craft at anchor, comes a green trumpet-shaped body, which now fixes itself by the lesser end of its frame, and then works its cilia like a steamer moored to a pier, but with its paddles in full swing. This is the *Stentor*, or Trumpet-animalcule, which can move itself or detach its frame from fixed objects at will, as you have just seen. In reality it resembles a Bell-animalcule *minus* a stalk, and as you note when it does attach itself, the cilia of its head-extremity begin to work at once and to create the currents which sweep the food particles by the score into the mouth. For like a wise animalcule, the Stentor rests that it may eat, and thus differs from hundreds of its smaller neighbours which are ever on the move, and which pass their existence, like some units of human kind, in one perpetual state of bustle. You observe that Stentor is coloured green. The colour is imparted by the same matter —chlorophyll—that you saw in the plant *Volvox*, or that you discern in every green leaf. The animal may thus manufacture the substance of the plant, and defies chemistry to say where the animal world and animal powers end, or where the plant world and plant functions truly begin.

Stentor is off on its tour after a brief respite, and our Bell-animalcules for a time appear to have the field to themselves. Softly; here is another being which comes rapidly upon the scene. Now it appears in full view; and a moment later, with aggravating intent, has swiftly sped out of view. Again it comes into the microscopic circle of our acquaintance, and fixing itself by its tail like Stentor, expands certain curious organs placed on its head, and like the latter animalcule creates a stir in its neighbourhood by the currents it excites. Watch those head-organs closely. You seem to see two revolving wheels. But things are not what they seem in the present case. The "wheels" are two round bodies which are absolutely stationary, and the revolving appearance is produced by the continuous and regular motion of the cilia with which they are provided. The illusion is produced much in the same way as when looking at the golden grain of autumn you appear to see the corn-stalks rushing in waves across the field when the light winds stir the stalks. Each stalk simply bends in its turn, just as each cilium moves in regular order and in its due sequence to produce the "wheel" before you. But the older naturalists called them Wheel-animalcules, through a belief that the "wheels" did revolve, and by this name, as well as by that of the *Rotifera*, they are still known. The being you are looking at is the *Rotifer vulgaris*, or common Wheel-animalcule itself. And now and then you will see other species of the class flit, like the ghosts of animalcules, across the field of vision. You can see through and through their bodies; and if the animalcule will only remain passive for a minute, you can learn a lesson in comparative anatomy with the greatest ease. The Wheel-animalcules are always to be known by these wheel-like heads. Then you note that within their bodies are contained systems of organs which Stentor and the Bell-heads want. You can trace the movements of the jaws, working like hammers on an anvil in the Rotifer, and now and then you see the general contraction of the body produced by muscular action, and curious movements of the internal organs as well. Altogether the Wheel-animalcules are beings of high structure. Your textbook of zoology will tell you that they possess a big nervous mass, certain sense-organs, eye-spots, a system of vessels for water-circulation, a complete digestive system, and a perfect provision of muscles. And if you care to pursue your study of them further, I will promise you a rich harvest of intellectual delight.

Such study, however, must be left for another day. I may only at present tell you that they were first discovered by old Leeuwenhoek, a Dutch observer, and a famous grinder of microscope-glasses. It was Leeuwenhoek who, in 1675, first beheld the Bell-animalcules, and in 1702, he first saw the Wheel-animalcules in some coloured water which had collected in a gutter of his house-roof. At the present day we know a good deal about the Rotifers, the list of species yearly increases, and the fascination of the study does not diminish on closer acquaintance with their life and habits. Within their family circle are tube-builders and house-constructors; the lady Rotifers exhibit the superiority to their partners already alluded to; and last of all, they seem to possess a vitality past comprehension as to its limits, and beyond explanation as to its details. In nature the Rotifers are dried up from their pools by the heat of the summer sun, and as mere mummified dust-specks they are blown about by the summer winds. You may dry them as they lie on your microscope-slide, till not a trace of motion remains, and you may keep them thus dried and parched for days, weeks, months, or even years. Yet, after such desiccation and drying, if you but add a drop of water, or place them therein, the functions of life are renewed and resumed with vigour, as if no epoch of Rip Van

Winkleism, with its awakening to a new life, had taken place. In what condition the organs, systems, and tissues of the Wheel-animalcules exist during their mummy-life, physiology does not yet explain; and how this suspended animation, simulating death, can persist for such lengthened periods with certainty of perfect revival, zoologists do not profess to make clear. But the facts are before you in all their wondrous significance, and you may profitably ponder upon life in a new aspect if you will. Should another Horace Smith appear wanting another mummy-subject for a poetic address, he may find one more wondrous far than that of Belzoni's Exhibition in the Rotifer and its history, and may dedicate his highest poetic aspirations to the celebration of the animalcule's startling return from dryness and barrenness to the activity of existence.

The "green mantle" of the pool teems with both animal and plant life in its lower aspects, as a glance at a fragment of *conferva* will show. But the shadows begin to gather and the light to fail, and what further study you feel inclined to pursue amidst weeds and water-fleas, must be left for another day. I can promise you, at least, an over-abundance of material for many days to come. One more peep at the microscope-field, and we shall put away our studies in pond-life for to-day. By the hundred, gathered on the margins of the delicate green cells that compose the confervæ of the pond's surface, you behold the *Diatomaceæ* and their neighbours—those lowest plants with the beautiful flinty envelopes, marked and sculptured in a thousand ways and forms. It is the study of a lifetime to figure and describe, and still more to understand, these lowest beings in their true nature; and forsooth we must pass them by to-day, with a glance at the varied form and beauteous structure. You also see the *Amœba*—that speck of protoplasm, affording a text for many a valued lesson in your zoology class-room—gliding, like Proteus of old, from one form to another, ever shifting its shape, and well-nigh as unstable as the water in which it lives. A mere speck of protoplasm is this Amœba; but when you think you have mastered the problem of vitality, let me recommend you to place your eye to the microscope, to watch the acts of an Amœba, to look through and through the living speck, and then to say if, after all, the theory of the class-room brings you nearer to the solution of the question "What is life?"

The Caddis-worms are in the phial at your elbow. And they deserve a word in passing. That is the larva or grub of the Alder-fly, dear to the heart of the angler. You see, by aid of the lens, its jaws, its six feet, and its seven pairs of curious gill-plumes, adapting it for an aquatic type of breathing. Here are your true Caddis-worms, well-known to Aristotle himself, and near relations of the big dragon-flies that sweep continually over the pond yonder. Gluing together bits of sticks, fragments of gravel, and grains of sand, and other odds and ends to be picked up in its native waters, these baby-insects pass their time in the active pursuit of the water-fleas, and live merrily enough in the bed of the clear-running brooks around. When maturity and its cares dawn upon the Caddis-worms, the mouth of the case is closed by a silken grating, spun, as are the threads which bind its materials together, from a silken gland placed in the mouth. Then the case ruptures, and the winged insect, having passed through its chrysalis state in the silent retirement of its abode, appears on the scene, henceforth discarding the waters and leading the aerial life of its kind. To watch the Caddis-worms is, in truth, no uninteresting study for part of a summer holiday.

Now let us push our phials and microscope aside. You had no idea the time would pass so quickly; and you have been interested in a very superficial glance at the polity of the pond.

It is always so in science studies which a love of nature may tempt you to pursue. You will no longer move about "in worlds not realized," as Wordsworth puts it. One glimpse of nature but leads to a deeper sight and to nearer looking; and your nature-studies bring with them the delight in a world fair to see, but fairer still when more truly known. But I am tempted to moralize, and you have no need of such counsel. We shall not exhaust the pond yet awhile; for there are water-spiders to see, and the newts wait to be watched. But to-day's labours are over, and we may shake hands and say " well done " over to-day's work. Come: we shall stroll round the garden and see the moon rise, and to-morrow we shall again "go a-fishing."

INDEX.

A

Adipocere, 26
Algæ, 235
Alternation of generations, 89
Amœba, 250
Arachnidans, 98
Aram, Eugene, case of, 30
Arden, Enoch, 13
Australia, zoology of, 211, *et seq.*

B

Baleen. *See* Whalebone
Barnacle, Autobiography of, 176
Bell-animalcules, 245
Bennett, 6
Blood-stains, tests for, 3, *et seq.*
Blowing of whales, 121
Bone-setting, 59

C

Caddis-worms, 250
Carbonic acid gas, 193
Chamisso, 90
Chlorophyll, 193, 234
Clotho, a spider, 112
Condé, Prince of, 11
Cooper, Sir Astley, 9
Crime and science, 1
Cumberland, Duke of, 9
Cuttlefishes, giant, 218, *et seq.*
Cyclops, 241
Cypris, 243

D

Daphnia, 244
Darwin, 126, 127, 128, 178
Dawn of life, animalcule, 160
Diatoms, 249
Dugongs, 133

E

Electric ray, 174
Eozoön, 160
Epeira, a spider, 106, 107, 108, 109

F

Fasting, 138
Fishes, giant, 226
Fly, autobiography of, 194
Food, 138; rules for taking, 139; of plants, 143
Foraminifera, 164
Fossil, oldest, 159
Fossil whales, 136

INDEX

G

Galton, 1
Ghosts of science, 148
Giants, 215; human, 227, *et seq.*
Gills of fishes, 172
Globe-animacule. *See* Volvox

H

Hair-dyes, injurious effects of, 53
Homology, 124
Hydra, 81

I

Identification, cases of, 22, *et seq.*

J

Jamrach's, At, 64, *et seq.*
Jelly-fishes, 71
Jessopp, Dr., 157

K

Kangaroos, 203

L

Leaves, 187
Lost and missing, 22
Lyons Mail, story of, 39

M

Macropus, 205
Manatees, 133
Marsupials. *See* Kangaroos
Medical By-ways, 43
Milk as a food, 141
Mind, influence of, on disease, 54, 55
Missing persons, 22
Mussels, 114

N

Nauplius, 182
Nicolai of Berlin, 149

O

Opossums, 210

P

Parkman, Dr., case of, 31
Patch, Mr., case of, 9
Peripatus, 114
Pinna, 116
Placoid scales, 170
Polity of a pond, 233
Pond life, 233
Presumption of death, 13

Q

Quack medicines, 46, *et seq.*

R

Rays, 168
Rhytina, 134
Rudimentary organs, 130

S

Science and ghosts, 148
Science and crime, 1
Sea-acorn, 179
Sea-cows, 133
Sea-horses, 209
Sensations, 153, 154, 155
Sensitive plant, 190
Sirenia, 133
Skates and rays, 168
Sperm whale, 132
Spiders, 96, *et seq.*
Starvation, 153, *et seq.*
Stentor, 246
Suicide and homicide, 11
Survivorship, 13, 17

T

Tendrils, 191
Thread-cells, 81
Threads and thrums, 96

U

Underwoods, case of, 17

V

Veins of leaves, 192
Venus' Flytrap, 189
Volvox, 238
Vorticellæ, 245

W

Walsh, Caroline, case of, 27
Water as a food, 140
Water-fleas, 240, *et seq.*
Waterloo Bridge murder, 33
Whalebone, 123 ; origin of, 126
Whales, 118
Wheel-animalcules, 247
Wings, movements of, in fly, 201

Z

Zeuglodon, 137
Zoophytes, 87
Zoospores, 239

THE END.

www.ingramcontent.com/pod-product-compliance
Lightning Source LLC
Chambersburg PA
CBHW031350230426
43670CB00006B/492